Finite Difference Fundamentals in MATLAB

Mohammad Nuruzzaman

Electrical Engineering Department
King Fahd University of Petroleum & Minerals
Dhahran, Saudi Arabia

CREATESPACE
4900 LaCross Road
North Charleston, SC 29406
www.createspace.com

Dr. Mohammad Nuruzzaman
Electrical Engineering Department
King Fahd University of Petroleum and Minerals
KFUPM BOX 1286
Dhahran 31261, Saudi Arabia
Email: nzaman@kfupm.edu.sa, nzaman@ymail.com, or mzamandr@gmail.com
Web Link: http://faculty.kfupm.edu.sa/EE/NZAMAN/

ISBN-10: 1-4848-4538-2
ISBN-13: 978-1484845387

Printed in the United States of America

This book is printed on acid-free paper.

To my parents

Mohammad Shamsul Haque & Nurbanu Begum

Other titles by the author:

1. M. Nuruzzaman, "*Digital Image: Theories, Algorithms, and Applications*", June, 2012, CreateSpace, Washington.
2. M. Nuruzzaman, "*Digital Audio Fundamentals in MATLAB*", July, 2010, CreateSpace, California.
3. M. Nuruzzaman, "*Modern Approach to Solving Electromagnetics in MATLAB*", January, 2009, BookSurge Publishing, Charleston, South Carolina.
4. M. Nuruzzaman, "*Signal and System Fundamentals in MATLAB and SIMULINK*", July, 2008, BookSurge Publishing, Charleston, South Carolina.
5. M. Nuruzzaman, "*Electric Circuit Fundamentals in MATLAB and SIMULINK*", October, 2007, BookSurge Publishing, Charleston, South Carolina.
6. M. Nuruzzaman, "*Technical Computation and Visualization in MATLAB for Engineers and Scientists*", February, 2007, AuthorHouse, Bloomington, Indiana.
7. M. Nuruzzaman, "*Digital Image Fundamentals in MATLAB*", September, 2005, AuthorHouse, Bloomington, Indiana.
8. M. Nuruzzaman, "*Modeling and Simulation in SIMULINK for Engineers and Scientists*", January, 2005, AuthorHouse, Bloomington, Indiana.
9. M. Nuruzzaman, "*Tutorials on Mathematics to MATLAB*", March, 2003, AuthorHouse, Bloomington, Indiana.

Preface

"Finite difference fundamentals in MATLAB" is devoted to the solution of numerical problems employing basic finite difference (FD) methods. In today's world numerical analysis is part and parcel in every branch of science and engineering. Industrial problems apply rigorous numerical techniques too, one of which is FD. A natural question is why to study FD? Classically established theories and tools solve certain class of scientific and engineering problems because the solving techniques suffer from assumption, limitation, or constraint. FD also has its limitations. FD results may not be solely accurate. Despite that, degree of FD accuracy in computing is quite high. It is better to have some solution rather than none. Else FD can be an alternative to traditional computing. Nevertheless in today's hi-tech trend whatever machine interface or computer based device we use inherits or implements FD based concepts or terminologies.

The reader might question why to study FD in MATLAB? MATLAB (abbreviation for matrix laboratory) as a computing software is attracting more and more scientific and engineering communities. Built-in functions embedded in MATLAB do not require reprogramming an already solved problem, nor does clumsy compiling often encountered in base language such as in FORTRAN or C. Facilitating MATLAB study tools on FD make this text perfect for self-learners. The spectrum of MATLAB whether computing or graphing is huge truly speaking several volumes are required to get the full extent of the package. We intend to introduce the fundamental FD computing and graphing through academic approach in MATLAB.

We live in the era of globalization which slowly changing the problem solving tactic. Internet and cell phones are empowering individuals literally digital democracy is evolving in education sector. Classroom teachers can not touch on all sorts of instructional materials or teaching tools because of time constraint or any other reason. A supplemental tool definitely helps learners of science and engineering fellows to solve their own problems the way they want in this regard the text would be a perfect read. FD computing linking to an archetype reveals the intrinsic of numerical technique which is a salient feature of the text. Besides intricacy of two dimensional computing and double summation analytical expression can be much reduced if matrix oriented computing is exercised. Hand-on playing of FD end results indeed engages students – this is what the text is about.

Chapter 1 presents a brief introduction to MATLAB's getting-started features. Chapter 2 addresses finite difference in one dimension. Chapter 3 merely demonstrates the finite difference computing and graphing in two dimensions. A meaningful application of finite difference is in ordinary differential equation which is considered in chapter 4. Partial differential equation is widely applied in advanced science and engineering problems which we focus in chapter 5. Moreover appendices A through G explain finite difference applications, relevant coding, function, or embedded graphing tool to the context of MATLAB.

My words of acknowledgement are due to the King Fahd University of Petroleum and Minerals (KFUPM). I am especially appreciative of library facilities, finite difference reading materials, and MATLAB software that I received from the university.

Mohammad Nuruzzaman

Table of Contents

Chapter 5
Finite Difference in Partial Differential Equations

Appendices

Chapter 1

Introduction to MATLAB

MATLAB is a computing software, which provides the quickest and easiest way to compute scientific and technical problems and visualize the solutions. As worldly standard for simulation and analysis, engineers, scientists, and researchers are becoming more and more affiliated with MATLAB. The general questionnaires about MATLAB platform before one gets started with are the contents of this chapter. Much of the MATLAB computational style presupposes that the element to be handled is a vector or matrix. Our explanation highlights the following:

- MATLAB features found in its opened command window
- The easiest and quickest way to get started in MATLAB beginning from scratch
- Frequently encountered questions while working in MATLAB environment
- Relevant introductory topics and forms of assistance about MATLAB

1.1 What is MATLAB?

MATLAB is mainly a scientific and technical computing software whose elaboration is matrix laboratory. The command prompt of MATLAB (>>) provides an interactive system. In the workspace of MATLAB, most data element is dealt as a matrix without dimensioning. The package is incredibly advantageous for the matrix-oriented computations. MATLAB's easy-to-use platform enables us to compute and manipulate matrices, perform numerical analyses, and visualize different variety of one/two/three dimensional graphics in a matter of second or seconds without conventional programming as conducted in FORTRAN, PASCAL, or C.

1.2 MATLAB's opening window features

If you do not have MATLAB installed in your personal computer, contact MathWorks (owner and developer, www.mathworks.com) for the installation CD. If you know how to get in MATLAB and its basics, you can skip the chapter. Assuming the package is installed in your system, run MATLAB from the Start of the Microsoft Windows. Let us get familiarized with MATLAB's opening window features. Figure 1.1(a) shows a typical firstly opened MATLAB window. Depending on the desktop setting or MATLAB version, your MATLAB window may not look like the figure 1.1(a) but descriptions of the features by and large are appropriate.

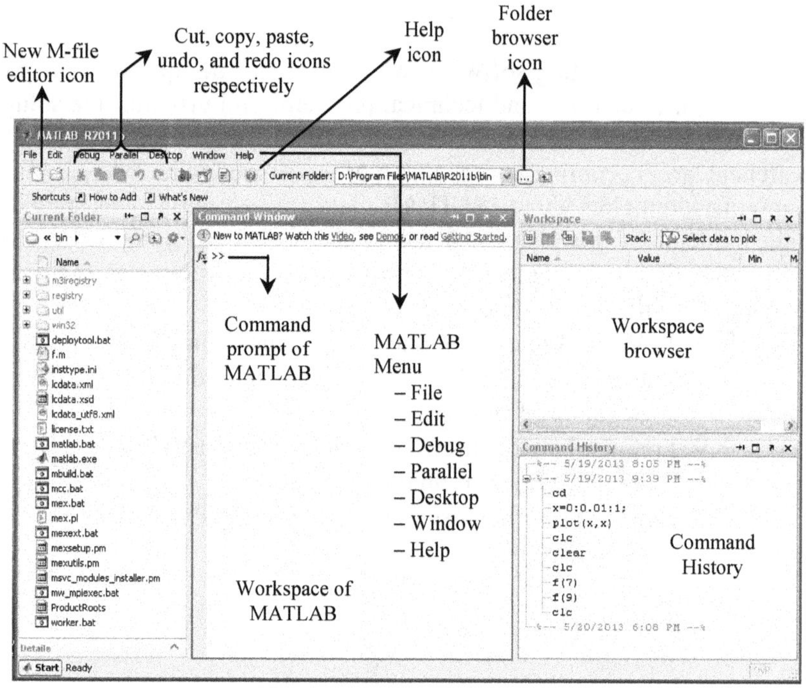

Figure 1.1(a) Typical features of MATLAB's firstly opened window

◆◆ Command prompt of MATLAB

Command prompt means that you tell MATLAB to do something from here. As an interactive system, MATLAB responds to user through this prompt. MATLAB cursor will be blinking after >> prompt once you open MATLAB that says MATLAB is ready to take your commands. To enter any command, type executable MATLAB statements from keyboard and to execute that, press the Enter key (the symbol ↵ is for the 'Hit the Enter Key' operation). Relative location of the command prompt is seen in figure 1.1(a).

❖❖ MATLAB Menu

MATLAB is supplied with seven submenus namely File, Edit, Debug, Parallel, Desktop, Window, and Help. Each submenu has its own features. Use the mouse to click different submenus and their brief descriptions are as follows:

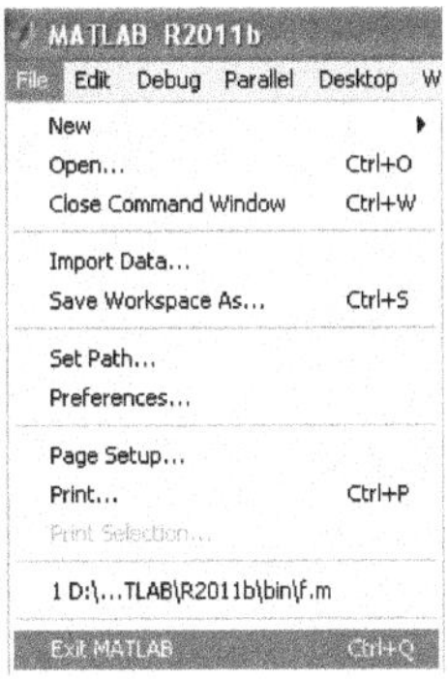

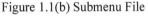

Figure 1.1(b) Submenu File

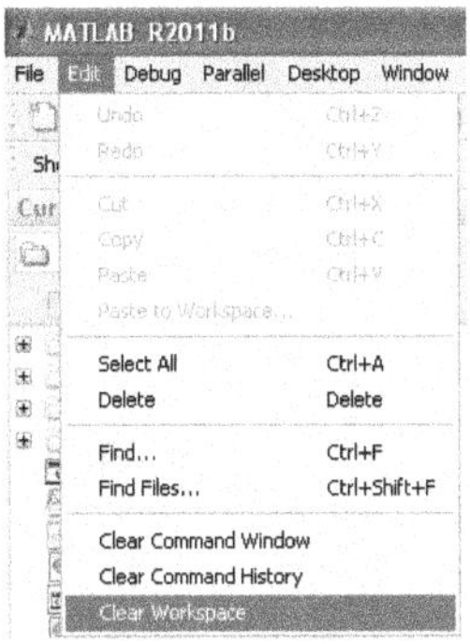

Figure 1.1(c) Submenu Edit

Submenu File: It (figure 1.1(b)) opens a new M-file, figure, model, or Graphical User Interface (GUI) layout maker, opens a file which was saved before, loads a saved workspace, imports data from a file, saves the workspace variables, sets the required path to execute a file, prints the workspace, and keeps the provision for changing the command window property.

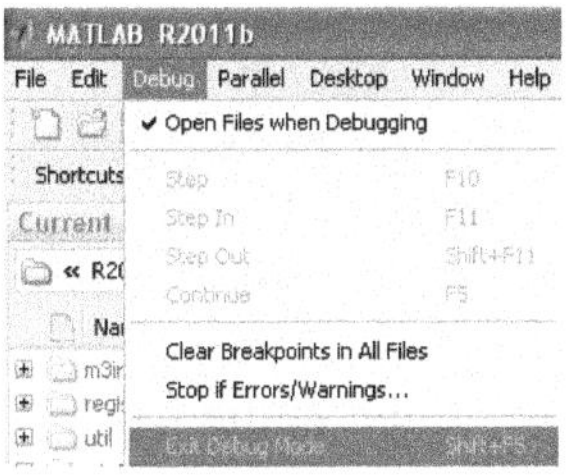

Figure 1.1(d) Submenu Debug

Submenu Edit: The second submenu Edit (figure 1.1(c)) includes cutting, copying, pasting, undoing, and clearing operations. These operations are useful when you frequently work at the command prompt.

Submenu Debug: The submenu Debug (figure 1.1(d)) is mainly related with the text mode or M-file programming.

Submenu Parallel: This submenu (figure 1.1(e)) provides necessary links or tools for parallel computing.

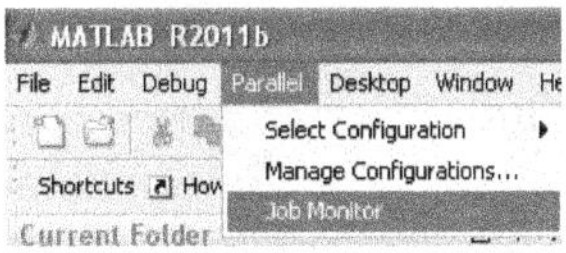

Figure 1.1(e) Submenu Parallel

Submenu Desktop: The fifth submenu Desktop (figure 1.1(f)) is equipped with control on command window or its subwindow opening options for example workspace browser of figure 1.1(a) will remain opened or not – this sort of option.

Submenu Window: You may open some graphics window from MATLAB command prompt or running some M-files. From the sixth submenu Window (figure 1.1(g)), one can see how many graphics window under MATLAB are open and can switch from one window to other by clicking the mouse to the required window.

Submenu Help: MATLAB holds abundant help facilities. The last submenu shows Help (figure 1.1(h)) in different ways. Latter in this chapter, we mention how one gets specific help. The submenu also provides the easiness to get connected with the MathWorks Website provided that your system is connected to internet.

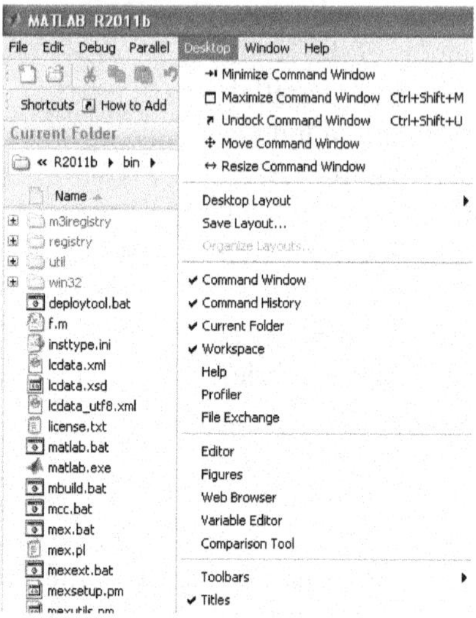

Figure 1.1(f) Submenu Desktop

♦♦ Icons

Available icons are shown in the icon bar (down the menu bar) of the figure 1.1(a). Frequently used operations such as opening a new file, opening an existing file, getting help, etc are found in the icon bar so that the user does not have to go through the menu bar over and over.

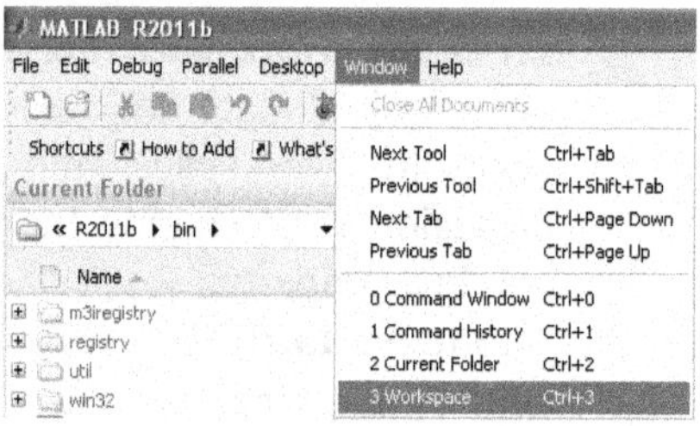

Figure 1.1(g) Submenu Window

♦♦ MATLAB workspace

Workspace (figure 1.1(a)) is the platform of MATLAB where one executes MATLAB commands. During execution of commands, one may have to deal with some input and output variables. These variables can be one-dimensional array, multi-dimensional array, characters, symbolic objects, etc. Again to deal with graphics window, we have texts, graphics, or object handles. Workspace holds all those variables or handles for you. As a subwindow of the figure 1.1(a), the browser exhibits the types or properties of

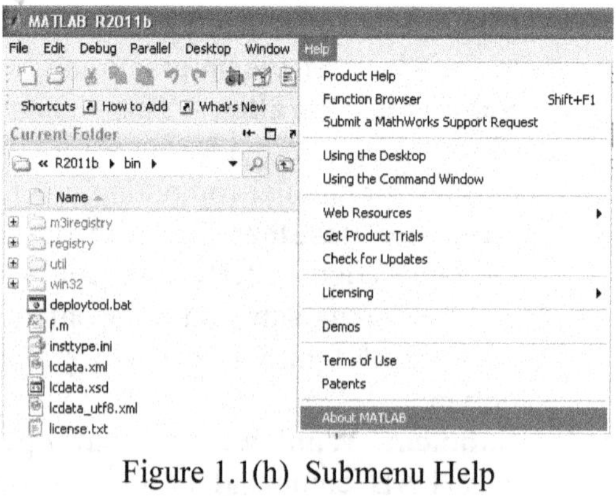

Figure 1.1(h) Submenu Help

those variables or handles. If the browser is not seen in the opening window of MATLAB, click the Desktop down Workspace in the menu bar to bring the subwindow (figure 1.1(f)).

◆◆ MATLAB command history

There is a subwindow in the figure 1.1(a) called Command History which holds all previously used commands at the command prompt. Depending on the desktop/laptop setting, it may or may not appear during the opening of MATLAB. If it is not seen, click the Command History in pulldown menu of the figure 1.1(f) under the Desktop.

1.3 How to get started in MATLAB?

New MATLAB users face a common question how one gets started in MATLAB. This tutorial is for the beginners in MATLAB. Here we address the terms under the following bold headings.

◆◆ How one can enter a vector/matrix

The first step is the user has to be in the command window of MATLAB. Look for the command prompt >> in the command window. One can type anything from the keyboard at the command prompt. Row or column matrices are termed as vectors. We intend to enter the row matrix $R=[2 \quad 3 \quad 4 \quad -2 \quad 0]$ into the workspace of MATLAB. Type the following from the keyboard at the command prompt:

```
>>R=[2 3 4 -2 0]
```

← Arial font set is used for executable commands in the text i.e. R⇔R

There is one space gap between two elements of the matrix R but no space gap at the edge elements. All elements are placed under the [ ]. Press Enter key after the third brace] from the keyboard and we see

```
R =
        2   3   4  -2   0
>>
```

← command prompt is ready again

It means we assigned the row matrix to the workspace variable R. Whenever we call R, MATLAB understands the whole row matrix. Matrix R is having five elements. Even if the R had 100 elements, it would understand the whole matrix that is one of many appreciative features of MATLAB. Next we wish to enter the column matrix $C=\begin{bmatrix} 7 \\ 8 \\ 10 \\ -11 \end{bmatrix}$. Again type the following from the keyboard at the blinking cursor:

```
>>C=[7;8;10;-11] ↵
```

you will see (↵ means 'Press the Enter Key'),

```
C =
      7
```

```
        8
       10
      -11
>>
```
← command prompt is ready again

This time we also assigned the column matrix to the workspace variable C. For the column matrix, there is one semicolon ; between two consecutive elements of the matrix C but no space gap is necessary. As another option, the matrix C could have been entered by writing C=[7 8 10 -11]'. The operator ' of the keyboard is the matrix transposition operator in MATLAB. As if you entered a row matrix but at the end just the transpose operator ' is attached. After that the rectangular matrix $A=\begin{bmatrix} 20 & 6 & 7 \\ 5 & 12 & -3 \\ 1 & -1 & 0 \\ 19 & 3 & 2 \end{bmatrix}$ is to be entered:

```
>>A=[20 6 7;5 12 -3;1 -1 0;19 3 2] ↵
```
you will see,

```
A =

    20   6   7
     5  12  -3
     1  -1   0
    19   3   2
```

Two consecutive rows of A are separated by a semicolon ; and consecutive elements in a row are separated by one space gap. Instead of typing all elements in a row, one can type the first row, press Enter key, the cursor blinks in the next line, type the second row, and so on.

♦♦ How one can use the colon and the semicolon operators

The operators semicolon ; and colon : have special significance in MATLAB. Most MATLAB statements and M-file programming use these two operators almost in every line. Vector generation is easily performed by the colon operator no matter how many elements we need. Let us carry out the following at the command prompt to see the importance of the colon operator:

```
>>A=1:4 ↵
```
you will see,

```
A =

     1   2   3   4
```
← We created a vector A or row matrix where A=[1 2 3 4]

Interact with MATLAB for an incremental vector by the following:

```
>>R=1:3:10 ↵
```
you will see,

```
R =

     1   4   7   10
```
← We created a vector or row matrix R whose elements form an arithmetic progression with first element 1, last element 10, and common difference or increment 3

Vector with decrement can also be generated:

```
>>C=[0:-2:-10]' ↵
```
you will see,

```
C =
        0
       -2
       -4
       -6
       -8
      -10
```

← We created a vector or column matrix C whose consecutive elements have the decrement 2 with the first element 0 and the last element −10

MATLAB also generates vectors whose elements are decimal numbers. Let us form a row matrix R whose first element is 3, last element is 6, and increment is 0.5 and which we accomplish as follows:

```
>>R=3:0.5:6 ↵
```

you will see,

```
R =
    3.0000    3.5000    4.0000    4.5000    5.0000    5.5000    6.0000
```

You may need to stretch your command window to see output like above. Then what is the use of the semicolon operator? Append a semicolon at the end in the last command and execute that:

```
>>R=3:0.5:6; ↵
```

you will see,

```
>>
```

← Assignment is not shown

Type R at the command prompt and press Enter:

```
>>R ↵

R =
    3.0000    3.5000    4.0000    4.5000    5.0000    5.5000    6.0000
```

It indicates that the semicolon operator prevents MATLAB from displaying the contents of workspace variable R (called suppression command).

◆◆How one can call a built-in MATLAB function

In MATLAB thousands of M-files or built-in function files are embedded. Acquaintance on description of the function, the numbers of input and output arguments, and the class or type of the arguments is mandatory in order to execute a built-in function at the command prompt. Let us start with a simplest example. We intend to find $\sin x$ for $x=\frac{3\pi}{2}$ which should be −1. The MATLAB counterpart (appendix B) of $\sin x$ is sin(x) where x can be any real or complex number in radians and can be a matrix too. The angle $\frac{3\pi}{2}$ is written as 3*pi/2(π is coded by pi) and let us perform it as follows:

```
>>sin(3*pi/2) ↵

ans =
    -1
```

By default the return from any function is assigned to workspace ans. If you wish to assign the return to S, you would write S=sin(3*pi/2);.

As another example, let us factorize the integer 84 (84=2×2×3×7). The MATLAB built-in function **factor** finds the factors of an integer and the implementation is as follows:

```
>>f=factor(84) ↵

f =
        2   2   3   7
```

The output of the **factor** is a row matrix which we assigned to workspace f in fact the f can be any user-supplied variable. Thus you can call any other built-in function from the command prompt provided that you have the knowledge about the calling of inputs to and outputs from the function.

◆◆ How one can open and execute an M-file

This is the most important start up for the beginners. An M-file can be regarded as a text or script file. A collection of executable MATLAB statements are the contents of an M-file. Ongoing discussion made you familiarize with entering a matrix, computing a sine value, and factorizing an integer. These three executions took place at the command prompt. They can be executed from an M-file as well. This necessitates opening the M-file editor. Referring to the figure 1.1(b), you find the link for the M-file editor as File → New → Script or M-file and click it to see the new untitled M-file editor. Another option is click the New M-file editor icon of figure 1.1(a).

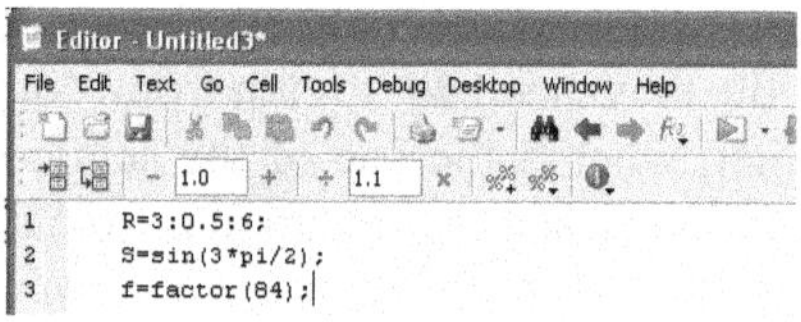

Figure 1.2(a) Last three executed statements are typed in the M-file editor of MATLAB

However after opening the new M-file editor, we typed the last three executable statements in the untitled file as shown in the figure 1.2(a). The next step is to save the untitled file by clicking the Save icon or from the File Menu of the M-file editor window. Figure 1.2(b) presents the File Save dialog window. We typed the File name of the figure 1.2(b) as **test** (type after deleting Untitled, can be any name of your choice) in the window. The M-file has the file extension .m but we do not type .m only the file name is enough. After saving the file, let us move on to the MATLAB command prompt and conduct the following:

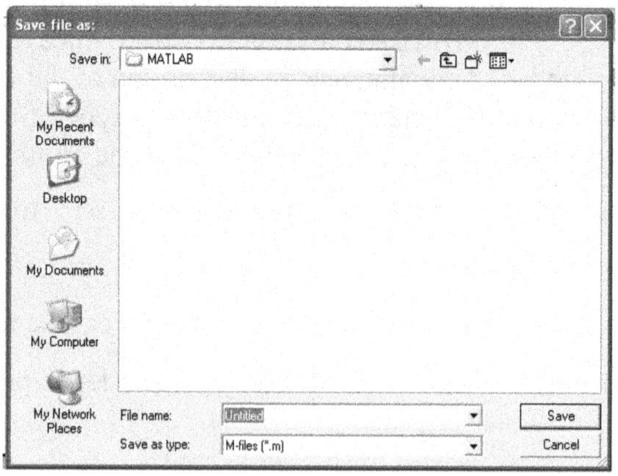

Figure 1.2(b) Save dialog window for naming the M-file

```
>>test ↵
>>        ← command prompt is ready again
```

It indicates that MATLAB executed the M-file by the name **test** and is ready for the next command. We can check calling the assignees whether the previously performed executions occurred exactly as follows:

```
>>R ↵

R =
     3.0000   3.5000   4.0000   4.5000   5.0000   5.5000   6.0000
>>S ↵                                >>f ↵

S =                                  f =
     -1                                        2    2    3    7
```

The last returns are the same ones what we found before. Thus one can run any executable MATLAB statements in an M-file.

The reader might ask in which folder or path the file **test** was saved. Figure 1.1(a) shows one slot for the **Current Folder** in the upper middle portion of the window for example the shown one is **D:\Program Files\MATLAB\R2011b\bin**. That is the location of your saved file. If you want to save the M-file in other folder or directory, change your path by clicking the folder browser icon (figure 1.1(a)) before saving the file. When you call the **test** or any other file from the command prompt of MATLAB, the command prompt must be in the same directory where the file is in or its path must be defined to MATLAB.

♦♦ Input and output arguments of a function file

MATLAB is supplied with numerous M-files. Some files are executed without any return and some return results which are called function files (appendix F). You have seen the use of function **sin(x)** which has one input argument **x**. The statement **test(x,y)** means that the **test** is a function file which has two input arguments – **x** and **y**. Again the **test(x,y,z)** means the

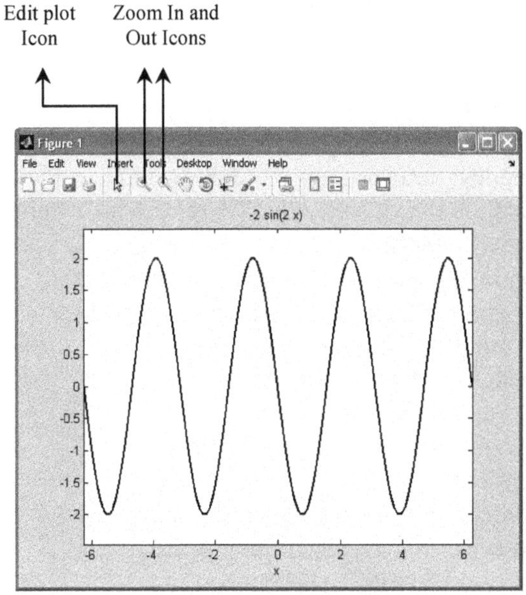

Figure 1.2(c) Graph of $-2\sin 2x$ versus x

test is a function file which needs three input arguments – **x**, **y**, and **z**. Similar style also follows for the return but under the third bracket. The **[a,b]=test(x,y)** means there are two output arguments from the **test** which are **a** and **b** and the **[a,b,c]=test(x,y)** means three returns from the **test** which are **a**, **b**, and **c**.

♦♦ How one can plot a graph

MATLAB is very convenient for plotting different sorts of graphs. The graphs are plotted either from a mathematical expression or from some data.

Let us plot the function $y = -2\sin 2x$. The MATLAB function **ezplot** plots y versus x type graph taking the expression as its input argument. The MATLAB code (appendix B) for the $-2\sin 2x$ is **-2*sin(2*x)**. The functional code is input argumented by using quote hence we conduct the following at the command prompt:

```
>>ezplot('-2*sin(2*x)') ↵
```

Figure 1.2(c) presents the outcome from above execution. The window in which the graph is plotted is called the MATLAB figure window. Any graphics is plotted in the figure window, which has its own menu (such as File, Edit, etc) as seen in the figure 1.2(c).

1.4 Some queries about MATLAB environment

Users need to know the answers of some questions when they start working at MATLAB. Some MATLAB environment related queries are presented in the following.

How to change the numeric format?

When you perform any computation at the command prompt, the output is returned up to four decimal display due to short numeric format which is the default one. There are other numeric formats too. To reach the numeric format dialog box, the clicking operation sequence is MATLAB command window ⇒ **File** ⇒ **Preferences** ⇒ **Command Window** ⇒ **Text Display** ⇒ **Numeric Format** (select from the popup menu e.g. **long**).

How to change the font or background color settings?

One might be interested to change the background color or font color while working in the command window. The clicking sequence is MATLAB command window ⇒ **File** ⇒ **Preferences** ⇒ **Colors**.

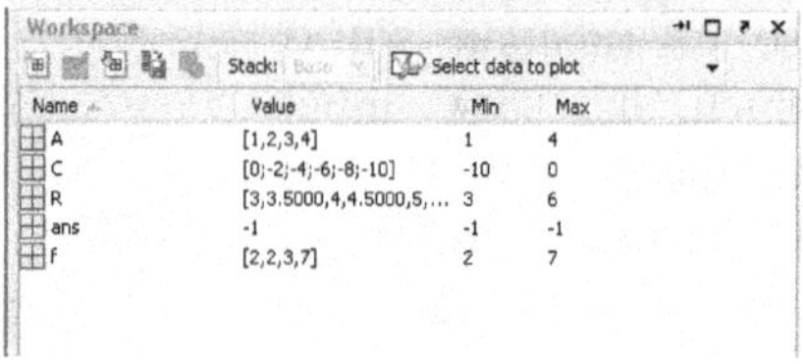

Figure 1.2(d) Workspace browser displays variable information

How to delete some/all variables from the workspace?

In order to delete all variables present at the workspace, the clicking sequence is MATLAB command window ⇒ Edit ⇒ Clear Workspace (figure 1.1(c)). If you want to delete a particular workspace variable, select the concern variable by using the mouse pointer in the workspace browser (assuming that it is open like the figure 1.2(d)) and then rightclick ⇒ delete. See section 1.2 for bringing the workspace browser in front in case it is not opened.

How to clear workspace but not the variables?

Once you conduct some sessions at the command prompt, monitor screen keeps all interactive sessions. You can clear the screen contents without removing the variables present in the workspace by the command clc or performing the clicking operation MATLAB command window ⇒ Edit ⇒ Clear Command Window (figure 1.1(c)).

How to know the current path?

In the upper portion of the figure 1.1(a), the Current Folder bar is located that indicates in which path the command prompt is or execute cd (abbreviation for the current directory) at the command prompt.

How to see different variables in the workspace?

There are two ways of viewing this – either use the command who or look at the workspace browser (like figure 1.2(d)) which displays information about workspace variables for example R is the name of the variable holding some values. One can view, change, or edit the contents of a variable by doubleclicking the concern variable situated in the workspace browser as conducted in Microsoft Excel.

How to enter a long command line?

MATLAB statements can be too long to fit in one line. Giving a break in the middle of a statement is accomplished by the ellipsis (three dots are called ellipsis). We show that considering the entering of the vector x=[1:3:10] as follows:

```
>>x=[1:3: . . . ↵
        10] ↵
x =
        1   4   7   10
```

Typing takes place in two lines and there is one space gap before the ellipsis.

Editing at the command prompt

This is advantageous specially for them who work frequently in the command window without opening an M-file. Keyboard has different arrow keys marked by ← ↑ → ↓. One may type a misspelled command at the command prompt causing error message to appear. Instead of retyping the entire line, press uparrow (for previous line) or downarrow (for next line) to edit the MATLAB statement. Or you can reexecute any past statement this way.

For example we generate a row vector 1 to 10 with increment 2 and assign the vector to x. The necessary command is x=1:2:10. Mistakenly you typed x+1:2:10. The response is as follows:

```
>>x+1:2:10 ↵
??? Undefined function or variable 'x'.
```

You discovered the mistake and want to correct that. Press ↑ key to see,

```
>>x+1:2:10
```

Edit the command by going to the + sign by using the left arrow key or mouse pointer. At the prompt, if you type x and press ↑ again and again, you see used commands that start with x.

Saving and loading data

User can save workspace variables or data in a binary file having the extension .mat. Suppose you have the matrix $A=\begin{bmatrix} 3 & 4 & 8 \\ 0 & 2 & 1 \end{bmatrix}$ and wish to save the A in a file by the name data.mat. Let us carry out the following:

```
>>A=[3 4 8;0 2 1]; ↵          ← Assigning the A to A
```

Now move on to the workspace browser (figure 1.2(d)) and you see the variable A including its information located in the subwindow. Bring the mouse pointer on the A, rightclick the mouse, and click the Save As. The Save dialog window appears and type only data (not the data.mat) in the slot of File name. If it is necessary, you can save all workspace variables by using the same action but clicking File ⇒ Save Workspace As (figure 1.1(b)). One retrieves the data file by clicking the menu File ⇒ Import Data (figure 1.1(b)). Another option is use the command load data at the command prompt.

How to delete a file from the command prompt?

Let us delete just mentioned data.mat by executing the command delete data.mat at the command prompt.

How to see the data held in a variable?

Figure 1.2(d) presents some variable information in which you find R. Doubleclick the R or your variable in the workspace browser and find the matrix contents of R in a data sheet.

1.5 How to get help?

Help facilities in MATLAB are plentiful. One can access to the information about a MATLAB function in a variety of ways. Command help finds the help of a particular function file. You are familiar with the function sin(x) from earlier discussion and can have the command prompt help regarding the sin(x) as follows:

```
>>help sin ↵                  ← Function name without the argument

sin   Sine of argument in radians.
   sin(X) is the sine of the elements of X.

   See also asin, sind.
```

Overloaded methods:
  codistributed/sin

Reference page in Help browser
  doc sin

One disadvantage of this method is that the user has to know the exact file name of a function. For a novice, this facility may not be appreciative.

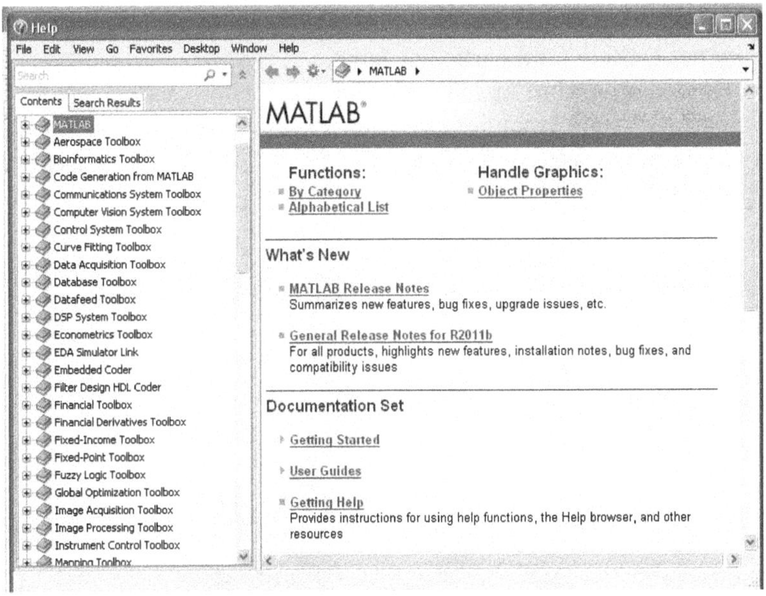

Figure 1.2(e) General Help Window of MATLAB

Casually we know the partial name of a function or try to check whether a function exists by that name. Suppose we intend to see whether any function by the name finite exists. We execute the following by the intermediacy of the command lookfor (no space gap between look and for) to see all possible functions bearing the file name finite or having the file name finite partly:

```
>>lookfor finite ↵

delsqdemo        - Finite Difference Laplacian
while            - Repeat statements an indefinite number of times.
isfinite         - True for finite elements.
isinf            - True for infinite elements.
realmax          - Largest finite floating point number.
ldl              - Block LDL' factorization for Hermitian indefinite matrices.
delsq            - Construct five-point finite difference Laplacian.
infline          - Generate data for infinite HG line.
     ⋮
```

The return may take few minutes so be patient. The return shows all possible matches of functions containing the word **finite**. Now the command **help** can be conducted to go through a particular one for example the first one is **delsqdemo** and we execute **help delsqdemo** to see its description at the command prompt.

In order to have window form help, click the Help icon of figure 1.1(a) and MATLAB responds with the opening Help window of the figure 1.2(e). As the figure shows, help is available by content or index. If you have some search word on finite difference, you search that through the **Search** of figure 1.2(e). This help form is better when one navigates MATLAB's capability not looking for a particular function.

Hidden algorithm or mathematical expression is often necessary in conducting MATLAB executions whose assistance we can have through the search option from MathWorks Website provided that the PC is connected to the Internet (figure 1.1(h)).

However we close the introductory discussion on MATLAB with this.

Chapter 2

Finite Difference in One Dimension

Subject matter in this chapter is to deal with very basics of finite difference (FD) associated to one dimensional function or data. Sample points and values are the foundation of finite difference which is a particular division of discrete mathematics. Finite difference plays a momentous role in numerical analysis and engineering mathematics that is undeniable in today's computer related ploys. The transform of one dimensional FD data to row/column matrix makes the study much easier. However the chapter highlights the following:

- Finite difference model pertaining to one dimensional function
- Implementational intricacy of one dimensional finite difference
- Available and programmable finite difference operators
- Plotting tools for one dimensional finite difference data

2.1 Model of one variable expression

In order to model a one dimensional expression mathematically, we first need to understand the conversion of a continuous function to its discrete counterpart. Most familiar one variable or dimensional function $f(x)$ like polynomial $x^2 - x + 3$, sinusoidal $2\sin 3x$, etc are always continuous never discrete. The continuity is of coarse with respect to x as well as $f(x)$.

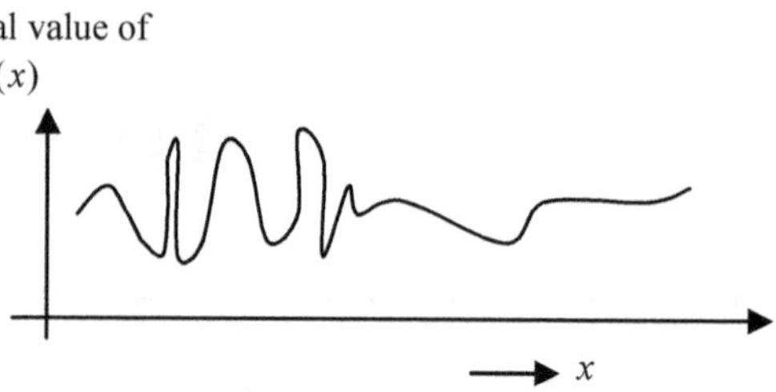

Figure 2.1(a) A typical function

Figure 2.1(a) shows a typical function $f(x)$ versus x variation. The meaning of continuous x is that its value can be any fractional or decimal for example x =0, x =0.00001, or x =1. Similar value for $f(x)$ is also likely. If $f(x)$ is represented by a definite function for example $f(x)=\sin x$, the continuous concept is well suited.

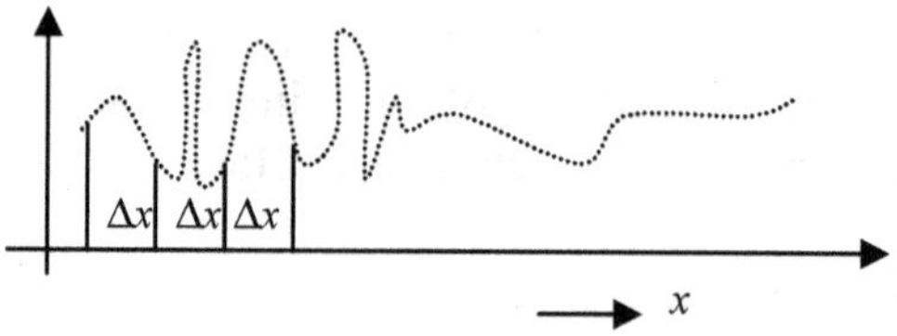

Figure 2.1(b) Discretization of the function in figure 2.1(a) along x

What if we have to deal with a function $f(x)$ which is not definite instead any value of the function within certain bound is likely? How do we process or manipulate this sort of function? In practical sense we consider the function values every after certain Δx rather than all values over the interval of x .

Introducing Δx to computing is termed as the finite difference (FD) approach. The Δx is called sample period or x resolution. In numerical analysis the Δx is often referred to as step size h – another synonym. The quantity x is just a variable which can be time, displacement, or other. The x is related to Δx as follows:

$$x = m\ \Delta x$$

where m is purely an integer and has no unit whereas x or Δx has the same unit for example meter in the case of displacement or sec in the case of time. Suppose the x represents time over the interval $0 \le x \le 2\,\text{sec}$ with Δx =0.5sec. Different x sample values are as follows:

$x \rightarrow 0$	0.5	1	1.5	2		all in sec
$m \rightarrow 0$	1	2	3	4		no unit – just integer

What can we say about the continuous x and discrete m? The x is just a linear function of m for a particular Δx.

Figure 2.1(b) depicts discretizing stratagem for the function in figure 2.1(a). The moment we introduce Δx, the $f(x)$ is no longer continuous that also becomes discrete. If the reader says, leave the $f(x)$ values unchanged, we may find $f(x)$ fractional. For a given resolution Δf on $f(x)$, it can be a function of integers too. Like x, we have also the linear relationship for the $f(x)$:

$$f(x) = p\ \Delta f$$

where p is an integer and units of $f(x)$ and Δf being the same.

Suppose the $f(x)$ represents distance over the range $0 \le f(x) \le 3meter$. By choosing Δf =0.6 meter, we get:

$f(x) \rightarrow 0$	0.6	1.2	1.8	2.4	3	all in meter
$p \rightarrow 0$	1	2	3	4	5	no unit – just integer

What can we conclude from these two illustrations? For a given resolution whether horizontal Δx or vertical Δf, each of x and $f(x)$ turns to linear function of integer to be precise the result of using finite difference. What if the actual value of x or $f(x)$ does not match the predecided Δx or Δf? Certainly that introduces some error which is the price of using FD technique. There are ways to make the error less for instance reduce the resolution, consider closest functional value, etc.

Now how can we fit these samples in a practical way? The solution is simple – put them in a row or column matrix that is

FD values of any continuous x with Δx over $x_1 \le x \le x_2$

results a row or column matrix and

FD values of any continuous $f(x)$ with Δf over $f_1 \le f(x) \le f_2$

results a row or column matrix or schematically

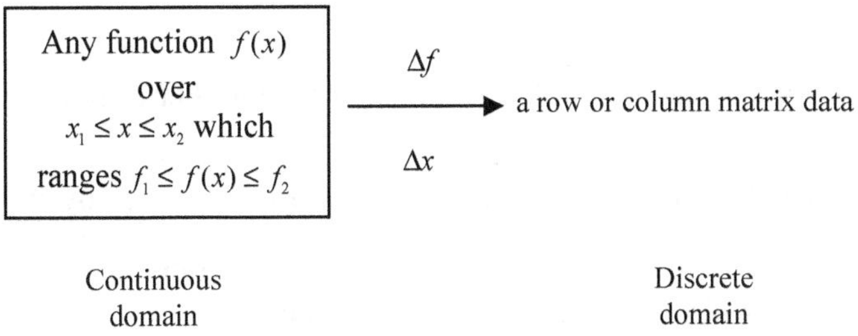

2.2 Implementing one dimensional FD

When thinking about the implementation of one dimensional FD, the first point should come in our mind is how to get the data? Usually scientific and engineering communities receive the FD data in following ways:

(a) from a mathematical relationship,
(b) data saved in a softcopy format,
(c) data after performing experiment that again can be in a softcopy form, and
(d) virtual generation of data by a computer program.

To contextualize above, we present the following examples.

Example 1:

This example presents how to get the FD data from a mathematical expression. You need first a functional relationship between x and $f(x)$ and then the resolution. Implement the FD data for $f(x)=x^2+3x+4$ with Δx =0.5 over $-2 \le x \le 2$.

From calculation one gets the following tabular data:

x	−2	−1.5	−1	−0.5	0	0.5	1	1.5	2
$f(x)$	2	1.75	2	2.75	4	5.75	8	10.75	14

From the x interval and Δx we first generate a row or column vector (section 1.3) and then write the scalar code (appendix B) of the $f(x)$ as follows:

```
>>x=-2:0.5:2; ↵
>>f=x.^2+3*x+4 ↵

f =
  2.0000 1.7500 2.0000 2.7500 4.0000 5.7500 8.0000 10.7500 14.0000
```

The interval beginning and ending bounds are also the bounds of the vector x and the increment of x vector is the Δx. The workspace f holds the $f(x)$ sample values. The x and f are user-chosen variables. If x is a row or column vector, so is the f.

Example 2:

Example 1 can be implemented from the number of points say with 9 points.

Under this circumstance we find the resolution Δx by using $\frac{x_2 - x_1}{N-1}$ where N is the required number of points and resolution Δx =(2−(−2))/(9−1) =0.5. The rest is similar to example 1. The same x vector could have been generated by linspace command without calculating the Δx which needs the syntax linspace(x_1 , x_2 , N) so complete execution is the following:

```
>>x=linspace(-2,2,9); ↵
>>f=x.^2+3*x+4; ↵
```

Example 3:

In the last two examples we just implemented the sample values of x. What if we need the index values i.e. m of section 2.1?

The integer m we obtain as follows: a vector from $\frac{x_1}{\Delta x}$ to $\frac{x_2}{\Delta x}$ with increment 1. For the example 1 we should be having –4 to 4 with increment 1 which needs the following implementation:

```
>>m=-2/0.5:2/0.5 ↵

m =
          -4   -3   -2   -1    0    1    2    3    4
```

Since the default increment in MATLAB is 1 that is why we did not include it in above generation and the m is a user-supplied variable which holds the m values as a row matrix.

Example 4:

Discretization is not applied on $f(x)$ in last examples. You either provide Δf or decide number of samples over $f_1 \le f(x) \le f_2$. Note that the number of samples must be equal to the number of m to be consistent with the coordinate. The f_1 and f_2 are the minimum and maximum values of $f(x)$ samples respectively hence $\Delta f = \frac{f_2 - f_1}{N-1}$. For the ongoing example we should have Δf =(14–1.75)/(9–1)=1.5313 which we implement as follows:

>>f1=min(f); ↵   ← f1⇔ f_1, f1 is user-chosen, appendix C.5 for min
>>f2=max(f); ↵   ← f2⇔ f_2, f2 is user-chosen, appendix C.5 for max
>>df=(f2-f1)/8 ↵   ← df⇔ Δf , df is user-chosen

```
df =
          1.5313
```

How do we determine integer $f[p]$ from $f(x)$? The answer is round $\frac{f(x)-f_1}{\Delta f}$ to its nearest integer as follows:

>>fp=round((f-f1)/df) ↵   ← fp⇔ $f[p]$, fp is user-chosen, appendix C.6 for round

```
fp =
          0    0    0    1    1    3    4    6    8
```

From the discrete $f[p]$ how do we reconstruct $f(x)$ (say $\hat{f}(x)$ is the reconstructed one from $f[p]$)? The $\hat{f}(x)$ is given by $f_1 + f[p]\,\Delta f$ and let us find it as follows:

```
>>f_hat=f1+fp*df ↵          ← f_hat⇔ f̂(x), f_hat is user-chosen

f_hat =
  1.7500 1.7500 1.7500 3.2813 3.2813 6.3438 7.8750 10.9375 14.0000
```

Are the $\hat{f}(x)$ and $f(x)$ of example 1 same? Of coarse not – that is the cost of discretization. If it is not, how do we find the error function $e(x)$ samples? The $e(x)$ is just $\hat{f}(x) - f(x)$ as found in the following:

```
>>e=f_hat-f ↵      ← e⇔ e(x), e is user-chosen

e =
     -0.2500 0 -0.2500 0.5313 -0.7188 0.5938 -0.1250 0.1875 0
```

Say $e[p]$ is the discrete version of $e(x)$. The mean square error (mse) is defined as $\frac{1}{N}\sum_{p}\{e[p]\}^2$ meaning square every sample in $e[p]$, sum them, and divide the sum by the total number of samples which should be 0.1475 for the ongoing example (same definition for $e(x)$ samples). We compute the error with the help of function **mse** which applies the syntax **mse(** $e[p]$ as a row or column matrix) so let us get it by:

```
>>mse(e) ↵

ans =
           0.1475
```

Example 5:

In this example we illustrate FD implementation when the sample data is saved in some file for instance in an Excel file like the figure 2.1(c).

The first step is to open the file in MATLAB with the help of function **xlsread** which applies the syntax **xlsread**(excel file name under quote). Figure 2.1(c) shown Excel file was saved by the name **Data1.xls** hence we call the file reader as follows:

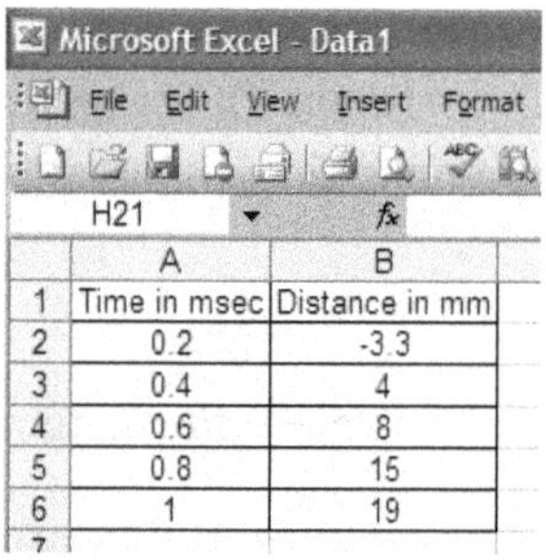

Figure 2.1(c) Some experimental data in an excel file

```
>>V=xlsread('Data1.xls') ↵

V =
```

```
    0.2000   -3.3000
    0.4000    4.0000
    0.6000    8.0000
    0.8000   15.0000
    1.0000   19.0000
```

Note that the soft file should be in the working path of MATLAB otherwise you get some file related error message. You may get the soft file from the email link of page ii. The V in the last execution is any user-chosen variable which holds the data as a rectangular matrix. Even if some texts are in the first row of the file in figure 2.1(c), MATLAB excludes that and picks just the data. In the V the first and second columns are the time and distance data respectively which we choose (appendix C.11) as follows:

```
>>x=V(:,1) ↵                              >>f=V(:,2) ↵

x =                                       f =
        0.2000                                   -3.3000
        0.4000                                    4.0000
        0.6000                                    8.0000
        0.8000                                   15.0000
        1.0000                                   19.0000
```

The x and f are user-chosen variables in above implementation which hold the figure 2.1(c) shown data both as a column matrix. If you want the data to be in a row matrix, transposition (section 1.3) helps us get that:

```
>>x=V(:,1)'; ↵                            >>f=V(:,2)'; ↵
```

Let us consider above row matrix for space reason. How do we relate the section 2.1 cited parameters? The Δx is 0.2 msec (the difference of elements in the x vector). Following earlier symbology, the m s we obtain as (elements of the x vector are divided by Δx):

```
>>m=x/0.2 ↵

m =
        1.0000    2.0000    3.0000    4.0000    5.0000
```

The f holds sample values of $f(x)$ from which f_1=–3.3 mm, f_2=19 mm, N= 5, and Δf =5.575 mm are implemented as follows:

```
>>f1=min(f); f2=max(f); N=length(f); df=(f2-f1)/(N-1) ↵

df =
        5.5750
```

The FD counterpart of $f(x)$ which is $f[p]$ should be:

```
>>fp=round((f-f1)/df) ↵

fp =
        0    1    2    3    4
```

The reconstructed $\hat{f}(x)$ we get as:

```
>>f_hat=f1+fp*df ↵

f_hat =
          -3.3000    2.2750    7.8500   13.4250   19.0000
```

Finally the mean square error is calculated as:

```
>>e=f_hat-f; mse(e) ↵

ans =
          1.0957
```

Example 6:

In this example we demonstrate how to work with virtually generated FD data by random variable generator of MATLAB. Well machine just generates random samples of $f(x)$, it is up to the reader how to link the data to x.

Suppose we intend to generate random samples each of uniform distribution within –2 mm and 10 mm over $0 \le x \le 2m\sec$ with $\Delta x = 0.5m\sec$.

The rand (appendix C.10) helps us get the samples. First we decide how many samples are over $0 \le x \le 2m\sec$ which is here $\frac{x_2 - x_1}{\Delta x}+1$ i.e. 5. We use the command 12*rand(1,5)-2 for row vector form. If the column vector form is sought, use the command 12*rand(5,1)-2. Let us see the machine response for the row vector:

```
>>f=12*rand(1,5)-2 ↵

f =
          7.1452    3.4776   -1.7780    7.8569    3.3364
```

Above f holds the $f(x)$ samples now if you wish to find m, $f[p]$, etc, examples 1-5 described computing or functions are equally applicable here.

2.3 Finite difference operators in MATLAB

MATLAB keeps provision for some built-in operators which we usually apply for summation, differentiation, and integration.

♦ Summation operator

Use of summation is common in FD related computing and the command sum (appendix C.9) is exercised to get the computing done, some examples of which are demonstrated in the following.

Example 1:

Suppose $\sum_{p=-2}^{2} p^2 = 10$ we intend to calculate.

We generate the p values as a row or column matrix (section 1.3), write the scalar code of p^2 for computing (appendix B), and use the command sum as follows:

>>p=-2:2; ↵ ← p⇔ p, p is user-chosen, holds values as a row matrix

```
>>f=p.^2; ↵    ← f is user-chosen, holds computed values as a row matrix
>>sum(f) ↵

ans =
        10
```

Example 2:

Not necessarily the p should be consecutive say $\sum pf[p]$=60 is to be implemented where p=[1 4 9] and $f[p]$=[−20 2 8].

Execute the following for the computation:

```
>>p=[1 4 9]; ↵ ← p⇔ p , p is user-chosen, holds values as a row matrix
>>f=[-20 2 8]; ↵ ← f⇔ f[p], user-chosen, holds values as a row matrix
>>sum(p.*f) ↵   ← .* is used for element by element multiplication

ans =
        60
```

The p can be even fractional or complex in last examples.

Example 3:

Let us compute the $\sum_{p=0}^{7} \frac{1}{p-3}$=0.25 subject to $p \neq 3$.

The singularity at p=3 makes the computing undefined because $\frac{1}{0}$ is infinity and machine can not handle the infinity. What is the solution? We generate the p vector as usual but exclude the p=3 from the vector:

```
>>p=0:7; ↵      ← p⇔ p , p is user-chosen, holds values as a row matrix
```

For exclusion, we determine the integer position index of p=3 by the find function (appendix C.7) as follows:

```
>>r=find(p==3) ↵              ← r is user-chosen variable

r =
      4
```

That is the 4th element in the p vector is p=3 which is stored in r. We form a vector from two vectors, the first of which is from 1 to (r-1)th elements of the p and second of which is from (r+1)th to last elements of the p. The two selections are conducted by p(1:r-1) and p(r+1:end) respectively and combined (appendix C.3) as follows:

```
>>p=[p(1:r-1) p(r+1:end)] ↵

p =
      0   1   2   4   5   6   7
```

As you see, the 3 is not present in the last p. Like the previous example we call the function as:

```
>>sum(1./(p-3)) ↵

ans =
```

```
0.2500
```

◆ Differential operator

Differential operator is of paramount importance in FD related computing. The function **diff** finds the differential of integer $f[p]$ or sampled $f(x)$ with the syntax **diff**($f[p]$ or $f(x)$ as a row or column matrix). Symbolically the Δ is tantamount to **diff**. How does it work? It provides successive difference of two samples but latter minus former. The return sample number by the **diff** is total sample number minus 1. There can be three possible cases:

Just differential of $f[p]$ or $f(x)$ samples:

Suppose we have sampled $f(x)$=[2.3 9.2 0 −3.3 −3.5]. The $\Delta f(x)$ should be [6.9 −9.2 −3.3 −0.2] which we implement as follows:

>>f=[2.3 9.2 0 -3.3 -3.5]; ↵ ← f⇔sampled $f(x)$, f is user-chosen
>>D=diff(f) ↵ ← D⇔ $\Delta f(x)$, D is user-chosen

```
D =
      6.9000   -9.2000   -3.3000   -0.2000
```

Say the $f(x)$ starts at p=0, then $\Delta f(x)$ index should be at 0, 1, 2, and 3 respectively.

Total differential for uniform Δx :

One might ask what about the discrete counterpart of $\frac{df(x)}{dx}$ symbolically which we write as $\frac{\Delta f(x)}{\Delta x}$? Since for uniform sampling the Δx is fixed, we just divide each element of $\Delta f(x)$ by the Δx.

Take the example 5 of section 2.2 from which x and $f(x)$ samples are available in **x** and **f** respectively. The 1st order discrete derivative of figure 2.1(c) shown data is the following:

>>D=diff(f)/0.2 ↵ ← D⇔$\frac{\Delta f(x)}{\Delta x}$, D is user-chosen

```
D =
      36.5000    20.0000    35.0000    20.0000
```

Each element in the last return must be in mm/msec unit.

Total differential for nonuniform Δx :

Under this circumstance we also need the x samples supposedly with nonuniform Δx say we have following sampled tabular data:

x (sec)	−2.1	−1.55	−0.9	−0.2	0	0.7	0.87	1.15	2
$f(x)$ (mm)	2	1.75	2	2.75	4	5.75	8	10.75	14

After entering the samples, we execute the computing as follows:

>>x=[-2.1 -1.55 -0.9 -0.2 0 0.7 0.87 1.15 2]; ↵ ←x⇔ x , x user-chosen

>>f=[2 1.75 2 2.75 4 5.75 8 10.75 14]; ↵ ← f⇔ $f(x)$, f is user-chosen

>>D=diff(f)./diff(x) ↵ ← D⇔ $\frac{\Delta f(x)}{\Delta x}$, D is user-chosen

```
D =
  -0.4545  0.3846  1.0714  6.2500  2.5000  13.2353  9.8214  3.8235
```

Above D holds the numerical derivative as a row matrix. The first element –0.4545 in above numerical differential we get from $\frac{1.75-2}{-1.55-(-2.1)}$, so as the others. The operator ./ in diff(f)./diff(x) is used to have element by element division.

♦ Integral operator

There is no hard and fast integral operator for FD because integration is valid for continuous functions. Earlier mentioned **sum** implements the $\int$..... Say we have to compute $\int_{x1}^{x2} f(x)dx$ by using the finite difference technique. Obviously the x interval is $x_1 \le x \le x_2$. User has to decide resolution Δx or number of samples N over the interval. Once known, the FD computing for the integration is $\Delta x \sum_m f(m\Delta x)$. First generate all x samples as a row or column vector, then use the scalar code (appendix B) to get $f(m\Delta x)$ values, and next apply the command **sum**. Let us see the following examples in this regard.

Example 1:

It is given that $\int_{x=-1}^{x=5} (-4x^2+8x-9)dx = -126$. Implement the integration by the FD method with 301 samples.

Clearly we have N=301, $x_1=-1$, and x_2=5 so $\Delta x = \frac{x_2 - x_1}{N-1}$ and execute the following:

>>N=301; ↵ ← N⇔ N , N is user-chosen

>>dx=(5-(-1))/(N-1); ↵ ← dx⇔ Δx , dx is user-chosen

>>x=-1:dx:5; ↵ ← x holds x samples as a row matrix, x user-chosen

>>f=-4*x.^2+8*x-9; ↵ ← f holds $f(m\Delta x)$ or $f(x)$ samples as a row matrix, f is user-chosen

>>dx*sum(f) ↵ ← Exercising $\Delta x \sum_m f(m\Delta x)$

```
ans =
        -126.9016
```

Example 2:

Think about $4\int_{x=-1}^{x=5} dx = 24$, how is it different from the example 1? No definitive x related expression is there in the integrand. If we choose 301 samples over $-1 \le x \le 5$, the value of each sample is constant or 4. We first generate (appendix C.8) necessary number of ones and then multiply by 4 to get the integrand samples, following is the complete execution:

```
>>N=301; ↵                 ← N⇔N
>>dx=(5-(-1))/(N-1); ↵     ← dx⇔Δx
>>x=-1:dx:5; ↵             ← x holds x samples as a row matrix
>>f=4*ones(1,N); ↵         ← f holds f(x) samples as a row matrix
>>dx*sum(f) ↵              ← Exercising Δx Σ_m f(mΔx)

ans =
        24.0800
```

Example 3:

When you have sample data like example 5 (make f data available) of section 2.2, the integration by FD method is the following:

```
>>0.2* sum(f) ↵

ans =
        8.5400             ← The return must be in mm-msec unit
```

Discrepancy and exception:

In example 2 the correct result is 24 but we found 24.08. Discrepancy is always there while using FD. How much relative error is associated? The answer is (24.08-24)/24×100=0.33% – extremely low indeed.

Expression related to singularities can be simulated to provide certain result. For example $\int_{x=2}^{x=5} \frac{1}{x-2} dx$ can not be perfectly computed by using FD because at $x=2$ the integrand is infinity. Nevertheless numeric sense objectivity is achieved by replacing the singular points on user-defined number. Instead of 0 we may set small quantity say 10^{-6}. By choosing 301 samples generate the x samples like we did for the other examples:

```
>>N=301; ↵                 ← N⇔N
>>dx=(5-2)/(N-1); ↵        ← dx⇔Δx
>>x=2:dx:5; ↵              ← x holds x samples as a row matrix
```

The singular point $x=2$ occupies the first element of x i.e. x(1). Assigning $2+10^{-6}$ to the first sample we get the modified samples as:

```
>>x(1)=2+1e-6; ↵              ← 1e-6⇔10^-6 , appendix B
>>f=1./(x-2); ↵               ← f holds f(x) samples as a row matrix

>>dx*sum(f) ↵                 ← Exercising Δx Σ_m f(mΔx)

ans =
        1.0006e+004
```

Above return indicates the FD computing result as 1.0006×10^4.

2.4 Theoretical numerical differences

The definition presented in section 2.3 is solely based on MATLAB built-in functions. Some analytical or theoretical computing needs the difference definition as provided in [2]. From sections 2.1 and 2.2, samples of x and $f(x)$ have the integer index coordinates m and p respectively let us commonly call those k and consider three consecutive samples as follows:

samples of x $\rightarrow$ $\cdots\ x[k-1] \quad x[k] \quad x[k+1]\ \cdots$

samples of $f(x)\rightarrow$ $\cdots\ f[k-1] \quad f[k] \quad f[k+1]\ \cdots$

Below tabular data we are going to apply for various differences:

x sample	-2	-1.5	-1	-0.5	0	0.5	1	1.5	2
$f(x)$ sample	2	1.75	2	2.75	4	5.75	8	10.75	14
FD index k	0	1	2	3	4	5	6	7	8

Enter the tabular data by:

```
>>x=-2:0.5:2; ↵
>>f=[2 1.75 2 2.75 4 5.75 8 10.75 14]; ↵
```

◆ Divided difference of the first order

Divided difference $\frac{\Delta f}{\Delta x}$ of the first order at the k-th sample is defined as $\frac{f[k+1]-f[k]}{x[k+1]-x[k]}$ so we get the following tabular differences on above data.

FD index k	0	1	2	3	4	5	6	7	8
$\frac{\Delta f}{\Delta x}$	-0.5	0.5	1.5	2.5	3.5	4.5	5.5	6.5	?

Its implementation is as follows:

```
>>D=diff(f)./diff(x) ↵

D =
   -0.5000   0.5000   1.5000   2.5000   3.5000   4.5000   5.5000   6.5000
```

Last D holds the $\frac{\Delta f}{\Delta x}$ where the D is a user-chosen variable. The difference at the last sample becomes undefined (?). If the reader demands equal sample number from the difference, one option is increase the data by one sample and by 0 and apply the **diff** as follows:

```
>>x1=-2:0.5:2.5; f1=[f 0]; ↵  ← The x1 and f1 are user-chosen, appendix C.3 for
                                  data accumulation
>>D=diff(f1)./diff(x1) ↵

D =
  -0.5000   0.5000   1.5000   2.5000   3.5000   4.5000   5.5000   6.5000 -28.0000
```

The 0 insertion occurs only in $f(x)$ samples. Notably the x samples are increased by appending one Δx i.e. the last bound becomes 2.5 instead of 2. The mark ? in the last table should be now –28, the last value in D.

◆ Forward difference of the first order

Forward difference $\Delta f(x)$ of the first order at the k-th sample is defined as $f[k+1]-f[k]$, following tabular differences are for ongoing data.

FD index k	0	1	2	3	4	5	6	7	8
$\Delta f(x)$	-0.25	0.25	0.75	1.25	1.75	2.25	2.75	3.25	?

Just apply the **diff** as follows:

```
>>D=diff(f) ↵

D =
  -0.2500   0.2500   0.7500   1.2500   1.7500   2.2500   2.7500   3.2500
```

Like the divided difference undefined situation appears at the 8th sample. You can make equal sample number by appending 0 to $f(x)$ samples:

```
>>f1=[f 0]; ↵               ← f1 is user-chosen
>>D=diff(f1) ↵

D =
  -0.2500   0.2500   0.7500   1.2500   1.7500   2.2500   2.7500   3.2500 -14.0000
```

Hence the 8th sample in last table which is undefined now should be –14.

◆ Backward difference of the first order

Backward difference $\Delta f(x)$ of the first order at the k-th sample is defined as $f[k]-f[k-1]$ so we get the following table for earlier data:

Index k	0	1	2	3	4	5	6	7	8
$\Delta f(x)$	?	-0.25	0.25	0.75	1.25	1.75	2.25	2.75	3.25

Its execution is the following:

```
>>D=diff(f) ↵

D =
   -0.2500   0.2500   0.7500   1.2500   1.7500   2.2500   2.7500   3.2500
```

The first sample here is undefined therefore the 0 appending in case equal sample number is sought occurs before:

```
>>f1=[0 f]; ↵
>>D=diff(f1) ↵

D =
   2.0000  -0.2500   0.2500   0.7500   1.2500   1.7500   2.2500   2.7500   3.2500
```

The first sample in the last table should be 2.

❖ Central difference of the first order

Central difference $\Delta f(x)$ of the first order at the k-th sample is defined as $f[k+1/2]-f[k-1/2]$ where $f[k+1/2]$ and $f[k-1/2]$ are the average values of $f[k]$ and $f[k+1]$ and $f[k]$ and $f[k-1]$ respectively. Suppose k is 2 for the ongoing data so $f[k+1/2]$ and $f[k-1/2]$ are (2.75+2)/2 and (2+1.75)/2 respectively hence $\Delta f(x)$=(2+2.75)/2–(2+1.75)/2=0.5. Similar computing provides the following tabular data:

FD index k	0	1	2	3	4	5	6	7	8
$\Delta f(x)$	?	0	0.5	1	1.5	2	2.5	3	?

Every difference needs 1 sample after and 1 sample before so two undefined differences evolve one at the beginning and one at the end, which you find in above table too. This difference requires slight programming tactic. Using a for loop (appendix C.4) and data accumulation technique we first compute the mean of two consecutive samples for the whole **f** as follows:

```
>>f2=[ ]; ↵
>>for k=1:length(f)-1, f2=[f2 (f(k)+f(k+1))/2]; end ↵
```

The **f2** is a user-chosen variable which holds the mean values as a row matrix. The **diff** is exercised on **f2** to get the central difference:

```
>>D=diff(f2) ↵

ans =
          0   0.5000   1.0000   1.5000   2.0000   2.5000   3.0000
```

The return sample number is 2 less than the sample number of **f**. In order to make equal sample number 0 padding before and after we carry out as follows:

```
>>f1=[0 f 0]; ↵
```

Identical for loop operation on **f1** is then performed:

```
>>f2=[ ]; ↵
>>for k=1:length(f1)-1, f2=[f2 (f1(k)+f1(k+1))/2]; end ↵
```

```
>>D=diff(f2) ↵

ans =

   0.8750  0   0.5000   1.0000   1.5000   2.0000   2.5000   3.0000  -5.3750
```

The ? marks in the last table for k =0 and k =8 should be filled with 0.875 and −5.375 respectively.

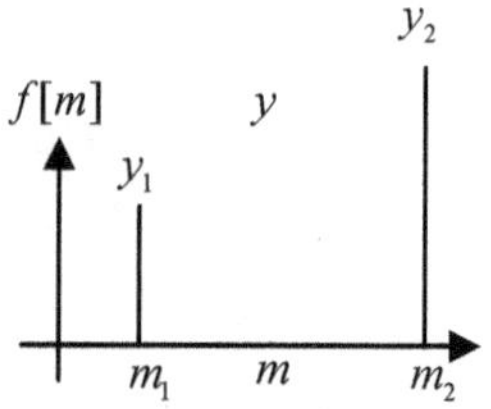

Figure 2.2(a) Two samples of a function

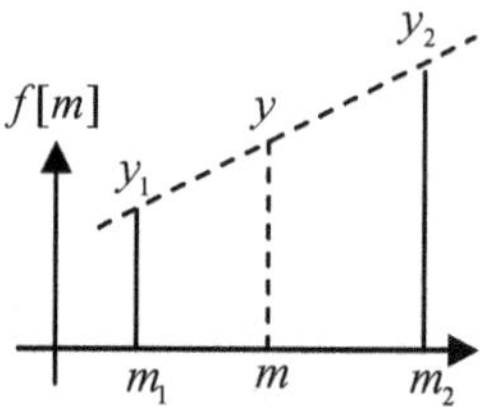

Figure 2.2(b) Linear interpolation of a discrete function from two sample values

2.5 Interpolation on one dimensional FD data

It goes without saying that FD computing is all about working on x and $f(x)$ samples subject to some resolution. Given a resolution, what are the ways to obtain intermediate samples of $f(x)$? That is why interpolation has to be drawn in. Figure 2.2(a) shows two samples of $f(x)$. If the $f[m]$ is required between m_1 and m_2 at some m, interpolation is applied. There are many methods to determine the interpolated values, out of which two namely nearest neighborhood and linear are addressed along with clue of others.

♦ Nearest neighborhood interpolation

In this scheme we have (m_1, y_1) and (m_2, y_2) and look for y over $m_1 \le m \le m_2$. If $m < \frac{m_1 + m_2}{2}$, $y = y_1$ else $y = y_2$. For example we have (1,5) and (2,7). What is y at m=1.1? Clearly the given coordinates are y_1=5, y_2=7, m_1=1, and m_2=2. The $\frac{m_1 + m_2}{2}$ is (1+2)/2 or 1.5 so y=5.

♦ Linear interpolation

Between the two known samples of figure 2.2(a), any sample over $m_1 \le m \le m_2$ is given by $y = \frac{y_2 - y_1}{m_2 - m_1}(m - m_1) + y_1$ and whose linear variation is seen in figure 2.2(b). Nearest neighborhood cited interpolated y should be $\frac{7-5}{2-1}(1.1-1)+5$ or 5.2 when linear interpolation is considered.

♦ MATLAB built-in function

The function interp1 conducts interpolations with syntax interp1(given m values as a row matrix, given $f[m]$ values as a row matrix, m as a row matrix for the value wanted at). Interpolation methods that are available in MATLAB are the nearest neighborhood, piecewise cubic spline, and shape preserving piecewise cubic whose MATLAB indicatory reserve words are nearest, spline, and cubic respectively. The reserve word is put as the fourth input argument to the interp1 but under a quote. Default method of the interp1 is the linear interpolation.

♦ Interpolation at a single point

As an example we have (m_1, y_1)=(4,3.7) and (m_2, y_2)=(5,6.3) and between the two samples some m=4.3 has the linearly interpolated $y=\frac{6.3-3.7}{5-4}(4.3-4)+3.7$=4.48. We wish to implement the interpolation.

Execute the following for the interpolation:

```
>>x=[4 5]; ↵        ← Given m1 and m2 are assigned to x as a row matrix, where x is user-chosen
>>y=[3.7 6.3]; ↵    ← Given y1 and y2 are assigned to y as a row matrix, where y is user-chosen
>>interp1(x,y,4.3) ↵    ← Calling the function

ans =
        4.4800          ← Value of the y we are looking for
```

For the same two points if we seek the nearest neighborhood interpolated value, the command would be interp1(x,y,4.3,'nearest') which results 3.7.

♦ Interpolation at multiple points

The function also keeps provision for multiple returns. Suppose we have four samples of $f(x)$ given as (4,3.7), (5,6.3), (6,–2), and (7,–7). The linearly interpolated values of the $f(x)$ at 4.3, 5.2, and 6.9 are 4.48, 4.64, and –6.5 respectively which we implement as follows:

```
>>x=[4 5 6 7]; ↵         ← Given horizontal points are assigned to x as a row matrix, where x is user-chosen
>>y=[3.7 6.3 -2 -7]; ↵ ← Given vertical points are assigned to y as a row matrix, where y is user-chosen
>>interp1(x,y,[4.3 5.2 6.9]) ↵        ← Points of interest are as a row matrix

ans =
        4.4800    4.6400   -6.5000     ← The return is also as a row matrix
```

You could have executed I=interp1(x,y,[4.3 5.2 6.9]); to hold the values to I where the I is a user-chosen variable. Should the reader need each interpolated value, the command I(1), I(2), or I(3) is exercised respectively. In case the nearest neighborhood method is sought, the command would be I=interp1(x,y,[4.3 5.2 6.9],'nearest');.

♦ Interpolation over a range of points

We may seek the interpolated values over a range of x values. For example starting from (4,3.7) and (5,6.3) with a step size 0.1 over the interval $4.1 \le m \le 4.6$, the linearly interpolated values are 3.96, 4.22, 4.48, 4.74, 5, and 5.26 for 4.1, 4.2, 4.3, 4.4, 4.5, and 4.6 respectively which we wish to implement.

This implementation is similar to earlier ones with the exception that the third input argument of interp1 is a range data which we feed by writing 4.1:0.1:4.6 and execute as follows:

```
>>x=[4 5]; ↵          ← Given m1 and m2 are assigned to x as a row matrix, where x
                                  is user-chosen
>>y=[3.7 6.3]; ↵      ← Given y1 and y2 are assigned to y as a row matrix, where y
                                  is user-chosen
>>yn=interp1(x,y,4.1:0.1:4.6) ↵  ← Calling the function with the 3rd input as a
                                                      range data
yn =
          3.9600    4.2200    4.4800    4.7400    5.0000    5.2600
```

In above execution the yn is a user-chosen variable which holds the return interpolated values as a row matrix respectively.

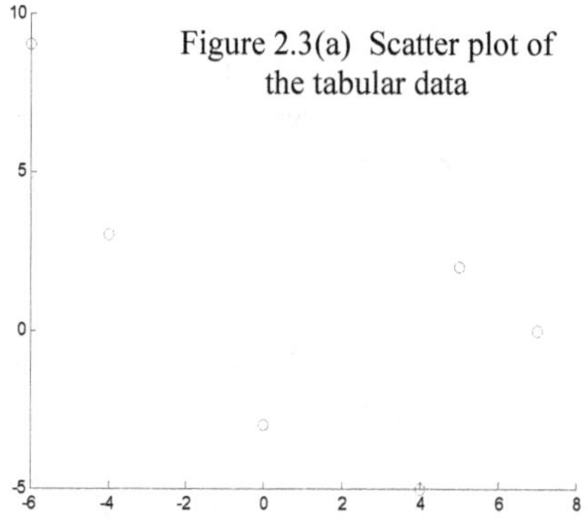

Figure 2.3(a) Scatter plot of the tabular data

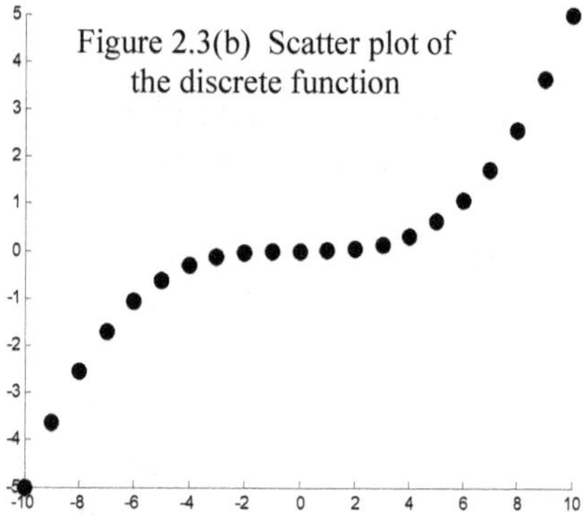

Figure 2.3(b) Scatter plot of the discrete function

2.6 Graphing one dimensional FD data

After making the FD or its derived data available, we may wish to see the data as a plot. Different kinds of graphs emerge depending on user-requirements, some of which are illustrated in the following.

◆ Scatter data plot using small circles

Instead of a continuous line, it is possible to have the graph in terms of bold dots or round circles like figure 2.3(a). The function **scatter** returns this sort of graph for which the common syntax is **scatter(** m data as a row matrix, $f[m]$ data as a row matrix, size of the circle, color of the circle). The function also accepts the first two input arguments. The size of the circle is any user-given integer number. The larger is the number, the bigger is the size for example 75, 100, etc.

Tabular data						
m	-6	-4	0	4	5	7
$f[m]$	9	3	-3	-5	2	0

Let us graph above tabular data as the scatter plot. The command we need is as follows:

```
>>m=[-6 -4 0 4 5 7]; ↵        ← Given m s are assigned to m, m is user-chosen
>>f=[9 3 -3 -5 2 0]; ↵        ← Given f[m] s are assigned to f, f is user-chosen
>>scatter(m,f) ↵
```

Upon execution of the command, we see the figure 2.3(a) in which the vertical and horizontal axes correspond to the $f[m]$ and m data respectively. The color of the circle is blue by default but any three element row matrix sets the user-defined color. The three element row matrix refers to red, green, and blue components respectively each one within 0 and 1. Black color means all zero, white means all 1, red means other two components zero, and so on.

The circle displayed in figure 2.3(a) is all empty but one fills the circle by using the reserve word **filled** under quote and included as another input argument to the **scatter**. Let us say we intend to scatter graph with circle size 100 and the circles should be filled with black color. The necessary command is **scatter(m,f,100,[0 0 0],'filled')**, graph is not shown for the space reason.

As another example the discrete function $f[m]=\frac{m^3}{200}$ over $-10 \le m \le 10$ is to be plotted with black circles of size 100 where m is integer. We form a row matrix **m** to generate the interval with start value −10, increment 1, and end value 10 by writing **m=-10:10;**. The scalar code of appendix B computes the $f[m]$ values and assigns those to workspace **f**. Following is the complete code which brings about the figure 2.3(b):

```
>>m=-10:10; f=m.^3/200; ↵
>>scatter(m,f,100,[0 0 0],'filled') ↵
```

♦ Plotting discrete data or function by vertical lines

There is another option by which we graph any discrete data using vertical lines proportionate to functional values. A discrete function may exist in two forms – data and expression based. The MATLAB function that graphs a discrete function or data is **stem** which has a syntax **stem(** m data as a row matrix, $f[m]$ data as a row matrix).

If we have some expression, first the sample values of the discrete function need to be calculated through the scalar code then the graphing is performed.

Let us plot the discrete function $f[m]=2^{-m}\cos m$ over the integer interval $-2 \le m \le 5$. Following commands are the implementation which results the figure 2.3(c):

```
>>m=-2:5; ↵
>>f=2.^(-m).*cos(m); ↵
>>stem(m,f) ↵
```

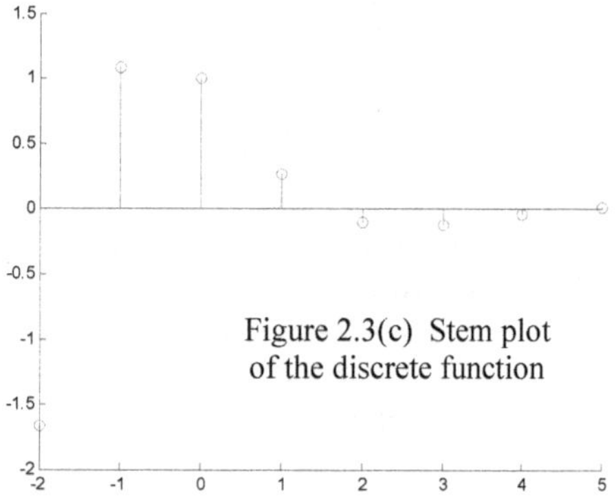

Figure 2.3(c) Stem plot of the discrete function

The user-chosen workspace m and f hold the eight integers from −2 to 5 and sample values of $f[m]$ both as a row matrix respectively. In figure 2.3(c) the horizontal and vertical axes refer to m and $f[m]$ data respectively.

By default the vertical line color of stem plot is blue. User-defined color of the vertical lines is obtainable by adding one more input argument to the **stem** mentioning the color type but under quote (r for red, g for green, b for blue, c for cyan, m for magenta, y for yellow, k for black, and w for white). If we wish to set the vertical line color as green for the graph of the figure 2.3(c), the command **stem(m,f,'g')** is exercised. The vertical line head circles can be filled by using the command **stem(m,f,'g','filled')** where **filled** is a reserve word placed under quote.

♦ Bar graph from some m - $f[m]$ data

Say we have year data $m=$ [1986 1987 1988 1989] (four consecutive years) and yield data $f[m]$=[6.6 4.5 5 7] (percentage yield from some stock) which we intend to use for plotting a bar graph.

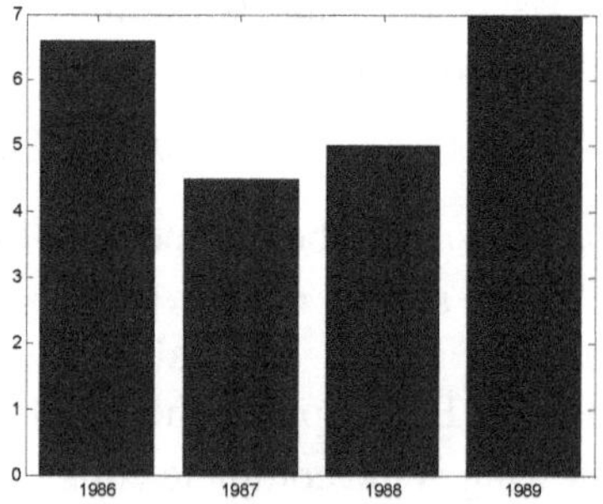

Figure 2.3(d) Bar graph of the year yield data

The command **bar** helps us graph the data with syntax **bar(** m data as a row matrix, $f[m]$ data as a row matrix). Following is the implementation:

```
>>m=[1986 1987 1988 1989]; ↵
>>f=[6.6 4.5 5 7]; ↵
>>bar(m,f) ↵
```

The last commands result the figure 2.3(d) in which the vertical and horizontal axes correspond to the $f[m]$ and m data respectively. The **m** and **f** are user-given variables which hold the m and $f[m]$ data both as a row matrix respectively. Note that every bar is placed symmetrically at its m index.

With the same syntax, the function **bar3** displays a three dimensional bar which we see in figure 2.3(e).

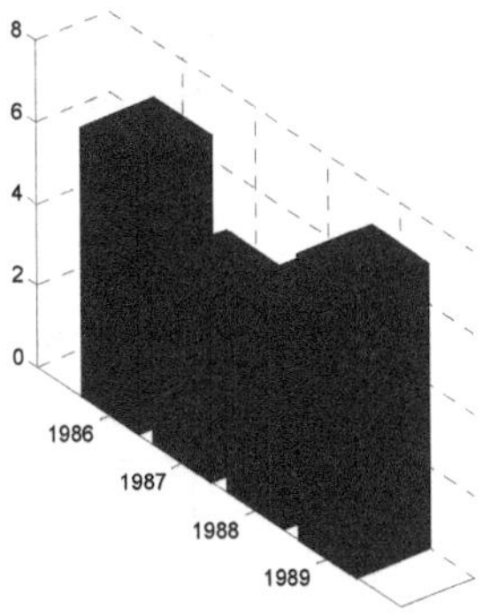

Figure 2.3(e) Three dimensional bar graph of the year yield data

♦ Stair case plot

The bars of the figure 2.3(d) can be placed consecutively and inbetween lines are removed which result the stair case plot like figure 2.3(f). With the syntax **stairs(**m data as a row matrix, $f[m]$ data as a row matrix) we get stair case type graphs.

Figure 2.3(b) shown functional scatter plot when needs to be displayed as a staircase requires the following codes with ongoing symbology:

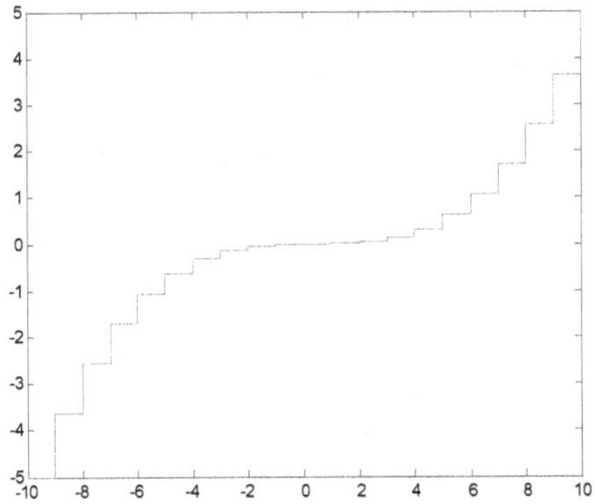

Figure 2.3(f) Stair case plot

```
>>m=-10:10; f=m.^3/200; ↵
>>stairs(m,f) ↵
```

Figure 2.3(f) is the outcome from above command in which the horizontal and vertical axes correspond to m and $f[m]$ data respectively.

2.7 Polynomial fitting of finite difference data

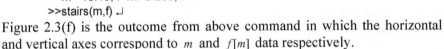

Starting from a given FD data we may seek for the best fit polynomial on the FD data. Suppose we have the samples of $f(x)$ at some x coordinates. Assume that these samples fit a n degree polynomial $\hat{f}(x) = c_n x^n + c_{n-1} x^{n-1} + \cdots + c_1 x + c_0$ where n is user-chosen. There are different problems related to the polynomial coefficients such that $|f(x) - \hat{f}(x)|^2$ is minimum. Some problems are demonstrated in the following. Optimization theory says that the user-chosen polynomial degree must be less than or equal to the number of data points minus 1 when unique solution is sought. If the degree requirement is not fulfilled, multiple solutions evolve.

♦ Example 1

Consider the following tabular data:

m	-2	-1	0	1	2	3
$f[m]$	9	3	-3	-5	2	0

Assuming a fourth degree polynomial, one finds the best fit polynomial in least square sense as $\hat{f}[m] = -0.4583m^4 + 0.6389m^3 + 4.125m^2 - 4.4008m - 3.9524$ which we intend to obtain.

The step we need is graph the given data as a continuous variation by using the function **plot** and apply the basic fitting tool of figure window to determine the best fit polynomial.

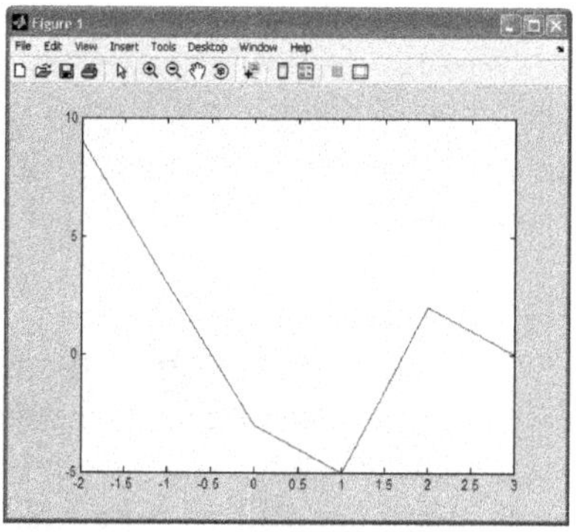

Figure 2.4(a) Plotting the tabular data – in continuous sense

Let us enter the tabular data as follows:

```
>>m=-2:3; ↵              ← Given m s are assigned to m, m is user-chosen
>>f=[9 3 -3 -5 2 0]; ↵   ← Given f[m] s are assigned to f, f is user-chosen
```

Call the function **plot** to see the response like figure 2.4(a):

```
>>plot(m,f) ↵
```

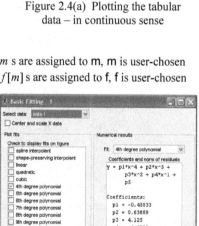

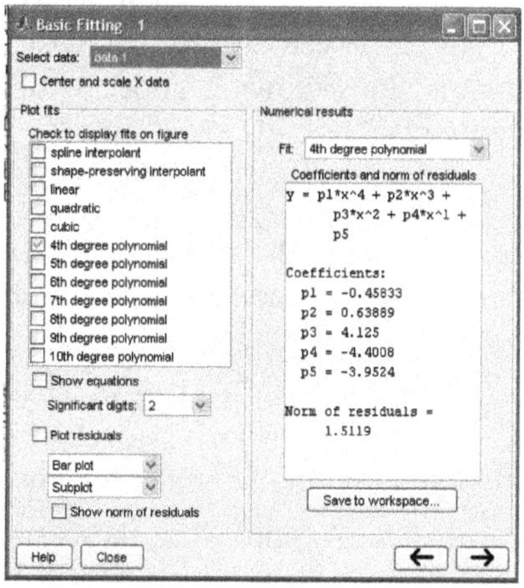

Figure 2.4(b) Prompt window of the Basic Fitting Tool

In figure 2.4(a) there is a **Menu** by name **Tools** in the menu bar of the window. If you click the **Tools**, you find an option **Basic Fitting** in dropdown menu. Click the option and the result is the left half of figure 2.4(b). Check the **4th degree polynomial** under the **Plot fits** of the prompt window. The figure window automatically updates. In the lower right portion of the prompt window, you find a pushbutton →. Click that and the right half of figure 2.4(b) appears before you. You find details of the polynomial in the right half of the figure. Symbol equivalence is the following: y⇔$\hat{f}[m]$, x⇔m, p1*x^4⇔$-0.4583m^4$, and so on. Note that the default variables are x and y instead of m and $\hat{f}[m]$ respectively. Reading off similarly from the screen we get the best fit polynomial as

$$\hat{f}[m] = -0.4583m^4 + 0.6389m^3 + 4.125m^2 - 4.4008m - 3.9524 .$$

♦ Example 2

In example 1 we wish to get control on the polynomial coefficients.

In figure 2.4(b) we find a button **Save to workspace** at the lower half window. Click the button and click OK in the Save prompt window. Variables are saved as a structure array fit by default name. You may choose another variable name in the Save prompt window. Call the default variable fit at the command prompt:

```
>>fit ↵

fit =
    type: 'polynomial degree 4'
   coeff: [-0.4583 0.6389 4.1250 -4.4008 -3.9524]
```

In order to extract the polynomial coefficients which are stored in coeff from above return, we may use fit.coeff and assign to some variable c as follows:

```
>>c=fit.coeff ↵

c =
           -0.4583    0.6389    4.1250   -4.4008   -3.9524
```

Then the c(1), c(2), etc give you control on the polynomial coefficients respectively.

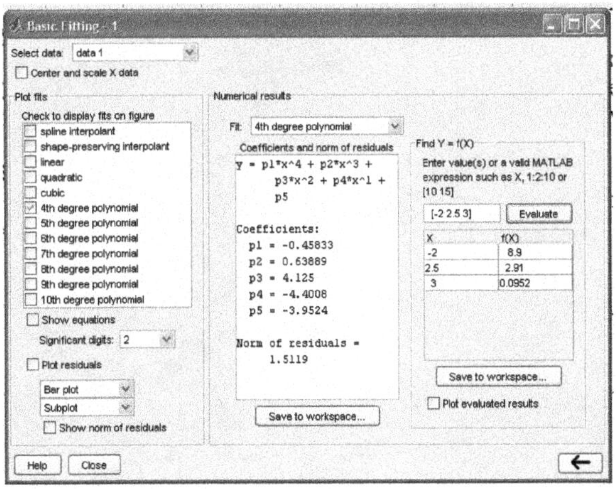

Figure 2.4(c) Extension of the Basic Fitting Tools

♦ Example 3

What if we need to plot both the original data and the polynomially approximated one?

When we checked the **4th degree polynomial** cited box in figure 2.4(b), the two data plots appear automatically. Even if you selected another degree e.g. 3rd, you would see the three curves plotted in the same window.

♦ Example 4

Suppose the $\hat{f}[m]$ functional values at some m for example at $m =$ −2, 2.5, and 3 are to be calculated. Employing the example 1 mentioned best fit polynomial we should get $\hat{f}[m]$=8.9, 2.91, and 0.0952 respectively.

In the lower right portion of prompt window in figure 2.4(b), you again find a pushbutton →. Click that one more time and be prompted with the extended window of figure 2.4(c). In the rightmost part of the figure you see the heading Find Y = f (X). The slot left to the Evaluate button initially is empty and we enter the m points as a row matrix by writing a three element row matrix [-2 2.5 3] and then click Evaluate. Below the button Evaluate you find the values calculated under the heading f(X) i.e. $\hat{f}[m]$. Corresponding X or m values are also seen in the window.

That brings an end to this chapter.

Exercises

1. A one variable function is given as $f(x) = -2.3x^3 + 3x - 9$ over $-1 \le x \le 4$. Determine the Δx if 6 sample points are chosen. What are the x sample values? What are the m values for the FD computing? What are the $f(x)$ sample values at those m s? Determine the f_1 and f_2 for the sampled $f(x)$, functional resolution Δf, and FD integer counterpart $f[p]$. Compute the FD reconstructed $\hat{f}(x)$ and the mean square error.
2. In question (1) now consider 11 sample points.
3. Write MATLAB codes to compute the following by using FD method: (a) $\sum_{p=-2}^{4}(2p^2 - p)$ (b) $\sum p^2 f^2[p]$ where p=[0 1 4 9] and $f[p]$=[5 −20 2 8] (c) $\sum_{p=-10}^{10} \frac{\pi}{\sqrt{|p-2|}}$, $p \ne 2$ (d) $\sum_{p=0}^{50} \frac{1+\ln|1+p|}{p^2+1}$ (e) $\sum_{m=-5}^{15} f(m\Delta x)$ over $-1 \le x \le 1$ where $f(x) = -3x^3 - 6x + 12$.
4. Compute each of the following integrations by using FD method: (a) $\int_{x=-3}^{x=2}(5x^2 - 6x + 5)dx$ choosing 401 samples (b) $\int_{x=-\pi}^{x=\pi}(1+\cos^2 x)dx$ choosing 301 samples (c) $\int_{x=0}^{x=0.5}(e^{-3x} + 2)dx$ choosing 401 samples (d) $-12\int_{x=-5}^{x=7} dx$ and relative error choosing 501 samples (e) $\int_{x=-5}^{x=5} \frac{1}{x+5}dx$ choose small quantity as 10^{-6} for singular point replacement and 401 samples.

x sample	−1	−0.5	0	0.5	1	1.5	2	2.5	3
$f(x)$ sample	12.1	15	17	19.7	20	23	27	28	30
FD index k	−2	−1	0	1	2	3	4	5	6

5. Based on above tabular data compute the following theoretical finite differences: (a) divided difference of the first order (b) forward difference of the first order (c) backward difference of the first order (d) central difference of the first order. Assume 0 padding wherever necessary.
6. Based on question (5) mentioned table determine the following subject to MATLAB defined difference: (a) just differential $\Delta f(x)$ (b) total differential $\frac{\Delta f(x)}{\Delta x}$ (c) total differential $\frac{\Delta f(x)}{\Delta x}$ for below tabular data.

x sample	−1.1	−0.55	0.1	0.35	1	1.25	2.1	2.5	3.8
$f(x)$ sample	12.1	17	19	19.7	21	23.2	27.2	28.2	30.2

7. Obtain the excel file **Data2.xls** through the email link of page ii and place the file in your working path of MATLAB. Make sure the data in the file

looks like figure E.2(a). Perform question (1) quoted FD computing for samples on the excel file data.

8. Generate random samples each of uniform distribution within –7 mm and 15 mm over $0 \le x \le 8m\sec$ with $\Delta x = 0.2m\sec$. Perform question (1) quoted FD computing on the random data.

9. Graph the question (1) mentioned FD data i.e. $f(x)$ versus x samples as (a) scatter round circle plot (b) vertical line plot (c) two dimensional bar plot (d) stair case plot (e) 3D bar plot.

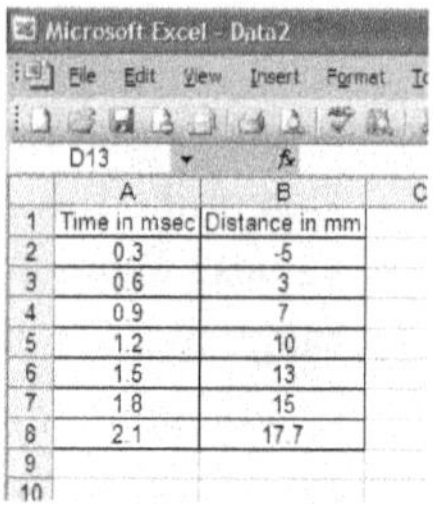

	A	B
1	Time in msec	Distance in mm
2	0.3	-5
3	0.6	3
4	0.9	7
5	1.2	10
6	1.5	13
7	1.8	15
8	2.1	17.7

Figure E.2(a) Some data in an excel file

10. Consider the data of Excel file in figure E.2(a) (see question 7). Determine the best fit polynomial if following degree is chosen (a) linear variation (b) 3rd order polynomial (c) 4th order polynomial subject to the units given.

11. In question (10) determine the best fit polynomial values at the same time points.

x sample	–1.1	–0.55	0.1	0.35	1	1.25	2.1	2.5	3.8
$f(x)$ sample	5.1	10	12	12.7	14	16.2	20.2	21.2	23.2

12. Following is based on above tabular data: (a) determine $f(x)$ at x =–1 by using the nearest neighborhood interpolation (b) in part (a) apply linear interpolation (c) determine $f(x)$ at x =–1, 0.75, and 3 by using the nearest neighborhood interpolation (d) in part (c) apply linear interpolation (e) determine $f(x)$ by using the nearest neighborhood interpolation with a step size 0.1 over $-1.1 \le x \le 3.8$ (f) in part (e) apply linear interpolation.

Answers:

(1) $\Delta x = 1$, $f_1 = -144.2$, $f_2 = -8.3$, $\Delta f = 27.18$, mse=29.0623

x	−1	0	1	2	3	4
m	−1	0	1	2	3	4
$f(x)$	−9.7	−9	−8.3	−21.4	−62.1	−144.2
$f[p]$	5	5	5	5	3	0
$\hat{f}(x)$	−8.3	−8.3	−8.3	−8.3	−62.66	−144.2

hint: sections 2.1 and 2.2

(2) $\Delta x = 0.5$, $f_1 = -144.2$, $f_2 = -7.7875$, $\Delta f = 13.6412$, mse=6.8144

x	m	$f(x)$	$f[p]$	$\hat{f}(x)$
−1	−2	−9.7	10	−7.7875
−0.5	−1	−10.2125	10	−7.7875
0	0	−9	10	−7.7875
0.5	1	−7.7875	10	−7.7875
1	2	−8.3	10	−7.7875
1.5	3	−12.2625	10	−7.7875
2	4	−21.4	9	−21.4287
2.5	5	−37.4375	8	−35.07
3	6	−62.1	6	−62.3525
3.5	7	−97.1125	3	−103.2762
4	8	−144.2	0	−144.2

(3) (a) `p=-2:4; f=2*p.^2-p; sum(f)`⇒63 (b) `p=[0 1 4 9]; f=[5 -20 2 8]; sum(p.^2.*f.^2)`⇒5648 (c) `p=-10:10; r=find(p==2); p=[p(1:r-1) p(r+1:end)]; f=pi./sqrt(abs(p-2)); sum(f)`⇒31.3613 (d) `p=0:50; f=(1+log(abs(1+p)))./(p.^2+1); sum(f)`⇒3.3302 (e) `m=-5:15; dx=2/(length(m)-1); x=-1:dx:1; f=-3*x.^3-6*x+12; sum(f)`⇒252 hint: section 2.3

(4) (a) 98.8402 (b) 9.4667 (c) 1.2622 (d) −144.288 and 0.2%
(e) 2.5007×10^4 hint: section 2.3

(5) Following tabular data:

(a) divided difference	5.8	4	5.4	0.6	6	8	2	4	-60
(b) forward difference	2.9	2	2.7	0.3	3	4	1	2	-30
(c) backward difference	12.1	2.9	2	2.7	0.3	3	4	1	2
(d) central difference	7.5	2.45	2.35	1.5	1.65	3.5	2.5	1.5	-14
FD index k	-2	-1	0	1	2	3	4	5	6

hint: section 2.4

(6) Following tabular data:

(a) $\Delta f(x)$	2.9	2	2.7	0.3	3	4	1	2
(b) $\dfrac{\Delta f(x)}{\Delta x}$	5.8	4	5.4	0.6	6	8	2	4
(c) $\dfrac{\Delta f(x)}{\Delta x}$	8.9091	3.0769	2.8	2	8.8	4.7059	2.5	1.5385

hint: section 2.3

(7) Δx =0.3 $m$sec, f_1=–5 mm, f_2=17.7 mm, Δf =3.7833 mm, mse=0.3774

x ($m$sec)	0.3	0.6	0.9	1.2	1.5	1.8	2.1
m	1	2	3	4	5	6	7
$f(x)$	–5	3	7	10	13	15	17.7
$f[p]$	0	2	3	4	5	5	6
$\hat{f}(x)$	–5	2.5667	6.35	10.1333	13.9167	13.9167	17.7

hint: sections 2.1 and 2.2

(8) x=0:0.2:8; N=length(x); f=22*rand(1,N)-7; f1=min(f); f2=max(f); df=(f2-f1)/(N-1); fp=round((f-f1)/df); f_hat=f1+fp*df; e=f_hat-f; mse(e)
hint: section 2.2

(9) dx=5/5; x=[-1:dx:4]; f=-2.3*x.^3+3*x-9;
(a) scatter(x,f) (b) stem(x,f) (c) bar(x,f) (d) stairs(x,f) (e) bar3(x,f)
Figures E.2(b), E.2(c), E.2(d), E.2(e), and E.2(f) respectively
hint: section 2.6

Figure E.2(b): Scatter Plot

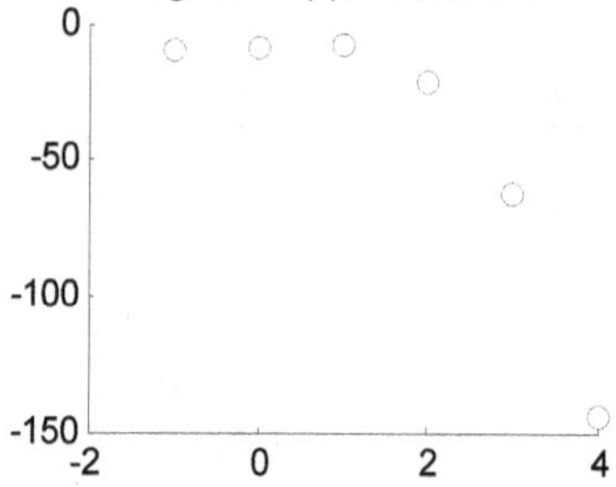

Figure E.2(c): Vertical Line Plot

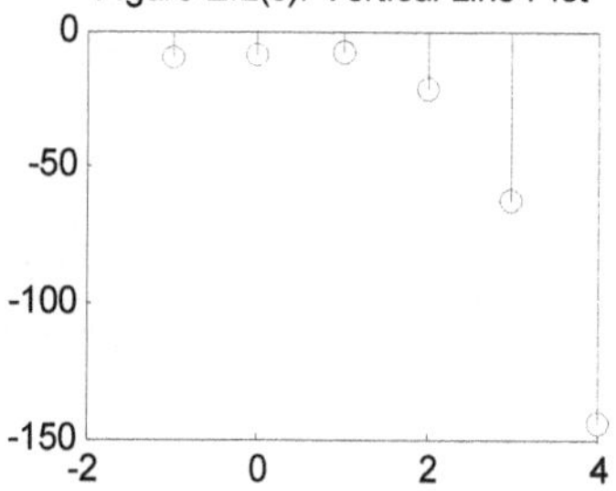

Figure E.2(d): Bar Plot

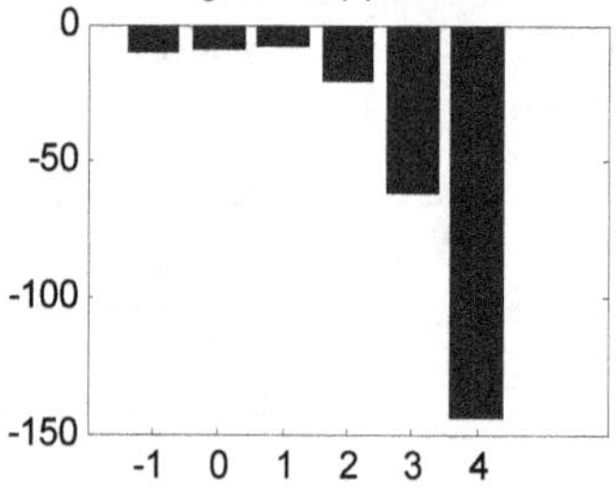

Figure E.2(e): Stair Case Plot

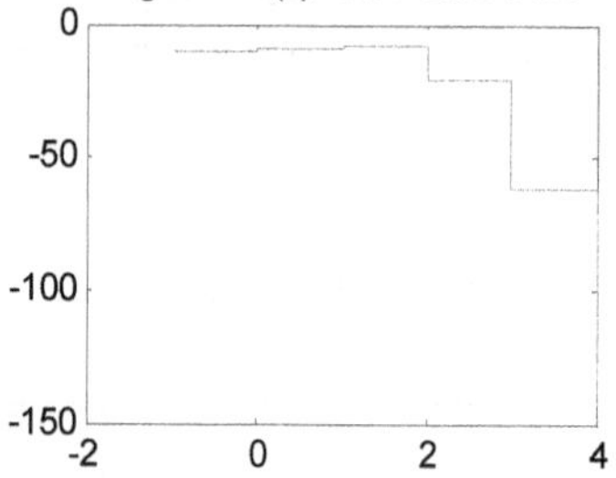

(10) (a) $\hat{f}[t]$=11.6786 t –5.3429

(b) $\hat{f}[t]$=4.8354 t^3 –22.2354 t^2 +41.1085 t –15.2571

(c) $\hat{f}[t]$=–3.6944 t^4 +22.5683 t^3 –50.9722 t^2 +59.0060 t –18.6429

where $\hat{f}[t]$ and t are in mm and msec respectively

Figure E.2(f): 3D Bar Plot

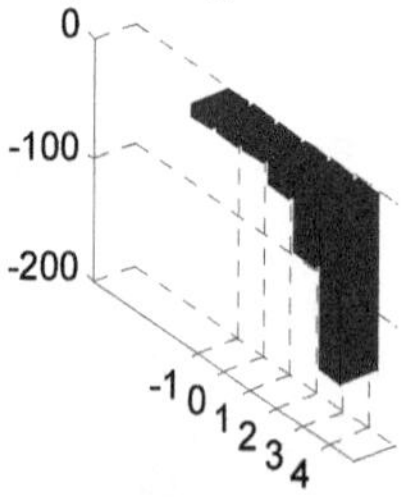

hint: section 2.7

(11) Following tabular data (t in msec and $\hat{f}[t]$ in mm):

t	(a) $\hat{f}[t]$	(b) $\hat{f}[t]$	(c) $\hat{f}[t]$
0.3	−1.8393	−4.7952	−4.9491
0.6	1.6643	2.4476	2.8067
0.9	5.1679	7.2548	7.2035
1.2	8.6714	10.4095	10.1017
1.5	12.1750	12.6952	12.6439
1.8	15.6786	14.8952	15.2543
2.1	19.1821	17.7929	17.6390

hint: section 2.7

(12) (a) 5.1 (b) 5.9909 (c) 5.1, 14, and 21.2 (d) 5.9909, 13.5, and 21.9692
(e) `interp1(x,y,-1.1:0.1:3.8,'nearest')` (f) `interp1(x,y,[-1.1:0.1:3.8])`
where `x` and `y` hold the x and $f(x)$ samples both as a row matrix respectively
hint: section 2.5

Chapter 3

Finite Difference in Two Dimensions

Despite this chapter is the extension of last chapter addressed topics, extra points or terminologies are very much essential to implement two dimensional finite difference (FD) problems. In one dimensional FD, basis vectors are either row or column in most calculations whereas in two dimensional counterpart frequently rectangular grid points are involved which make the computing somewhat complicated. A new understanding needs to be developed for which we highlight the following:

- Mathematical model of two variable expressions
- Links of two variable functions with grid point matrices
- Two dimensional FD analysis on various data availability
- Embeded tools for other mathematical operations on FD data

3.1 Model of two variable expression

Conversion of a one dimensional continuous function to its discrete counterpart is extended for the modeling. All-too-familiar two variable function $f(x,y)$ for example polynomial $x^2 - xy + 3y^2$, sinusoidal $2\sin 3(x+y)$, exponential e^{x+y}, etc are also continuous. The continuity is presently with respect to x, with respect to y, and with respect to $f(x,y)$.

◆ Independent variable discretization i.e. on x and y

Now discretization takes place both in x and in y directions which are the independent or basis variables. Let us say the continuous coordinate corresponding to any $f(x,y)$ is (x,y) where the x or y is not integer and each can assume any real number. For example x can be 1.9999, 2, or 2.0001. The x is written as $x = m\Delta x$ where the Δx is the sample period along x or horizontal direction. Similar writing is also applicable for the y i.e. $y = n\Delta y$ where the Δy is the sample period along y or vertical direction. The x or Δx has the same unit (e.g. meter) but the m does not have unit. Similar explanation is true for y, Δy, and n. The Δx and Δy are also called step size in x and y directions respectively.

Figure 3.1(a) depicts the whole strategy on the discretization. A rectangular area of size $x_0 \times y_0$ has the continuous domain variation over $0 \le x \le x_0$ and $0 \le y \le y_0$. Any point (x, y) in the continuous domain turns to integer coordinate (m, n) in the FD domain. Every bold dot in figure 3.1(a) represents one sample point.

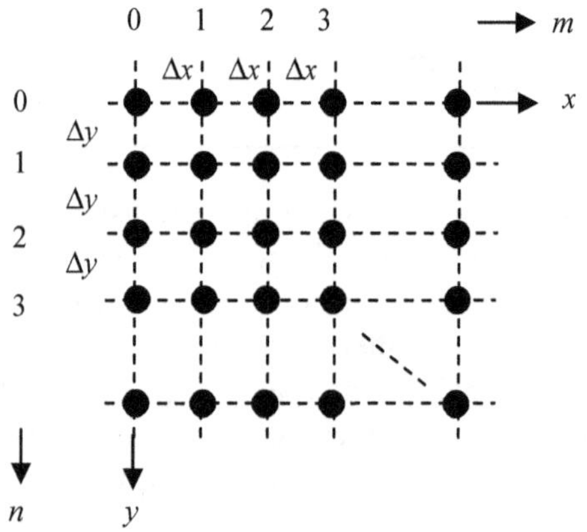

Figure 3.1(a) Link between the continuous and discrete coordinates of $f(x,y)$ due to FD

Suppose the continuous x and y have the intervals $0 \le x \le 8\mu m$ and $0 \le y \le 12\mu m$ respectively and $\Delta x = \Delta y = 2\ \mu m$ is chosen. The integer m varies from 0 to 4, so does n from 0 to 6 in other words the FD domain is over $0 \le m \le 4$ and $0 \le n \le 6$.

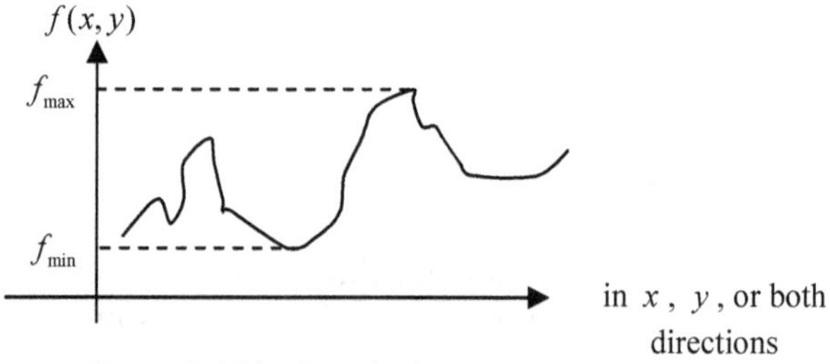

Figure 3.1(b) A typical $f(x,y)$ variation over some domain

♦ Functional discretization i.e. on $f(x,y)$

The Δx or Δy is solely related to continuous (x,y). What is about functional value resolution? Say the discretized $f(x,y)$ is labeled as $f[m,n]$. How do we derive the discrete $f[m,n]$ from continuous $f(x,y)$?

Finite difference study always works over finite range of $f(x,y)$. Any $f(x,y)$ may vary from some minimum to maximum say $f_{\min}$ to $f_{\max}$ respectively. Over a given domain you may check the functional value of $f(x,y)$ along x, y, or both directions but for sure the value is going to be between $f_{\min}$ and $f_{\max}$ as in figure 3.1(b).

Numerical example is the best for understanding a concept. Suppose the continuous $f(x,y)$ is changing from $f_{\min}$=0.1 $\mu W/\mu m^2$ (i.e. microwatts/ micrometer^2) to $f_{\max}$=0.9 $\mu W/\mu m^2$ over some x-y domain. Mathematically you may write the figure 3.1(b) cited variation as $0.1\mu W/\mu m^2 \leq f(x,y) \leq 0.9\mu W/\mu m^2$. The $f(x,y)$ at (x,y) can be any value e.g. 0.1999999 $\mu W/\mu m^2$, 0.2 $\mu W/\mu m^2$, or 0.20000001 $\mu W/\mu m^2$ – infinite possibilities. FD does not handle infinity like situation that brings the resolution on $f(x,y)$ drawn in.

Usually we consider some predecided levels for discretization of $f(x,y)$ and divide $f_{\max}-f_{\min}$ by the level number minus 1 and the result is the resolution on $f(x,y)$ say Δf. For instance if we decide 5 levels, then the $f(x,y)$ with $f_{\min}$=0.1 $\mu W/\mu m^2$ and $f_{\max}$=0.9 $\mu W/\mu m^2$ has functional resolution Δf=(0.9-0.1)/4=0.2 $\mu W/\mu m^2$. With this probable variations of $f(x,y)$ are restricted to 0.1, 0.3, 0.5, 0.7, and 0.9 (all in $\mu W/\mu m^2$).

Inbetween $f(x,y)$ values are approximated to the nearest discretized functional value. For example $f(x,y)$=0.21 $\mu W/\mu m^2$ is considered as 0.3 $\mu W/\mu m^2$. Slight functional value is lost due to this approximation but that is the price of using FD technique or discretization.

However the reconstructed functional value is computed from $\hat{f}(x,y) = f_{\min} + \Delta f \; f[m,n]$ with earlier $x = m\Delta x$ and $y = n\Delta y$. Note that the $\hat{f}(x,y)$, $f_{\min}$, $f_{\max}$, and Δf have the same unit (i.e. $\mu W/\mu m^2$) but the $f[m,n]$ does not have any unit and it is simply some integer number. In tabular form we show the link among $\hat{f}(x,y)$, Δf, and $f[m,n]$ for the numerical example as follows:

$\hat{f}(x,y)$ in $\mu W/\mu m^2$	Δf in $\mu W/\mu m^2$	$f[m,n]$ unitless
0.1		0
0.3		1
0.5	0.2	2
0.7		3
0.9		4

What can we say about last tabular representation? Continuous functional value of $f(x,y)$ i.e. 0.1-0.9 $\mu W/\mu m^2$ is linearly transformed to integer 0-4 with resolution Δf =0.2 $\mu W/\mu m^2$ and $f_{\min}$ =0.1 $\mu W/\mu m^2$.

In general functional resolution Δf is linked to $f(x,y)$ by $\Delta f = \frac{f_{\max} - f_{\min}}{L-1}$ where L is the user-chosen level number. The greater is the level number L, the better is the functional resolution.

Different notations are seen in the literature. For instance the $f[m,n]$ variation from 0 to 31 is mathematically written as $0 \le f[m,n] \le 31$ for 32 levels. As another notation [0,31] elucidates the same.

We summarize the following for a two dimensional continuous function which has to be discretized:

Continuous function $f(x,y)$ ⟹ Discrete function $f[m,n]$

over $0 \le x \le x_0$ and $0 \le y \le y_0$ with range $f_{\min} \le f(x,y) \le f_{\max}$

Subject to $x = m\Delta x$, $y = n\Delta y$, and $\hat{f}(x,y) = f_{\min} + \Delta f \; f[m,n]$

3.2 Rectangular matrix for 2D finite difference

Sections 2.1 and 3.1 are the prerequisite for this discourse. Here our objective is to establish a matrix link between a continuous function $f(x,y)$ and two dimensional finite difference derived $f[m,n]$.

Let us choose some $f(x,y)$ for this purpose say $f(x,y)=(x-y)^2$. The x-y domain and its sample periods are also essential so let it be $-0.5 \le x \le 1$, $-1 \le y \le 1$, Δx =0.5, and Δy =0.5.

For the given sample periods the x and y sample points both as a row matrix are [−0.5 0 0.5 1] and [−1 −0.5 0 0.5 1] respectively. The sample values of $f(x,y)$ are organized as follows:

$$x \rightarrow$$

$$y \downarrow \begin{bmatrix} f(-0.5,-1) & f(0,-1) & f(0.5,-1) & f(1,-1) \\ f(-0.5,-0.5) & f(0,-0.5) & f(0.5,-0.5) & f(1,-0.5) \\ f(-0.5,0) & f(0,0) & f(0.5,0) & f(1,0) \\ f(-0.5,0.5) & f(0,0.5) & f(0.5,0.5) & f(1,0.5) \\ f(-0.5,1) & f(0,1) & f(0.5,1) & f(1,1) \end{bmatrix}.$$

The samples of $f(x,y)$ evidently occupy a matrix in which the x and y coordinates are horizontally rightward and vertically downward respectively.

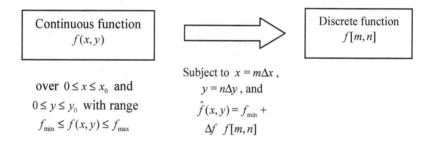

We followed this convention. You could choose another convention. In the first column of the matrix all we have is –0.5 in the position of x which is the first element of x sample points. Again in the first row we have only –1 in the position of y which is the first element of y sample points. Collecting only the x and only the y coordinates we get the following matrices:

$$X = \begin{bmatrix} -0.5 & 0 & 0.5 & 1 \\ -0.5 & 0 & 0.5 & 1 \\ -0.5 & 0 & 0.5 & 1 \\ -0.5 & 0 & 0.5 & 1 \\ -0.5 & 0 & 0.5 & 1 \end{bmatrix} \quad and \quad Y = \begin{bmatrix} -1 & -1 & -1 & -1 \\ -0.5 & -0.5 & -0.5 & -0.5 \\ 0 & 0 & 0 & 0 \\ 0.5 & 0.5 & 0.5 & 0.5 \\ 1 & 1 & 1 & 1 \end{bmatrix}.$$

What can we say about the last X and Y matrices? They are identical in size which is the size of $f(x,y)$ sample matrix. The X is formed from the repetition of only x point samples as a row matrix where the repetition is according to the number of y point samples. Again the Y is formed from the repetition of only y point samples as a column matrix where the repetition is according to the number of x point samples. Let us name the two matrices as grid or sample point matrices.

Having found the grid point matrices, computing of $f(x,y)$ takes place by replacing the x by X and the y by Y i.e.

$$f(X,Y) = (X-Y)^2 = \begin{bmatrix} (-0.5+1)^2 & (0+1)^2 & (0.5+1)^2 & (1+1)^2 \\ (-0.5+0.5)^2 & (0+0.5)^2 & (0.5+0.5)^2 & (1+0.5)^2 \\ (-0.5-0)^2 & (0-0)^2 & (0.5-0)^2 & (1-0)^2 \\ (-0.5-0.5)^2 & (0-0.5)^2 & (0.5-0.5)^2 & (1-0.5)^2 \\ (-0.5-1)^2 & (0-1)^2 & (0.5-1)^2 & (1-1)^2 \end{bmatrix} =$$

$$\begin{bmatrix} 0.25 & 1 & 2.25 & 4 \\ 0 & 0.25 & 1 & 2.25 \\ 0.25 & 0 & 0.25 & 1 \\ 1 & 0.25 & 0 & 0.25 \\ 2.25 & 1 & 0.25 & 0 \end{bmatrix}$$ which are the samples of $f(x,y)$.

Let us summarize the procedure in order to get sampled $f(x,y)$ from its expression in FD domain:

(a) generate x samples as a row matrix from given x variation and Δx,

(b) generate y samples as a column matrix from given y variation and Δy,

(c) repeat x samples according to the number of y samples to get X,

(d) repeat y samples according to the number of x samples to get Y, and

(e) perform $f(X,Y)$ operation to get the samples of $f(x,y)$.

◆ How to get $f[m,n]$ from sampled $f(x,y)$?

Suppose we have a rectangular matrix, it represents just samples of $f(x,y)$. In the matrix there is no information about Δx or Δy. From the sample matrix we determine the following:

f_{min} =minimum in the whole $f(x,y)$ sample matrix and

f_{max} =maximum in the whole $f(x,y)$ sample matrix.

For the ongoing example we have f_{min} =0 and f_{max} =4. The Δf needs L say L=3 so Δf =(4-0)/(3-1)=2. In order to get $f[m,n]$ we have to round the $\dfrac{f(X,Y)-f_{min}}{\Delta f}$ towards its nearest integer so $f(X,Y)=\begin{bmatrix} 0.25 & 1 & 2.25 & 4 \\ 0 & 0.25 & 1 & 2.25 \\ 0.25 & 0 & 0.25 & 1 \\ 1 & 0.25 & 0 & 0.25 \\ 2.25 & 1 & 0.25 & 0 \end{bmatrix}$

provides $f[m,n]$=round$\{\dfrac{f(X,Y)-0}{2}\}$=round$\{\begin{bmatrix} 0.125 & 0.5 & 1.125 & 2 \\ 0 & 0.125 & 0.5 & 1.125 \\ 0.125 & 0 & 0.125 & 0.5 \\ 0..5 & 0.125 & 0 & 0.125 \\ 1.125 & 0.5 & 0.125 & 0 \end{bmatrix}\}$= $\begin{bmatrix} 0 & 1 & 1 & 2 \\ 0 & 0 & 1 & 1 \\ 0 & 0 & 0 & 1 \\ 1 & 0 & 0 & 0 \\ 1 & 1 & 0 & 0 \end{bmatrix}$.

◆ How to get reconstructed $\hat{f}(x,y)$ from sampled $f[m,n]$?

The reconstructed $\hat{f}(x,y)$ is $f_{min}+\Delta f\ f[m,n]$ which becomes $\hat{f}(x,y)$= $0+2\begin{bmatrix} 0 & 1 & 1 & 2 \\ 0 & 0 & 1 & 1 \\ 0 & 0 & 0 & 1 \\ 1 & 0 & 0 & 0 \\ 1 & 1 & 0 & 0 \end{bmatrix}=\begin{bmatrix} 0 & 2 & 2 & 4 \\ 0 & 0 & 2 & 2 \\ 0 & 0 & 0 & 2 \\ 2 & 0 & 0 & 0 \\ 2 & 2 & 0 & 0 \end{bmatrix}$ for the numerical example.

◆ How to calculate the mean square error?

In sample space the mean square error (mse) is defined as $\dfrac{1}{M\times N}\sum_x \sum_y [f(x,y)-\hat{f}(x,y)]^2$ where M and N are the numbers of columns and rows of $f(x,y)$ samples, which is tantamount to averaging all elements on matrix elements of $[f(x,y)-\hat{f}(x,y)]^2$.

For the numerical example we get the $f(x,y)-\hat{f}(x,y)$ samples as $\begin{bmatrix} 0.25 & -1 & 0.25 & 0 \\ 0 & 0.25 & -1 & 0.25 \\ 0.25 & 0 & 0.25 & -1 \\ -1 & 0.25 & 0 & 0.25 \\ 0.25 & -1 & 0.25 & 0 \end{bmatrix}$ hence mse=$[0.25^2+(-1)^2+0.25^2+0^2+0^2+\ldots]/20$= 0.2813 where M=4 and N=5.

♦ How to get alike convention on coordinates?

Concerning the figure 3.1(a) the coordinate convention is not identical with commonly exercised one. The reason for doing so is to comply with the machine convention. Figure 3.2(a) depicts the conventional one. In the samples of $f(x,y)$ the rows are alright but the columns have to be flipped vertically in order to get the sample values complying the conventional coordinate. For the ongoing numerical example we should be having $f(x,y)$ samples or $f(X,Y)$ as

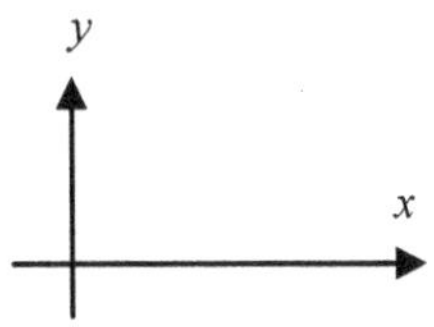

Figure 3.2(a) Common coordinate convention

$$\begin{bmatrix} 2.25 & 1 & 0.25 & 0 \\ 1 & 0.25 & 0 & 0.25 \\ 0.25 & 0 & 0.25 & 1 \\ 0 & 0.25 & 1 & 2.25 \\ 0.25 & 1 & 2.25 & 4 \end{bmatrix}$$ according to the conventional coordinate system.

3.3 Implementing two dimensional FD

Whatever implementation we conducted on 1D FD in section 2.2 can be performed on a two dimensional counterpart. Since complexity is increased because of added dimension, extra function is necessary for the implementation. Following examples are demonstrated in this context.

Example 1 – 2D FD from mathematical expression:

In the last section we presented one numerical example which we intend to implement. The five step procedure to compute the $f(x,y)$ samples is also applicable here.

The function meshgrid returns the grid point matrices (i.e. X and Y) with the syntax [user-supplied variable for X ,user-supplied variable for Y]=meshgrid(x sample points as a row matrix, y sample points as a row matrix). After obtaining the X and Y matrices, the $f(X,Y)$ is calculated by scalar code of appendix B. Straightforwardly we implement the last section quoted numerical example as follows:

```
>>x=-0.5:0.5:1; ↵              ← x samples are assigned to x, x is user-chosen
>>y=-1:0.5:1; ↵                ← y samples are assigned to y, y is user-chosen
>>[X,Y]=meshgrid(x,y) ↵        ← Generation of grid point matrices, X⇔X , Y⇔Y ,
                                  X and Y are user-chosen
X =
     -0.5000    0    0.5000    1.0000
     -0.5000    0    0.5000    1.0000
     -0.5000    0    0.5000    1.0000
     -0.5000    0    0.5000    1.0000
     -0.5000    0    0.5000    1.0000
Y =
     -1.0000  -1.0000  -1.0000  -1.0000
```

```
   -0.5000  -0.5000  -0.5000  -0.5000
         0        0        0        0
    0.5000   0.5000   0.5000   0.5000
    1.0000   1.0000   1.0000   1.0000
```

Scalar code computes the samples of $f(x,y)$ which we assign to f where f is user-chosen:

```
>>f=(X-Y).^2 ↵

f =

    0.2500    1.0000    2.2500    4.0000
         0    0.2500    1.0000    2.2500
    0.2500         0    0.2500    1.0000
    1.0000    0.2500         0    0.2500
    2.2500    1.0000    0.2500         0
```

The two dimensional discrete function $f[m,n]$ needs $f(x,y)|_{\min}$ and $f(x,y)|_{\max}$ in sample space. Compute them by the following:

>>f1=min(min(f)); ↵ ← f1⇔ $f(x,y)|_{\min}$, f1 is user-chosen

>>f2=max(max(f)); ↵ ← f2⇔ $f(x,y)|_{\max}$, f2 is user-chosen

Moreover we need the level number L and functional resolution Δf so execute the following:

>>L=3; df=(f2-f1)/(L-1); ↵ ← L⇔ L, df⇔ Δf , L and df are user-chosen

Hence computing for $f[m,n]$ requires:

>>fmn=round((f-f1)/df) ↵ ← fmn⇔ $f[m,n]$, fmn is user-chosen

```
fmn =

     0     1     1     2
     0     0     1     1
     0     0     0     1
     1     0     0     0
     1     1     0     0
```

Then the reconstructed $\hat{f}(x,y)$ samples we obtain by $f_{\min} + \Delta f \; f[m,n]$:

>>f_hat=f1+df*fmn ↵ ← f_hat⇔ $\hat{f}(x,y)$, f_hat is user-chosen

```
f_hat =

     0     2     2     4
     0     0     2     2
     0     0     0     2
     2     0     0     0
     2     2     0     0
```

The error samples due to FD are $f(x,y) - \hat{f}(x,y)$ hence carry out the following:

>>e=f-f_hat ↵ ← e⇔ $f(x,y) - \hat{f}(x,y)$, e is user-chosen

```
e =

    0.2500   -1.0000    0.2500         0
         0    0.2500   -1.0000    0.2500
    0.2500         0    0.2500   -1.0000
```

```
   -1.0000    0.2500         0    0.2500
    0.2500   -1.0000    0.2500         0
```

Finally mean square error is computed by:

```
>>mse(e) ↵

ans =
        0.2813
```

Example 2 – 2D FD on random or virtual data:

This example addresses how to get FD data of $f(x,y)$ virtually by random variable generator of MATLAB.

Suppose we intend to generate random samples of $f(x,y)$ each of uniform distribution within $-2\,V$ and $2\,V$ based on step sizes $\Delta x = 0.5mm$ and $\Delta y = 1mm$ over $0 \le x \le 2mm$ and $-2 \le y \le 3mm$.

The two step sizes provide the sample numbers by $\frac{x_2 - x_1}{\Delta x} + 1$ and $\frac{y_2 - y_1}{\Delta y} + 1$ which we get as 5 and 6 in x and y directions respectively (since x_2=2 and x_1=0 from $0 \le x \le 2mm$ and y_2=3 and y_1=–2 from $-2 \le y \le 3mm$). In accordance with figure 3.1(a) convention the row and column numbers in $f(x,y)$ samples are 6 and 5 respectively.

The **rand** also keeps provision for generating rectangular matrices so samples between 0 and 1 are obtained from **rand(6,5)**. The $-2\,V$ to $2\,V$ mapping takes place by **4*rand(6,5)-2**. See the machine random response for $f(x,y)$ samples in the following:

```
>>f=4*rand(6,5)-2 ↵          ← f holds f(x,y) samples, f is user-chosen

f =
    1.8005   -0.1741    1.6873   -0.3589   -1.4444
   -1.0754   -1.9260    0.9528    1.5746   -1.1889
    0.4274    1.2856   -1.2949   -1.7684   -1.2051
   -0.0561   -0.2212   -0.3772   -0.5885    0.4152
    1.5652    0.4617    1.7419    1.2527   -0.9112
    1.0484    1.1677    1.6676   -1.9606   -1.2047
```

The Δx and Δy or x - y intervals are not known from above samples.

Example 3 – 2D FD on user-supplied samples:

When sample data of $f(x,y)$ is stored in some soft file, how do you work with that? That answer you get by going through this example.

Figure 3.2(b) shows an excel file containing some sample data of $f(x,y)$.

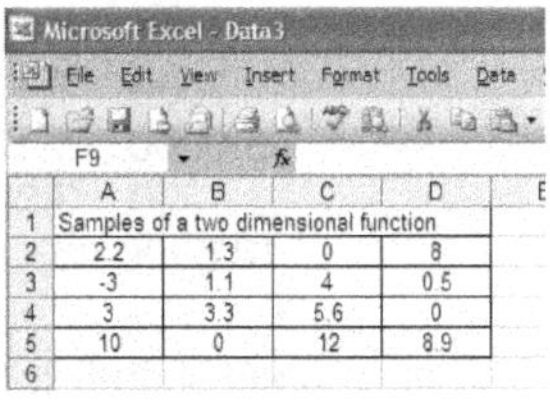

	A	B	C	D
1	Samples of a two dimensional function			
2	2.2	1.3	0	8
3	-3	1.1	4	0.5
4	3	3.3	5.6	0
5	10	0	12	8.9
6				

Figure 3.2(b) Samples of some $f(x,y)$ in an excel file

The file name is **Data3.xls**. Obtain the file, place it in your working path of MATLAB, and execute the following (example 5 of section 2.2):

```
>>f=xlsread('Data3.xls') ↵
```
← f holds $f(x,y)$ samples, f is user-chosen

```
f =

    2.2000    1.3000         0    8.0000
   -3.0000    1.1000    4.0000    0.5000
    3.0000    3.3000    5.6000         0
   10.0000         0   12.0000    8.9000
```

Note that above f just contains the samples of $f(x,y)$, there is no information about the step sizes or intervals.

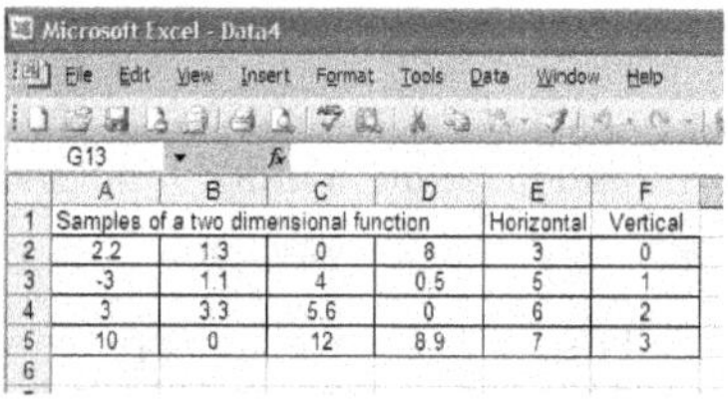

	A	B	C	D	E	F
1	Samples of a two dimensional function				Horizontal	Vertical
2	2.2	1.3	0	8	3	0
3	-3	1.1	4	0.5	5	1
4	3	3.3	5.6	0	6	2
5	10	0	12	8.9	7	3
6						

Figure 3.2(c) Samples of figure 3.2(b) with step size information

Referring to figure 3.2(c) the step size information is provided by appending two more column data. The **Horizontal** and **Vertical** in the figure correspond to x and y sample points respectively. After obtaining the figure 3.2(c) shown file (**Data4.xls**) and placing it in working path, carry out the following:

```
>>V=xlsread('Data4.xls') ↵
```
← V holds all data, V is user-chosen

```
V =

    2.2000    1.3000         0    8.0000    3.0000         0
   -3.0000    1.1000    4.0000    0.5000    5.0000    1.0000
    3.0000    3.3000    5.6000         0    6.0000    2.0000
   10.0000         0   12.0000    8.9000    7.0000    3.0000
```

In above V, the first four, fifth, and sixth columns are $f(x,y)$, x point, and y point samples respectively. Let us pick the samples by the following:

For $f(x,y)$ samples:

```
>>f=V(:,1:4) ↵
```
← f holds $f(x,y)$ samples, f is user-chosen

```
f =

    2.2000    1.3000         0    8.0000
   -3.0000    1.1000    4.0000    0.5000
    3.0000    3.3000    5.6000         0
   10.0000         0   12.0000    8.9000
```

For x point samples:

```
>>x=V(:,5) ↵

x =

     3
```

For y point samples:

```
>>y=V(:,6)

y=

     0
```

```
     5          1
     6          2
     7          3
```

Now you may generate the grid point matrices (i.e. the X and Y matrices) by using [X,Y]=meshgrid(x,y) if it is necessary for FD related analysis like example 1.

Note that the coordinate convention of figure 3.1(a) is observed and the meshgrid works even for non uniform x or y sample points.

Example 4 – Samples in conventional coordinate system:

In this text most machine exercised problems follow figure 3.1(a) convention on 2D FD data. If the reader persists in conventional coordinate system, the function flipud (appendix C.12) can be exercised. If we consider the example 1 FD data, the conventional coordinate $f(x,y)$ data is obtained as follows:

```
>>f=flipud((X-Y).^2) ↵

f =

    2.2500    1.0000    0.2500         0
    1.0000    0.2500         0    0.2500
    0.2500         0    0.2500    1.0000
         0    0.2500    1.0000    2.2500
    0.2500    1.0000    2.2500    4.0000
```

3.4 Implementing double summation

Primarily we need two sum functions (appendix C.9) to conduct double summation. Last three section illustrated grid point matrices are essential to generate sample values particularly when we have functional computing. The $\Sigma\Sigma$ indicates sum of all elements in the sample matrix. Let us see the following examples.

Example 1 – Summation from integer mathematical expression:

Suppose $\sum_{q=0}^{4} \sum_{p=-2}^{2} (p^2+q)^2 = 520$ we intend to calculate.

First we generate the summation variables (i.e. p and q) as a row or column matrix (section 1.3):

```
>>p=-2:2; ↵   ← p holds p values as a row matrix, p is user-chosen
>>q=0:4; ↵    ← q holds q values as a row matrix, q is user-chosen
```

Then we generate the grid point matrices (like X and Y of previous sections) by using meshgrid as follows:

```
>>[P,Q]=meshgrid(p,q); ↵   ← P and Q are user-chosen that hold the matrices
```

Scalar code (appendix B) on summation expression i.e. $(p^2+q)^2$ by using P and Q provides the functional sample matrix upon which two sum functions are exercised:

```
>>f=(P.^2+Q).^2; ↵                ← f is user-chosen which holds computed
                                    values as a rectangular matrix
>>sum(sum(f)) ↵

ans =
        520
```

Example 2 – Summation from decimal type mathematical expression:

Suppose in sample space $\sum_y \sum_x f(x,y)$=992.75 is to be computed where $f(x,y)$ samples are obtained from $(x^2+y^2)^2$ with step sizes $\Delta x = 0.5mm$ and $\Delta y = 1mm$ over $0 \le x \le 2mm$ and $-2 \le y \le 3mm$.

Involvement of decimal calculation does not change the procedure of example 1 so execute the following:

```
>>x=0:0.5:2; ↵   ← x holds x values as a row matrix, x is user-chosen
>>y=-2:3; ↵      ← y holds y values as a row matrix, y is user-chosen
>>[X,Y]=meshgrid(x,y); ↵          ← X and Y are user-chosen that hold the
                                    grid point matrices
>>f=(X.^2+Y.^2).^2; ↵             ← f is user-chosen which holds computed
                                    values as a rectangular matrix
>>sum(sum(f)) ↵

ans =
        992.7500
```

Example 3 – Summation from sample values:

No extra manipulation is required; apply two sum functions when sample values in the form of a rectangular matrix are given. For instance figure 3.2(b) shown data is available in workspace variable f (example 3 of last section). Execute sum(sum(f)) to see 56.9 at the command prompt which is equivalent to $\sum_y \sum_x f(x,y)$ in sample space.

Example 4 – Summation with variable exclusivity:

Let us compute $\sum_{q=-2}^{2} \sum_{p=0}^{7} \frac{1}{(p-3)(q+1)}$=0.2083 subject to $p \ne 3$ and $q \ne -1$.

In section 2.3 we have demonstrated how to simulate one variable singularity, this example is the extension on two variables. Maintaining similar symbology we perform the following:

```
>>p=0:7; ↵ ← p⇔p , p is user-chosen, holds p values as a row matrix
>>q=-2:2; ↵ ← q⇔q , q is user-chosen, holds q values as a row matrix
```

Integer position index r1 for p=3 in p by the function find is obtained as:

```
>>r1=find(p==3); ↵                ← r1 is user-chosen variable
```

Integer position index r2 for q=−1 in q by the function find is obtained as:

```
>>r2=find(q==-1); ↵               ← r2 is user-chosen variable
```

Exclude the singular index and form a row vector again using the other elements in p:

```
>>p=[p(1:r1-1) p(r1+1:end)]; ↵
```

Similar exclusion is also applicable for q:

```
>>q=[q(1:r2-1) q(r2+1:end)]; ↵
```

Form the grid point matrices (P and Q) from above p and q:

```
>>[P,Q]=meshgrid(p,q); ↵
```

Compute the functional samples employing above grid point matrices:

```
>>f=1./(P-3)./(Q+1); ↵
```

Finally apply double summation for the result:

```
>>sum(sum(f)) ↵

ans =
        0.2083
```

3.5 Double integration by FD method

General form of a double integration is $\int_{y=y_1}^{y=y_2}\int_{x=x_1}^{x=x_2} f(x,y)dxdy$ understandably the $f(x,y)$ domain is over $x_1 \le x \le x_2$ and $y_1 \le y \le y_2$. By choosing some Δx and Δy, we approximate the integration by double summation $\Delta x \Delta y \sum\sum f(m\Delta x, n\Delta y)$ where the symbols have ongoing meanings. In order to proceed in MATLAB basically we follow last section quoted double summation i.e. grid point matrix generation is mandatory for samples on the integrand. Let us see the following integrals.

Example 1:

Implement the integration $\int_{y=-1}^{2}\int_{x=0}^{1}(x+y)^2\, dxdy$ =5.5 by using FD method with step sizes Δx =0.01 and Δy =0.01.

Let us enter the given step size specifications:

```
>>dx=0.01; dy=0.01; ↵
```

← dx⇔ Δx , dy⇔ Δy , dx and dy are user-chosen

Generate only x and only y sample points as follows:

```
>>x=0:dx:1; ↵
>>y=-1:dy:2; ↵
```

Then generate the grid point matrices by:

```
>>[X,Y]=meshgrid(x,y); ↵
```

After that compute the given function sample values by:

```
>>f=(X+Y).^2; ↵

>>I=dx*dy*sum(sum(f)) ↵

I =
        5.5938
```

← Implementing $\Delta x \Delta y \sum\sum f(m\Delta x, n\Delta y)$

← I is a user-chosen variable

Due to FD computing how much percentage error is involved? The answer is (5.5938–5.5)/5.5×100%=1.705% – negligible indeed.

Example 2:

Single variable integrand for instance $\int_{y=-1}^{2}\int_{x=0}^{1} x^2\, dxdy = 1$ is also handled similarly, the Δx and Δy are the same as in example 1.

Example 1 executions are applicable completely except the functional code which is now f=X.^2; and results 1.0184 following the implementation.

Example 3:

Implement the integration $\int_{y=-1}^{2}\int_{x=0}^{1} (x+y)^2\, dxdy = 5.5$ by using FD method and choosing 301 and 401 sample points in x and y directions respectively.

You may generate the x and y sample points by using linspace (example 2 of section 2.2) and do so by:

```
>>x=linspace(0,1,301); ↵
>>y=linspace(-1,2,401); ↵
```

Although Δx and Δy are not used in last command lines, we do need them in the summation calculation hence execute the following:

```
>>dx=1/300; dy=3/400; ↵
```

The rest computing is similar to that of example 1 therefore we have:

```
>>[X,Y]=meshgrid(x,y); ↵
>>f=(X+Y).^2; ↵
>>I=dx*dy*sum(sum(f)) ↵

I =

        5.5451
```

Example 4:

Constant integrand needs the function ones as exercised in example 2 of section 2.3. Say $\int_{y=-1}^{2}\int_{x=0}^{1} dxdy = 3$ subject to $\Delta x = 0.01$ and $\Delta y = 0.01$ is to be implemented by using the FD method.

From the Δx and x interval we find the number of sample points in x direction as (1-0)/0.01+1 or 101 so the computer execution is the following:

```
>>M=(1-0)/0.01+1; ↵        ← M is user-chosen, holds number of samples along x
>>N=(2-(-1))/0.01+1; ↵     ← N is user-chosen, holds number of samples along y
```

Unlike one dimensional counterpart the integrand $f(x,y) = 1$ needs to be generated in both the x and y directions thereby requiring a rectangular matrix of ones whose dimension is assessed by the M and N:

```
>>f=ones(M,N); ↵           ← f is user-chosen, holds the rectangular matrix of ones
```

The Δx and Δy are needed for the summation so get them by:

```
>>dx=(1-0)/(M-1); dy=(2-(-1))/(N-1); ↵
```

>>I=dx*dy*sum(sum(f)) ⏎ ← Computing the integration

| =
 3.0401

3.6 Discrete 2D gradient or differentiation

In sections 2.3 and 2.4 one dimensional gradient or difference definitions are found. Here those definitions are extended to two dimensions. In order to determine the gradient we start from integer $f[m,n]$ or $f(x,y)$ samples. In either function we acquire a rectangular matrix of coarse the resolution information must be known (i.e. Δx and Δy).

Given information may appear in two forms – values of $f[m,n]$ or $f(x,y)$ as a rectangular matrix and expression of $f(x,y)$. Say any FD point p has the coordinate (m,n), the surrounding grid points have the coordinates as shown below as far as figure 3.1(a) is concerned:

● ● ● ● ●

● ●$(m-1,n-1)$ ●$(m,n-1)$ ●$(m+1,n-1)$ ●

● ●$(m-1,n)$ p●(m,n) ●$(m+1,n)$ ●

● ●$(m-1,n+1)$ ●$(m,n+1)$ ●$(m+1,n+1)$ ●

● ● ● ● ●

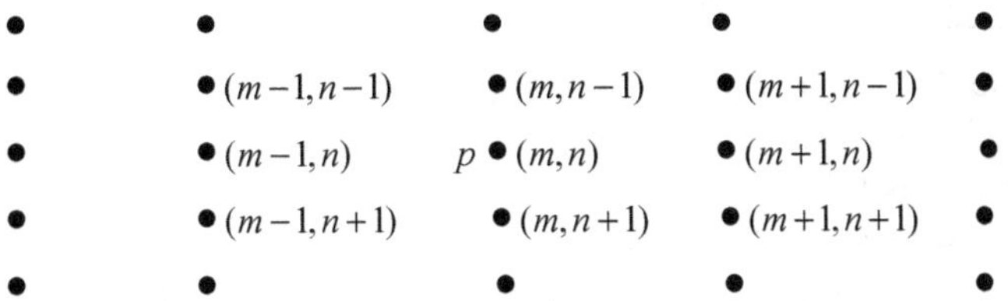

● represents one grid point

Out of the four difference definitions, let us consider the forward difference of the first order:

m directed gradient: $G_m = \dfrac{\Delta f[m,n]}{\Delta m} = f[m+1,n] - f[m,n]$,

n directed gradient: $G_n = \dfrac{\Delta f[m,n]}{\Delta n} = f[m,n+1] - f[m,n]$, and

magnitude gradient: $G = \sqrt{G_m^2 + G_n^2}$.

The two gradients are actually linked to its continuous counterparts $\dfrac{\partial f(x,y)}{\partial x}$ and $\dfrac{\partial f(x,y)}{\partial y}$ respectively.

If second order gradient is sought, the expressions we need are the following:

m directed gradient: $G_{2m} = f[m+2,n] - 2f[m+1,n] - f[m,n]$,

n directed gradient: $G_{2n} = f[m,n+2] - 2f[m,n+1] - f[m,n]$, and

magnitude gradient: $G_2 = \sqrt{G_{2m}^2 + G_{2n}^2}$.

In continuous counterpart of the first order derivative, the $\frac{\partial f(x,y)}{\partial x}$ is infinite if the $f(x,y)$ changes abruptly at some x for example 0 to 1 at $x=1$. But in discrete mathematics we do not handle infinity. We just get a large number at x where the abruptness occurs. The G_m, G_n, and G can be written as $G_m[m,n]$, $G_n[m,n]$, and $G[m,n]$ with the same coordinate convention indicating another discrete function respectively. Following examples illustrate the computing on the 2D gradient.

◆ Example 1: m/n directed first order gradient on $f[m,n]$

Let us choose $f[m,n]=\begin{bmatrix} 9 & 45 & 43 & 9 \\ 4 & 32 & 45 & 6 \\ 8 & 21 & 34 & 6 \end{bmatrix}$ for the computing. Applying the presented expressions, the first order two gradients are computed as $G_m=$ $\begin{bmatrix} 36 & -2 & -34 \\ 28 & 13 & -39 \\ 13 & 13 & -28 \end{bmatrix}$ and $G_n=\begin{bmatrix} -5 & -13 & 2 & -3 \\ 4 & -11 & -11 & 0 \end{bmatrix}$ respectively.

The diff of section 2.3 we apply for gradient finding which is also applicable for a two dimensional function or rectangular matrix. Let us enter the $f[m,n]$ to f as follows:

```
>>f=[9 45 43 9;4 32 45 6;8 21 34 6]; ↵
```

The diff is applied following the transposition of $f[m,n]$ (which is conducted by ' operator) in order to get the G_m:

```
>>Gm=diff(f')' ↵                    ← Gm⇔ Gm, Gm is user-chosen

Gm =

        36    -2   -34
        28    13   -39
        13    13   -28
```

Two transposition operators are applied in last execution because the diff operates over columns. For the G_n, the diff is applied directly without any transposition which we get by:

```
>>Gn=diff(f) ↵                      ← Gn⇔ Gn, Gn is user-chosen

Gn =

        -5   -13     2    -3
         4   -11   -11     0
```

But one problem is there in computation of $G=\sqrt{G_m^2+G_n^2}$ due to non-identical sizes of G_m and G_n which will be taken care of later.

◆ Example 2: From the samples of $f(x,y)$

Samples of $f(x,y)$ can be obtained from mathematical expression, supplied data, or virtual generation (section 3.3). Divided difference of the first order (section 2.4) needs the Δx and Δy information. Suppose $f(x,y)=(x+y)^2$ is defined over $0 \le x \le 2$ and $-1 \le y \le 1$ with Δx =0.4 and Δy = 0.5. We wish to determine $\frac{\Delta f}{\Delta x}$ and $\frac{\Delta f}{\Delta y}$ whose continuous counterparts are $\frac{\partial f(x,y)}{\partial x}$ and $\frac{\partial f(x,y)}{\partial y}$ respectively.

When a mathematical expression is given, we make the samples of $f(x,y)$ available through the use of grid points:

```
>>x=0:0.4:2; ↵              ← x holds x values as a row matrix, x is user-chosen
>>y=-1:0.5:1; ↵             ← y holds y values as a row matrix, y is user-chosen
>>[X,Y]=meshgrid(x,y); ↵    ← X and Y are user-chosen that hold the grid point
                                                        matrices
>>f=(X+Y).^2; ↵
```

Therefore the samples of $f(x,y)$ are available in workspace f. The $\frac{\Delta f}{\Delta x}$ finding is similar to that of G_m in example 1 but the Δx has to be fed as follows:

```
>>dx=0.4; ↵                 ← dx⇔ Δx , dx is user-chosen
>>Gx=diff(f')'/dx ↵         ← Gx⇔ Δf/Δx , Gx is user-chosen

Gx =
          -1.6000  -0.8000        0   0.8000   1.6000
          -0.6000   0.2000   1.0000   1.8000   2.6000
           0.4000   1.2000   2.0000   2.8000   3.6000
           1.4000   2.2000   3.0000   3.8000   4.6000
           2.4000   3.2000   4.0000   4.8000   5.6000
```

Similar computing for $\frac{\Delta f}{\Delta y}$ results the following:

```
>>dy=0.5; ↵                 ← dy⇔ Δy , dy is user-chosen
>>Gy=diff(f)/dy ↵           ← Gy⇔ Δf/Δy , Gy is user-chosen

Gy =
          -1.5000  -0.7000   0.1000   0.9000   1.7000   2.5000
          -0.5000   0.3000   1.1000   1.9000   2.7000   3.5000
           0.5000   1.3000   2.1000   2.9000   3.7000   4.5000
           1.5000   2.3000   3.1000   3.9000   4.7000   5.5000
```

Note that the size of $f(x,y)$ samples is 6×5 (column by row) while the nature of computing causes one column less for $\frac{\Delta f}{\Delta x}$ and one row less for $\frac{\Delta f}{\Delta y}$.

◆ Example 3: Equality in sample of $f(x,y)$ and its FD derivative

In example 1 or 2 the FD derivative matrix size is not equal to that of the $f[m,n]$ or $f(x,y)$. For making equal size there are two options depending on the application – repeat the last row or column and pad the $f(x,y)$ by necessary 0, both of which are addressed based on example 1 in the following.

By repeating third column and second row one should get $G_m = \begin{bmatrix} 36 & -2 & -34 & -34 \\ 28 & 13 & -39 & -39 \\ 13 & 13 & -28 & -28 \end{bmatrix}$ and $G_n = \begin{bmatrix} -5 & -13 & 2 & -3 \\ 4 & -11 & -11 & 0 \\ 4 & -11 & -11 & 0 \end{bmatrix}$ respectively. You may get them by (appendix C.3 for row or column appending and assuming that example 1 variables are in the workspace):

For G_m:

```
>>Gm=[Gm Gm(:,3)] ↵

Gm =
        36   -2  -34  -34
        28   13  -39  -39
        13   13  -28  -28
```

For G_n:

```
>>Gn=[Gn;Gn(2,:)] ↵

Gn =
        -5  -13    2   -3
         4  -11  -11    0
         4  -11  -11    0
```

We have chosen the same variables **Gm** and **Gn** again in above execution, another variable could have been chosen in each case. Having found the G_m and G_n, the magnitude gradient is $G = \begin{bmatrix} 36.3456 & 13.1529 & 34.0588 & 34.1321 \\ 28.2843 & 17.0294 & 40.5216 & 39 \\ 13.6015 & 17.0294 & 30.0832 & 28 \end{bmatrix}$ which requires (appendix B for coding) just the following:

```
>>G=sqrt(Gm.^2+Gn.^2) ↵

G =
      36.3456  13.1529  34.0588  34.1321
      28.2843  17.0294  40.5216  39.0000
      13.6015  17.0294  30.0832  28.0000
```

Again one may choose 0 padding to f. In that case zeroes (appendix C.8) equal to the numbers of rows and columns are appended respectively as follows:

```
>>f1=[f zeros(3,1)]; ↵        ← f1 is user-chosen, holds padded f by 3 zeroes along column
>>Gm=diff(f1')' ↵             ← Two transpositions are required for Gm

Gm =
      36   -2  -34   -9
      28   13  -39   -6
      13   13  -28   -6
>>f2=[f;zeros(1,4)]; ↵        ← f2 is user-chosen, holds padded f by 4 zeroes along row
>>Gn=diff(f2) ↵               ← No transposition is necessary
```

```
Gn =
      -5  -13    2   -3
       4  -11  -11    0
      -8  -21  -34   -6
```

♦ Example 4: Higher order FD derivative

Suppose we intend to find the second order m directed FD derivative for example 1 mentioned $f[m,n]$.

Assign the first order result to some variable and apply the FD derivative again as follows:

```
>>Gm=diff(f')'; ↵             ← For the first order derivative
>>G2m=diff(Gm')' ↵            ← G2m is user-chosen, holds the 2nd order derivative

G2m =
     -38  -32
     -15  -52
       0  -41
```

Keep in mind that each time we take forward derivative on $f[m,n]$, one column is reduced for G_m and one row is reduced for G_n. For a second order derivative two columns or rows are lost.

♦ Example 5: Built-in gradient operator

There is an embedded function called **gradient** which operates in a slight different way. At the beginning and ending elements the function computes the forward difference whereas the inside elements are treated based on the central difference (section 2.4).

Example 1 quoted $f[m,n]$ has the first row [9 45 43 9]. Both edge elements are 9 so the m directed gradient at those positions should be 45–9 and 9–43 respectively. At the element 45, the gradient value is (43–9)/2=17. Continuing this way we get the first order m directed gradient as [36 17 −18 −34]. For the whole $f[m,n]$ we should have $G_m = \begin{bmatrix} 36 & 17 & -18 & -34 \\ 28 & 20.5 & -13 & -39 \\ 13 & 13 & -7.5 & -28 \end{bmatrix}$.

Likewise calculation along n direction yields $G_n = \begin{bmatrix} -5 & -13 & 2 & -3 \\ -0.5 & -12 & -4.5 & -1.5 \\ 4 & -11 & -11 & 0 \end{bmatrix}$.

The **gradient** needs two output arguments with the syntax [G_m, G_n]= gradient($f[m,n]$) so call it as follows:

```
>>[Gm,Gn]=gradient(f) ↵

Gm =
     36.0000  17.0000  -18.0000  -34.0000
     28.0000  20.5000  -13.0000  -39.0000
     13.0000  13.0000   -7.5000  -28.0000

Gn =
     -5.0000  -13.0000    2.0000   -3.0000
```

```
   -0.5000  -12.0000   -4.5000   -1.5000
    4.0000  -11.0000  -11.0000         0
```

3.7 Interpolation on two dimensional FD data

Section 2.5 addresses one dimensional counterpart. Starting from integer $f[m,n]$ or $f(x,y)$ samples, objective of two dimensional (2D) interpolation is to obtain intermediate samples based on some resolution or step size. Each of the methods explained in section 2.5 has the extension in two dimensions.

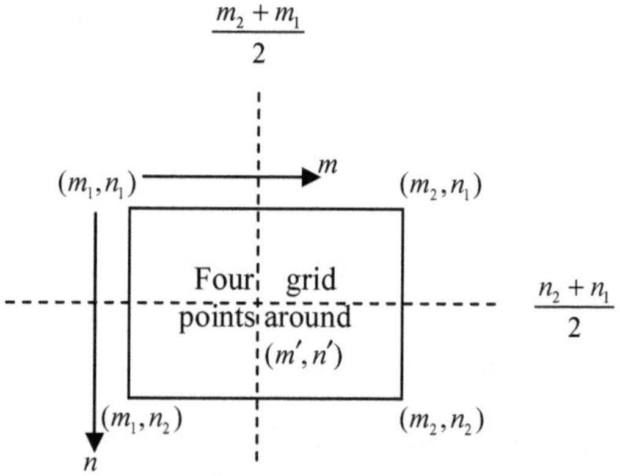

Figure 3.3(a) Squarely formed four grid points in 2D FD domain

Grid point coordinate of a discrete function $f[m,n]$ is integer. Figure 3.3(a) depicts the (m',n') inside a square formed by four grid points in 2D FD domain. The (m',n') is assumed to be fractional. Suppose we need $f[m',n']$ which inevitably involves 2D interpolation. There is no absolute guarantee that $f[m',n']$ value obtained this way is close to the actual one however better results are achieved due to an interpolation.

We wish to address the theory of nearest neighborhood and bilinear interpolations as a basic introduction.

♦ Nearest neighborhood interpolation

The fractional (m',n') lies within the squarely formed four integer coordinates (m_1,n_1), (m_2,n_1), (m_2,n_2), and (m_1,n_2) as pointed out in figure 3.3(a). In this scheme we approximate the wanted $f[m',n']$ to the closest of the four functional values. Mathematically the approximation is carried out as follows:

if $m' \geq \frac{m_2+m_1}{2}$, then $m' = m_2$

else $m' = m_1$ and

if $n' \geq \frac{n_2+n_1}{2}$, then $n'=n_2$

else $n'=n_1$.

Following numerical example demonstrates the nearest neighborhood interpolation.

Example:

By applying the nearest neighborhood interpolation, determine $f[m',n']$ on $f[m,n]$ of last section (example 1) at fractional (m',n')=(0.3,1.5).

The m' and n' coordinates lie between 0 and 1 and 1 and 2 respectively so m_1=0, m_2=1, n_1=1, and n_2=2. Comparing the m' and n' coordinates with $\frac{m_2+m_1}{2}$ and $\frac{n_2+n_1}{2}$ respectively, we get the nearest neighbor coordinate as (0,2) therefore $f[m',n']=f[0,2]$=8 (figure 3.1(a) shown convention is applied).

♦ Bilinear interpolation

Bilinear interpolation is derived from one dimensional counterpart. Figure 2.2(a) shows the interpolation from two sample values of a linear discrete function which at this time is applied in m and n directions of $f[m,n]$ that is why the term bilinear is associated.

Concerning the figure 3.3(a), squarely formed four grid points have the coordinates and functional values (m_1,n_1), (m_2,n_1), (m_2,n_2), and (m_1,n_2) and $f[m_1,n_1]$, $f[m_2,n_1]$, $f[m_2,n_2]$, and $f[m_1,n_2]$ respectively. We determine $f[m',n']$ at fractional (m',n') from these four grid points. Following expressions are exercised to calculate the bilinearly interpolated functional value:

linearity along $n=n_1$:

$$f[m',n_1]=\frac{f[m_2,n_1]-f[m_1,n_1]}{m_2-m_1}(m'-m_1)+f[m_1,n_1]$$

linearity along $n=n_2$:

$$f[m',n_2]=\frac{f[m_2,n_2]-f[m_1,n_2]}{m_2-m_1}(m'-m_1)+f[m_1,n_2]$$

linearity along $m=m'$:

$$f[m',n']=\frac{f[m',n_2]-f[m',n_1]}{n_2-n_1}(n'-n_1)+f[m',n_1]$$

Understandably above mathematical relationships are valid over $m_1 \leq m' \leq m_2$ and $n_1 \leq n' \leq n_2$.

Example:

Apply bilinear interpolation to determine the $f[m',n']$ at (m',n')=(0.3,1.5) for last section (example 1) mentioned $f[m,n]$.

From the coordinate of interest we find the neighboring functional values as $\begin{bmatrix} 4 & 32 \\ 8 & 21 \end{bmatrix}$ in given $f[m,n]$. Related coordinates and functional values are as follows: m_1=0, m_2=1, n_1=1, n_2=2, $f[0,1]$ =4, $f[1,1]$=32, $f[0,2]$=8, and $f[1,2]$=21 hence

$$f[m',n_1]=\frac{f[1,1]-f[0,1]}{1-0}(0.3-0)+f[0,1]=(32-4)(0.3)+4=12.4,$$

similarly,

$$f[m',n_2]=\frac{f[1,2]-f[0,2]}{1-0}(0.3-0)+f[0,2]=11.9,$$ and finally

$$f[m',n']=\frac{11.9-12.4}{2-1}(1.5-1)+12.4=12.15.$$

❖ MATLAB built-in function

The function interp2 conducts 2D interpolations which keeps a variety of options. A simple procedure is followed:

(1) From given m and n values, obtain the grid point matrices like section 3.2.

(2) Enter the given $f[m,n]$.

(3) From wanted (m',n') values, obtain the grid point matrices like step (1).

(4) Call the interp2 with five input argument syntax interp2(m directed grid point rectangular matrix, n directed grid point rectangular matrix, given $f[m,n]$ as a rectangular matrix, wanted m' directed grid point rectangular matrix, wanted n' directed grid point rectangular matrix) where the last two input arguments can be single element too. The return from the interp2 can be assigned to user-chosen variable fn which holds the interpolated $f[m',n']$.

(5) The default method chosen by the interp2 is bilinear interpolation. In case other methods are required, another input argument is appended with the interp2. Interpolation methods that are available in MATLAB are the nearest neighborhood, piecewise cubic spline, and shape preserving piecewise cubic whose MATLAB indicatory reserve words are nearest, spline, and cubic respectively, each of which is put under a quote.

❖ Interpolation at a single point by interp2

We demonstrated two numerical examples considering the $f[m,n]$ of last section. Let us enter the $f[m,n]$ to f as follows:

```
>>f=[9 45 43 9;4 32 45 6;8 21 34 6]; ↵
```

The matrix size of $f[m,n]$ says that the m and n intervals are $0 \le m \le 3$ and $0 \le n \le 2$ respectively upon which both variables as a row matrix are generated by:

```
>>m=0:3; ↵         ← m is user-chosen, holds all m s
>>n=0:2; ↵         ← n is user-chosen, holds all n s
```

Using the **meshgrid** of section 3.3, grid point matrices are generated by:

```
>>[M,N]=meshgrid(m,n); ↵
```

In above execution the M and N are user-chosen variables which hold the m and n directed grid point matrices respectively. Earlier we obtained $f[m',n']$ as 8 and 12.15 attributed to the nearest neighborhood and bilinear interpolations at (m',n')=(0.3,1.5) respectively which we get by:

For the nearest neighborhood interpolation:

```
>>fn=interp2(M,N,f,0.3,1.5,'nearest') ↵

fn =
         8
```

For the bilinear interpolation:

```
>>fn=interp2(M,N,f,0.3,1.5) ↵

fn =
         12.1500
```

♦ Interpolation at multiple points by interp2

Suppose for the ongoing $f[m,n]$, three $f[m',n']$s employing bilinear interpolation are 12.15, 25.72, and 26 at (m',n')=(0.3,1.5), (0.7,0.8), and (1.3,1.9) respectively which we intend to find.

Following is the execution:

```
>>mp=[0.3 0.7 1.3]; ↵ ← Given m′s are assigned to mp as a row matrix, where
                                   mp is user-chosen
>>np=[1.5 0.8 1.9]; ↵ ← Given n′s are assigned to np as a row matrix, where np
                                   is user-chosen
>>fn=interp2(M,N,f,mp,np) ↵        ← Calling the function on points of interest

fn =
         12.1500   25.7200   26.0000
```

The return is also as a row matrix. Should the reader need each interpolated value, the command fn(1), fn(2), or fn(3) is exercised respectively. In case the nearest neighborhood method were sought, the command would be fn=interp2(M,N,f,mp,np,'nearest');.

Interpolation along a row or column can also be handled this way for instance $f[m',n']$ over $1 \le n' \le 1.5$ with $\Delta n' = 0.125$ and m'=0.7 (assume bilinear interpolation) needs us to execute the following:

```
>>mp=0.7; ↵
>>np=1:0.125:1.5; ↵
>>fn=interp2(M,N,f,mp,np) ↵

fn =
        23.6000
        22.7875
        21.9750
        21.1625
        20.3500
```

The n' is in column direction that is why the return is as a column matrix.

◆ Interpolation over a domain by interp2

Instead of point set, an area can also be of interest. For the ongoing $f[m,n]$, the $f[m',n']$ is $\begin{bmatrix} 4 & 6.8 & 9.6 & 12.4 & 15.2 & 18 & 20.8 \\ 4.5 & 7.1125 & 9.725 & 12.3375 & 14.95 & 17.5625 & 20.175 \\ 5 & 7.425 & 9.85 & 12.275 & 14.7 & 17.125 & 19.55 \\ 5.5 & 7.7375 & 9.975 & 12.2125 & 14.45 & 16.6875 & 18.925 \\ 6 & 8.05 & 10.1 & 12.15 & 14.2 & 16.25 & 18.3 \end{bmatrix}$ over $0 \le m' \le 0.6$ and $1 \le n' \le 1.5$ with $\Delta m' = 0.1$ and $\Delta n' = 0.125$ by using bilinear interpolation which we wish to find.

When interpolation over a domain is required, it is mandatory that we generate the rectangular grid point matrices by employing the meshgrid therefore execute the following:

```
>>mp=0:0.1:0.6; ↵       ← Given m′s are assigned to mp as a row matrix, where
                                  mp is user-chosen
>>np=1:0.125:1.5; ↵  ← Given n′s are assigned to np as a row matrix, where np
                                  is user-chosen
>>[Mp,Np]=meshgrid(mp,np); ↵  ← Mp and Np hold m′ and n′ directed grid
                    point matrices respectively where Mp and Np are user-chosen
```

Eventually call the interpolator at points of interest:

```
>>fn=interp2(M,N,f,Mp,Np) ↵          ← fn holds f[m′,n′], fn is user-chosen

fn =
        4.0000  6.8000  9.6000 12.4000 15.2000 18.0000 20.8000
        4.5000  7.1125  9.7250 12.3375 14.9500 17.5625 20.1750
        5.0000  7.4250  9.8500 12.2750 14.7000 17.1250 19.5500
        5.5000  7.7375  9.9750 12.2125 14.4500 16.6875 18.9250
        6.0000  8.0500 10.1000 12.1500 14.2000 16.2500 18.3000
```

◆ Note on the interpolator

(1) When any (m',n') falls out of the given domain, the return is an undesirable character which we call not a number (NaN).

(2) Multiplicity of $\Delta m'$ or $\Delta n'$ should be maintained while exercising the range data for example on $\Delta m'=0.4$ the interval $0 \le m' \le 3$ can not be appropriately covered whereas $\Delta m'=0.3$ can.

(3) Whatever computing we performed on $f[m,n]$ can be conducted on the samples of $f(x,y)$.

3.8 Graphing two dimensional FD data

As we have been exercising, two dimensional FD data takes the form of a rectangular matrix. After making the $f(x,y)$ or FD rectangular matrix available (section 3.3), decide what kind of plot you need. In the sequel we explain a number of plotting tools on FD data or expression. It is important to quote that graphing functions for expression and sampled data are different.

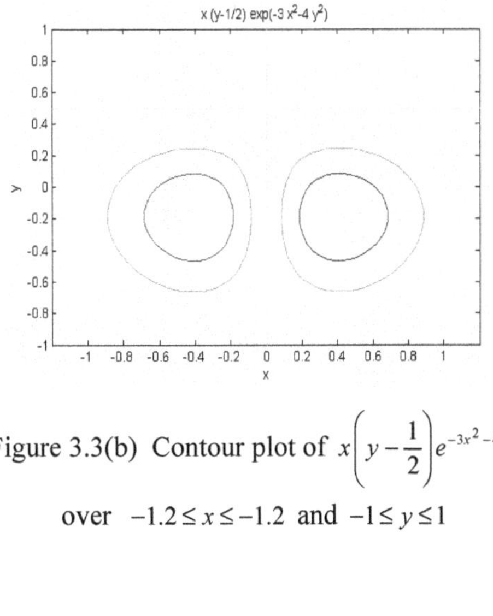

Figure 3.3(b) Contour plot of $x\left(y-\frac{1}{2}\right)e^{-3x^2-4y^2}$

over $-1.2 \le x \le -1.2$ and $-1 \le y \le 1$

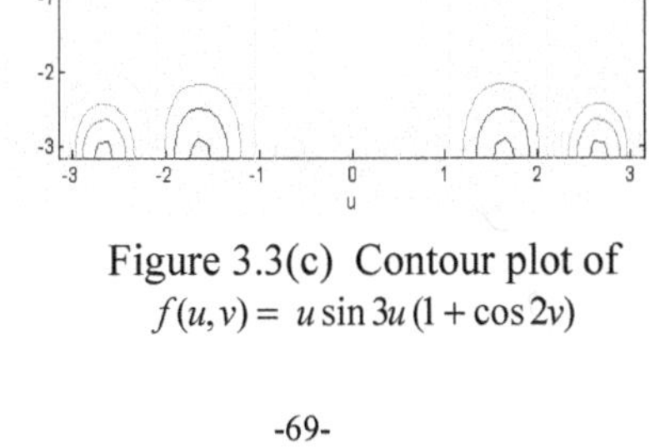

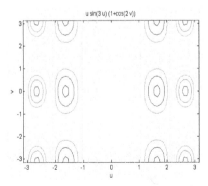

Figure 3.3(c) Contour plot of $f(u,v)=\ u\sin 3u\,(1+\cos 2v)$

❖ Contour plot from $f(x,y)$ expression

Contour plot of $f(x,y)$ versus x and y is basically a three dimensional plot but graphed on a two dimensional convenience. By mathematical definition any closed curve is termed as a contour. When a contour is graphed in a computer, curves connected by the lines of same functional values are called a contour.

MATLAB function **ezcontour** (abbreviation for easy contour) graphs a contour plot from the expression of $f(x,y)$. Syntax for the plot is ezcontour(vector code of $f(x,y)$ under quote – appendix B, x interval bounds as a two element row matrix, y interval bounds as a two element row matrix). The default intervals that **ezcontour** conceives for the x and y are $-2\pi \le x \le 2\pi$ and $-2\pi \le y \le 2\pi$ respectively. The contours so displayed by the **ezcontour** are color curves.

We intend to contour graph the function $f(x,y) = x\left(y - \frac{1}{2}\right)e^{-3x^2-4y^2}$ over the domain formed by $-1.2 \le x \le 1.2$ and $-1 \le y \le 1$.

Having gone through the syntax, one easily carries out:

```
>>ezcontour('x*(y-1/2)*exp(-3*x^2-4*y^2)',[-1.2,1.2],[-1,1]) ↵
```

Figure 3.3(b) presents the graph. Looking into the contour plot, it is very difficult to know the value of a contour (i.e. the functional value of $f(x,y)$). Moreover the contours are displayed in terms of color curves. One needs to know the color scale which should indicate the value of the contour at any x and y, and for which we execute the command **colorbar** at the command prompt. Upon execution we must find a color bar attached with the contour plot which indicates the color code values (not shown for the space reason).

Contours filled by various colors are viewed by the function **ezcontourf** (the last letter is f, syntax is the same as that of **ezcontour**) as follows (graph is not shown for the space reason):

```
>>ezcontourf('x*(y-1/2)*exp(-3*x^2-4*y^2)',[-1.2,1.2],[-1,1]) ↵
```

The functional expression automatically appears on top of the graph. However we include one more example on graphing a contour in the following.

Example:

Let us contour plot the $f(u,v) = u\sin 3u\,(1+\cos 2v)$ over the domain formed by $-\pi \le u \le \pi$ and $-\pi \le v \le \pi$. Now our independent variables are other than x and y. Following command plots the contour of figure 3.3(c):

```
>>ezcontour('u*sin(3*u)*(1+cos(2*v))',[-pi,pi]) ↵
```

Alphabetically u comes first, and then does v which is why v and u follow the y and x traces respectively. Since the two intervals are identical, mentioning one of them in the input argument is enough.

❖ Surface plot for $f(x, y)$

Surface plot of $f(x, y)$ versus x and y is a three dimensional one for which we apply the MATLAB function **ezsurf** with the syntax **ezsurf**(vector code of the $f(x, y)$). Considering the function $f(x, y) = -8(x^2 + y^2)$, we execute the following to display figure 3.3(d):

```
>>ezsurf('-8*(x^2+y^2)') ↵
```

The z axis of figure 3.3(d) corresponds to the functional values of $f(x, y)$. The plotter puts surface on the default domain formed by $-2\pi \le x \le 2\pi$ and $-2\pi \le y \le 2\pi$. User-defined domains are entered by a four element row matrix that contains the lower bound of x, upper bound of x, lower bound of y, and upper bound of y respectively.

Whatever surfaces are plotted by the **ezsurf** can be plotted by another variant called **ezmesh**. The difference between the **ezsurf** and **ezmesh** is that the former drops a surface and the latter drops a net or mesh proportionately to the z axis or $f(x, y)$ value. Three more examples are included in the following.

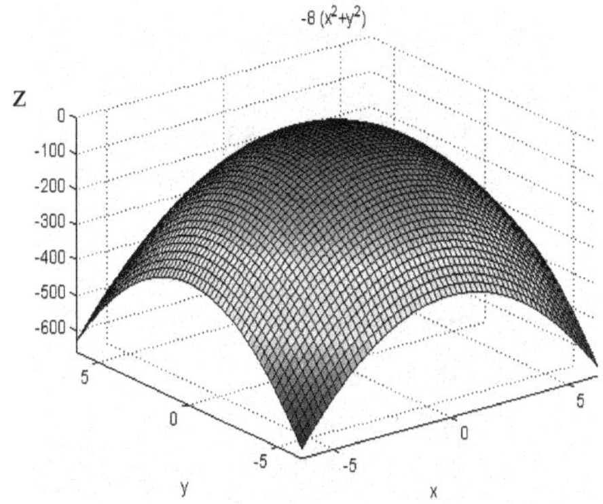

Figure 3.3(d) Surface plot of $-8(x^2 + y^2)$

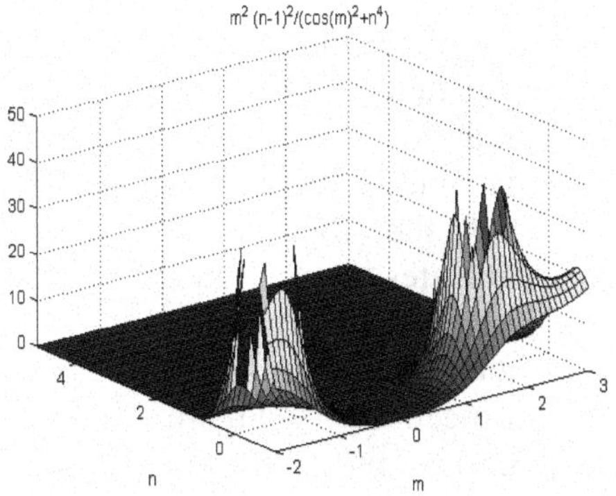

Figure 3.4(a) Surface plot of $\frac{m^2(n-1)^2}{\cos^2 m + n^4}$

Example 1:

Let us plot the surface of the figure 3.4(a) for different independent variable function $f(m, n) =$

$\frac{m^2(n-1)^2}{\cos^2 m + n^4}$ over the domain formed by $-2 \le m \le 3$ and $-1 \le n \le 5$ as follows:

```
>>ezsurf('m^2*(n-1)^2/(cos(m)^2+n^4)',[-2,3,-1,5]) ↵
```

Bounds of m and n are put as a four element row matrix in above.

Example 2:

A parametric surface defined by two parameters u and v takes the form $x = f(u,v)$, $y = g(u,v)$, and $z = h(u,v)$ which can be plotted by **ezsurf** too.

Let us say we have the parametric surface expression $x = 2u - v$, $y = e^{-u-v}$, and $z = \cos(4u + v)$ and wish to plot the surface over the parametric intervals $-2 \le u \le 3$ and $0 \le v \le \pi$ and do so by:

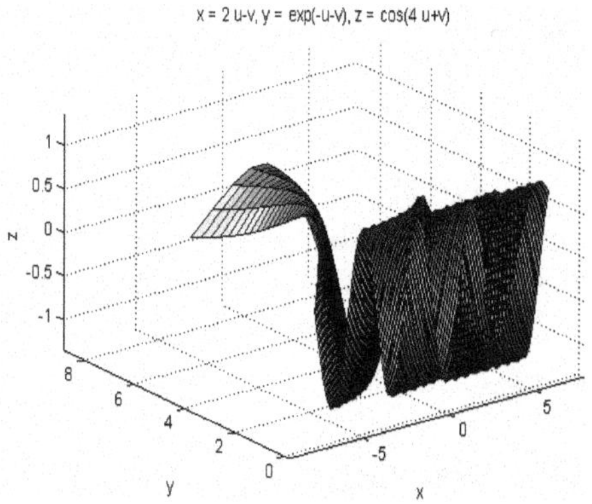

Figure 3.4(b) Surface plot on $x = 2u - v$, $y = e^{-u-v}$, and $z = \cos(4u + v)$

```
>>x='2*u-v'; ↵                  ← Assigning f(u,v) to x
>>y='exp(-u-v)'; ↵              ← Assigning g(u,v) to y
>>z='cos(4*u+v)'; ↵             ← Assigning h(u,v) to z
>>ezsurf(x,y,z,[-2 3 0 pi]) ↵         ← Calling the function
```

The first three input arguments of the **ezsurf** are the parametric equations and the fourth one indicates the parametric interval bound description respectively. Figure 3.4(b) presents the parametric surface plot.

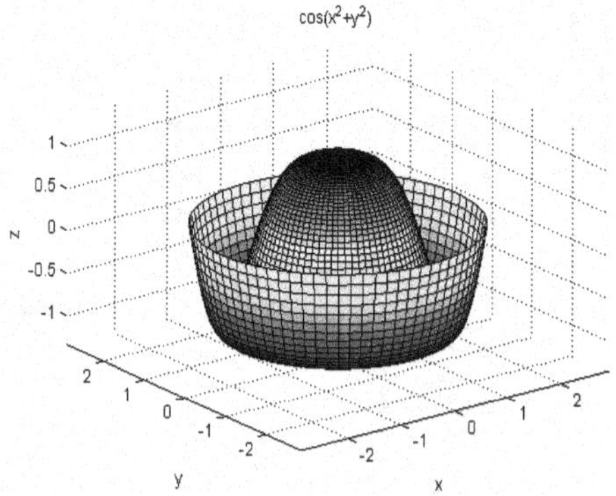

Figure 3.4(c) Surface plot of $\cos(x^2 + y^2)$ on a circular domain regarding x and y

Example 3:

The examples

we mentioned so far consider rectangular domains regarding x and y. What if we wish to plot the surface on x and y over a circular disc domain.

To demonstrate that plot the surface for a function $f(x, y) = \cos(x^2 + y^2)$ on a circular disk domain over $-\frac{\pi}{2} \le x \le \frac{\pi}{2}$ and $-\frac{\pi}{2} \le y \le \frac{\pi}{2}$ by using the following command:

```
>>ezsurf('cos(x^2+y^2)',[-pi/2,pi/2],'circ') ↵
```

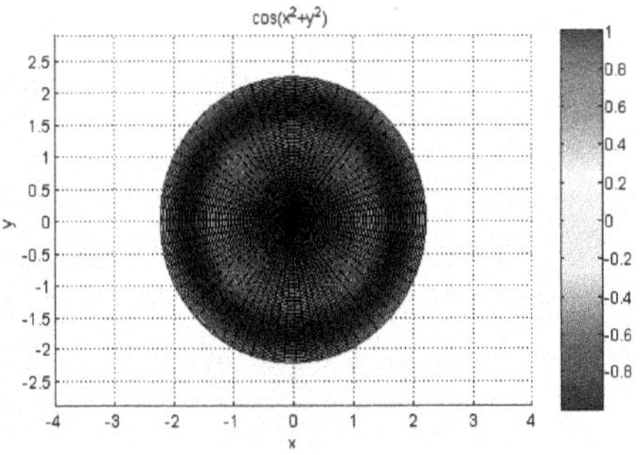

Figure 3.4(d) Top view of the surface plot of figure 3.4(c) with gray intensity scale

We obtain the surface plot like figure 3.4(c) from above execution. Of the three input arguments, the first, second, and third represent the function $f(x, y)$, the rectangular domain bounds of x and y (since both are identical, coding one is sufficient) as a row matrix, and the reserve word **circ** under quote respectively.

Since the surface plot represents visually a three dimensional object on a two dimensional screen, there are infinite views of the three dimensional object depending on the angle you look at. If we wish to see the top view of the surface plot with equal axes and intensity scale like figure 3.4(d), employ the following commands: **view(0,90), axis equal, colorbar**. The command **view** sets the viewing angle of plot and the angle set **0-90** means top view.

Table 3.A Data for a contour plot:

	$x \rightarrow$ -2	-1	0	1	2	3
y ↓ -1	10	10	10	10	10	10
0	0	2	2	2	2	0
1	-9	-9	-9	-9	-9	0
2	3	3	3	3	3	3

♦ Contour plot from sampled $f(x,y)$ data

We not only graph contour from a symbolic expression but also can plot contours from tabular or matrix data by virtue of the command **contour**. The function takes three input arguments, the first, second, and third of which are the x axis variation vector as a row matrix, the y axis variation vector as a row matrix, and the sampled functional values of $f(x,y)$ as a rectangular matrix respectively. The command **clabel** (abbreviation for contour label) attaches value of contour on the graph which is more indicative.

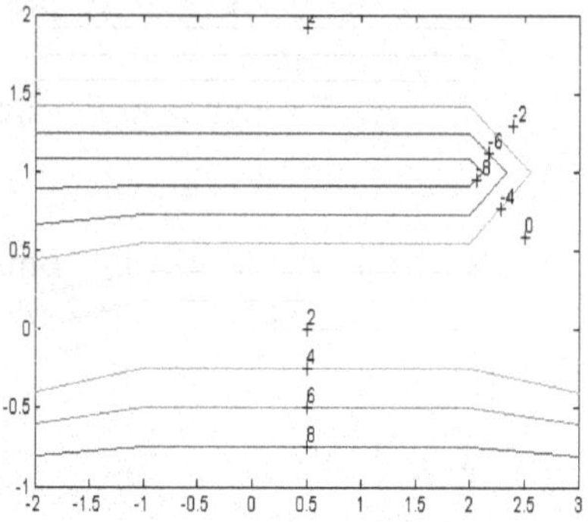

Figure 3.5(a) Contour plot of the tabular data

Concerning the table 3.A, it contains the sample values of some $f(x,y)$ at x and y. In the table, the x and y vary from –2 to 3 and –1 to 2 respectively. The shaded cell in the table corresponds to $f(x,y)=f(2,1)=-9$. In order to graph contour from the data, the x, y, and $f(x,y)$ data must be available in the workspace so assign the functional values of $f(x,y)$ to some rectangular matrix f as shown below:

```
>>f=[10 10 10 10 10 10;0 2 2 2 2 0;-9 -9 -9 -9 -9 0;3 3 3 3 3 3]; ↵
>>x=-2:3; y=-1:2; ↵        ← Each vector with increment 1
>>clabel(contour(x,y,f)) ↵
```

The x and y variations must be as a row matrix which we assigned to the workspace **x** and **y** in above respectively. The last command line returns the figure 3.5(a).

Earlier we contoured the function $f(x,y)=x\left(y-\frac{1}{2}\right)e^{-3x^2-4y^2}$ over $-1.2\le x\le 1.2$ and $-1\le y\le 1$ and can do the same by using the **contour**.

The **ezcontour** automatically selects some step size but **contour** does not. User has to decide the step size (say 0.1 for each interval). Sample data of $f(x,y)$ as a rectangular matrix is made available by using the grid point matrices (section 3.3):

```
>>x=-1.2:0.1:1.2; y=-1:0.1:1; ↵
>>[X,Y]=meshgrid(x,y); ↵
>>f=X.*(Y-0.5).*exp(-3*X.^2-4*Y.^2); ↵
```

Hence sample data of $f(x,y)$ is available in **f**. However following line brings the graph of figure 3.3(b) with contour labeling in front (not shown for space reason):

```
>>clabel(contour(x,y,f)) ↵
```

♦ Surface plot from sampled $f(x,y)$ data

Like earlier mentioned **ezsuf** or **ezmesh**, MATLAB retains the provision for graphing a mesh or surface from sampled $f(x,y)$ data by means of the function **mesh** or **surf**. Both functions accept three input arguments – the x variation vector as a row matrix, the y variation vector as a row matrix, and the sampled $f(x,y)$ data as a rectangular matrix.

Let us consider the sampled $f(x,y)$ as $\begin{bmatrix} 9 & 8 & -4 & 3 & 6 \\ 4 & 9 & 5 & 1 & -3 \\ -3 & -6 & -2 & 0 & 4 \\ 7 & -5 & 2 & 3 & -3 \end{bmatrix}$ in which the row and column variations correspond to $0.5 \le x \le 2.5$ and $0.2 \le y \le 1.4$ respectively. The x and y variation vectors must correspond to the sample values of $f(x,y)$ or the rectangular matrix elements. Since there are 5 columns along the row direction, we must choose 5 points over $0.5 \le x \le 2.5$ i.e. the row vector corresponding to x should be [0.5 1 1.5 2 2.5]. Again there are 4 rows in the column direction, the interval $0.2 \le y \le 1.4$ must be split as [0.2 0.6 1 1.4]. Placed below is the implementation of the surface plot which results in figure 3.5(b):

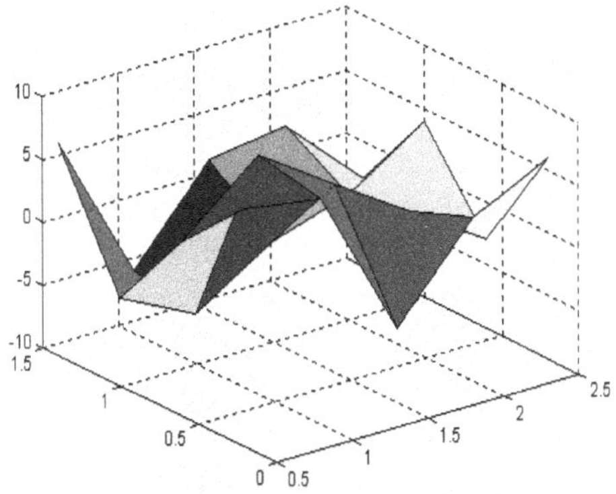

Figure 3.5(b) Surface plot from the sampled $f(x,y)$ data

```
>>f=[9 8 -4 3 6;4 9 5 1 -3;-3 -6 -2 0 4;7 -5 2 3 -3]; ↵
>>x=[0.5 1 1.5 2 2.5]; y=[0.2 0.6 1 1.4]; ↵
>>surf(x,y,f) ↵
```

In above execution the first line is to assign the $f(x,y)$ sample data to **f**, so is the second line to **x** and **y** for the x and y directed vectors respectively. The third line calls the function for graphing.

The reader may execute **mesh(x,y,f)** to see the mesh plot for the problem. The functions merely graph the surface or mesh without labeling.

Surface plot is obtainable from functional expressions too. In the contour plot we made the sampled data available for the function $f(x,y) = x\left(y - \frac{1}{2}\right)e^{-3x^2-4y^2}$ to the workspace **f**. You need to reexecute the commands to have the **x**, **y**, and **f**. Our objective is to surface graph this function for which the necessary command is **surf(x,y,f)** or **mesh(x,y,f)**, graph is not shown for the space reason.

◆ Intensity image plot from sample data

Starting from $f[m,n]$ or $f(x,y)$ samples, one may need to display the data as an intensity image. Usually in this type of plot we get a large dimension matrix like 200×200, 400×400, or more. The data in the matrix must be between 0 and 1 in order to see the intensity image. The 1 and 0 represent white and black respectively. Values other than 1 and 0 are gray.

Figure 3.5(c) Plot of $f(x,y)$ as a gray intensity image

Any given samples in the form of a rectangular matrix are linearly mapped (minimum and maximum to 0 and 1 respectively) between 0 and 1 by using the function mat2gray (abbreviation for matrix to (2) gray level). The function imshow displays the mapped data as a gray image when the matrix is its input argument.

For instance we intend to show the $f(x,y)=\sin c(x^2+y^2)$ as a gray intensity image over the domain $-2 \le x \le 2$ and $-1 \le y \le 1$ subject to step sizes $\Delta x = 0.02$ and $\Delta y = 0.02$.

Computing $f(x,y)$ samples needs the generation of grid point rectangular matrices as explained in section 3.3:

```
>>x=-2:0.02:2; ↵        ← Generating the x points as a row matrix
>>y=-1:0.02:1; ↵        ← Generating the y points as a row matrix
>>[X,Y]=meshgrid(x,y); ↵   ← X and Y hold x and y directed grid point
                              matrices respectively
>>f=sinc(X.^2+Y.^2); ↵     ← f holds the samples of f(x,y), appendix B
>>imshow(mat2gray(f)) ↵
```

Last line command brings the intensity image of figure 3.5(c) in front in which the x and y directions are also shown.

◆ Plotting 1D FD data from 2D counterpart

Just now we made $f(x,y)=\sin c(x^2+y^2)$ samples available to f. Say $f(x,y)$ over $-1 \le y \le 1$ for $x=1.1$ needs to be plotted.

We first determine integer index for $x=1.1$ in the x vector by find function (appendix C.7) and then select the particular column from f however following is the complete execution:

```
>>I=find(x==1.1); ↵     ← I holds the integer index, I is user-chosen
>>fp=f(:,I); ↵          ← fp holds the column, fp is user-chosen
>>plot(y,fp) ↵          ← For plotting, y holds data for −1 ≤ y ≤ 1, graph not
                           shown for space reason
```

Above execution brings an end to this chapter.

Exercises

1. An area over the domain $-0.9cm \le x \le 4.5cm$ and $-1.6cm \le y \le 5.6cm$ is chosen to apply the FD technique with $\Delta x = 0.9\ cm$ and $\Delta y = 0.8\ cm$. What is the FD domain in integer coordinates? How many sample coordinates are in the domain? Do the same if each resolution is reduced to half.
2. Suppose a discrete two dimensional function $f[m,n]$ varies subject to $\Delta x =$ $0.5\ cm$ and $\Delta y = 0.6\ cm$ over the integer domain $-3 \le m \le 8$ and $-5 \le n \le 11$. What is the continuous domain? Do the same if the resolution is reduced to half.
3. Suppose $f(x,y) = 3xy^3 - x^3$ is to be computed based on FD method subject to $\Delta x = 0.3$ and $\Delta y = 0.5$ over $-0.5 \le x \le 0.7$ and $-1 \le y \le 1$. What are the grid point matrices? Which mathematical operation provides $f(x,y)$ samples employing the grid point matrices? Compute the samples employing the grid point matrices.
4. In question (3) determine f_{min}, f_{max}, and $f[m,n]$ if four levels are chosen as functional resolution. What are the FD reconstructed $\hat{f}(x,y)$ samples? Calculate the mean square error in the FD approximation. What will be the $\hat{f}(x,y)$ samples in conventional coordinate system?

$$\begin{pmatrix} 1.1 & 1.1 & 0.69 & 1 & 1 \\ 1 & 0.65 & 0.6 & 0.65 & 1 \\ 1 & 0.87 & 1 & 0.8 & 1 \\ 1 & 0.81 & 1.2 & 1 & 1 \\ 1.1 & 1.1 & 1 & 0.8 & 1 \\ 0.9 & 0.8 & 1.01 & 0.8 & 1 \\ 0.8 & 1 & 0.89 & 0.8 & 1 \\ 0.8 & 0.8 & 1 & 0.8 & 0.8 \end{pmatrix}$$

Figure E.3(a) Some $f(x,y)$ samples

5. In question (4) now the $f(x,y)$ samples are taken from the figure E.3(a). With $\Delta x = 0.4$ and $\Delta y = 0.6$, what is the $f(x,y)$ domain based on the convention of figure 3.1(a)?
6. Obtain the excel file Data5.xls through the email link of page ii and place the file in your working path of MATLAB. Make sure the data in file looks like figure E.3(b). In question (4) now $f(x,y)$ samples are taken from the

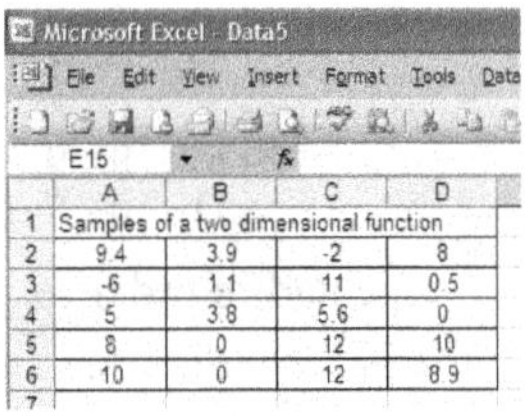

	A	B	C	D
1	Samples of a two dimensional function			
2	9.4	3.9	-2	8
3	-6	1.1	11	0.5
4	5	3.8	5.6	0
5	8	0	12	10
6	10	0	12	8.9
7				

Figure E.3(b) Some $f(x,y)$ samples in an excel file

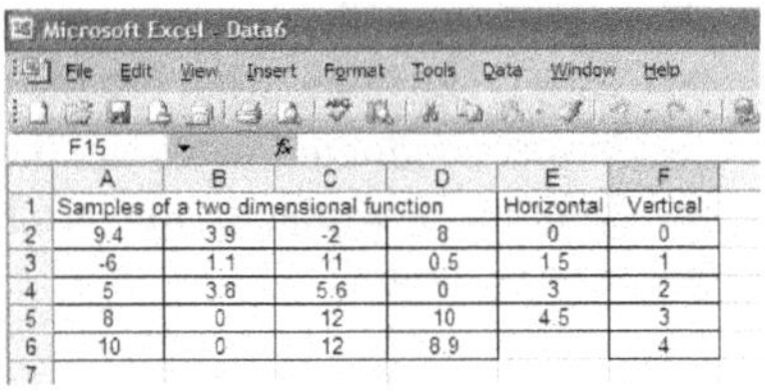

	A	B	C	D	E	F
1	Samples of a two dimensional function				Horizontal	Vertical
2	9.4	3.9	-2	8	0	0
3	-6	1.1	11	0.5	1.5	1
4	5	3.8	5.6	0	3	2
5	8	0	12	10	4.5	3
6	10	0	12	8.9		4
7						

Figure E.3(c) Samples of figure E.3(b) with domain information – right side figure

figure E.3(b). With Δx =0.3 and Δy =0.5, what is the $f(x,y)$ domain based on the convention of figure 3.1(a)?

7. What if the domain information in question (6) is given as in figure E.3(c)? Obtain the excel file Data6.xls which holds the data of figure E.3(c).
8. Generate random samples for $f(x,y)$ each of uniform distribution within $-7V$ and $15V$ with $\Delta x = 0.2mm$ and $\Delta y = 0.3mm$ over $0 \le x \le 8mm$ and $0 \le y \le 6mm$. Perform question (4) quoted FD computing on the random samples of $f(x,y)$ based on 12 level functional resolution.
9. Contemplate about the grid point matrices and write MATLAB codes to compute the following double summations by using FD method: (a) $\sum_{q=-1}^{3}\sum_{p=-2}^{4}(2qp^2 - 5pq)$ (b) $\sum_{q=-1}^{3}\sum_{p=-2}^{4}(p^2 - 10)$ (c) $\sum_{q=0}^{4}\sum_{p=-5}^{5}\frac{\pi}{(p+1)(q-1)}$, $p \ne -1$, $q \ne 1$ (d) $\sum_{n=-2}^{4}\sum_{m=-3}^{2} f(m\Delta x, n\Delta y)$ over $-1 \le x \le 1$ and $0 \le y \le 1.2$ where $f(x,y) = -3x^2 - 6yx + 12y$ (e) $\sum_{y}\sum_{x} f(n\Delta x, n\Delta y)$ over $0 \le x \le 1$ and $0 \le y \le 2$ where $f(x,y) = y^2 - 5yx$ with Δx =0.05 and Δy =0.1.
10. Compute each of the following integrations by using FD method: (a) $\int_{y=0}^{4}\int_{x=-3}^{x=2}(5yx^2 - 2xy + 5y^2)dxdy$ choosing 401 samples for each interval (b) $\int_{\varphi=0}^{2\pi}\int_{\theta=0}^{\pi}\sin(\theta+\varphi)d\theta d\varphi$ choosing 501 samples for each interval (c) $\int_{y=-1}^{y=2}\int_{x=0}^{x=0.5}(e^{-3xy}+1)dxdy$ choosing 401 samples for each interval (d) $-45\int_{y=3}^{4}\int_{x=-5}^{x=7}dxdy$ and relative error choosing 501 samples for each interval.
11. (a) Compute the m and n directed first order forward difference on $f[m,n] = \begin{bmatrix} 29 & 5 & 3 & 19 \\ 24 & 2 & 5 & 26 \\ 78 & 1 & 0 & 63 \\ 67 & 8 & 9 & 34 \\ 11 & 0 & 7 & 65 \end{bmatrix}$ (b) In part (a) if the last row or column is repeated in order to get the same size as $f[m,n]$ does, what are the forward differences? (c) In part (a) if zero padding is conducted, what are the forward differences? (d) In parts (b) and (c) compute the magnitude gradient (e) In part (a) now second order gradient is sought.
12. (a) Compute the x and y directed first order divided difference on $f(x,y) = y^2 - 5yx$ with Δx =0.25 and Δy =0.5 over $0 \le x \le 1$ and $0 \le y \le 2$ (b) In part (a) if the last row or column is repeated in order to get the same size as $f(x,y)$ does, what are the divided differences? (c) In part (a) if zero padding is conducted, what are the divided differences? (d) In parts (b) and (c) compute the magnitude gradient (e) In part (a) now second order gradient is sought.

13. In question (11) if we apply the MATLAB built-in gradient, what is the magnitude gradient?
14. In question (12) if we apply the MATLAB built-in gradient, what is the magnitude gradient?
15. Concerning the question (11) mentioned $f[m,n]$, obtain the following by applying interp2 of MATLAB: (a) $f[m',n']$ on the nearest neighborhood interpolation at (m',n')=(2.7,2.2) (b) in part (a) use bilinear interpolation (c) in part (a) for three points (2.7,2.2), (2.8,2.5), and (2.9,2.7) (d) in part (c) use bilinear interpolation (e) $f[m',n']$ based on bilinear interpolation with $\Delta n' = 0.1$ and m'=0.6 over $1.5 \le n' \le 2$ (f) $f[m',n']$ based on bilinear interpolation with $\Delta m' = 0.1$ and n'=0.6 over $1.5 \le m' \le 2$ (g) $f[m',n']$ based on bilinear interpolation with $\Delta m' = 0.1$ and $\Delta n' = 0.1$ over $1.2 \le m' \le 2$ and $1.5 \le n' \le 2$ (h) in part (g) apply the nearest neighborhood interpolation.
16. Consider $f(x,y) = e^{-x-y} - 5x + 3y$ over $0 \le x \le 3$ and $0 \le y \le 4$. Make the samples of $f(x,y)$ available subject to Δx =1 and Δy =1 by using grid point matrices in MATLAB. Exercise the interp2 of MATLAB to calculate the following: (a) $f(x',y')$ on the nearest neighborhood interpolation at (x',y') = (2.7,2.2) (b) in part (a) use bilinear interpolation (c) in part (a) for three points (2.7,2.2), (2.8,2.5), and (2.9,2.7) (d) in part (c) use bilinear interpolation (e) $f(x',y')$ based on bilinear interpolation with $\Delta y' = 0.1$ and x'=0.6 over $1.5 \le y' \le 2$ (f) $f(x',y')$ based on bilinear interpolation with $\Delta x' = 0.1$ and y'=0.6 over $1.5 \le x' \le 2$ (g) $f(x',y')$ based on bilinear interpolation with $\Delta x' = 0.2$ and $\Delta y' = 0.2$ over $1.7 \le x' \le 2.6$ and $1.7 \le y' \le 2.6$ (h) in part (g) apply the nearest neighborhood interpolation.
17. Use MATLAB graphing function to conduct the following: (a) contour plot of $f(x,y) = e^{-x-y} - 5x + 3y$ over $0 \le x \le 3$ and $0 \le y \le 4$ (b) surface plot in part (a) (c) surface plot of $x = \sin(u+v)$, $y = u^2$, and $z = uv$ over $-5 \le u \le 5$ and $-\pi \le v \le \pi$ (d) surface plot of $\sin(x^2 + y^2)$ on a circular disk domain over $-\pi \le x \le \pi$ and $-\pi \le y \le \pi$ (e) top view of the surface plot in part (d) along with color or gray scale (f) intensity image of $f(x,y) = -12\sin(x+y)$ subject to Δx =0.05 and Δy =0.1 over $0 \le x \le 10$ and $0 \le y \le 15$.

Table 3.B Data for a contour or surface plot:

$y \downarrow$ \ $x \rightarrow$	-3	-1.5	0	1.5	3	4.5	6	7.5
-2	-20	10	10	10	10	-2	-3	-4
0	3	-20	2	2	2	-2	-3	-4
2	10	9	8	11	12	14	15	9
4	4	5	9	10	23	20	6	10
6	13	13	7	12	11	15	0	12

18. Using the data of table 3.B and exercising appropriate MATLAB function, obtain the following: (a) contour plot (b) surface plot.
19. In question (17) obtain the two dimensional plot: (a) for $y=2$ over $0 \le x \le 3$ in part (a) (b) $f(1,y)$ versus y over $0 \le y \le 4$ in part (a) (c) $f(5,y)$ versus y subject to Δy =0.1 over $0 \le y \le 15$ in part (f) (d) $f(x,10)$ versus x subject to Δx =0.05 over $0 \le x \le 10$.

Answers:

(1) $-1 \le m \le 5$, $-2 \le n \le 7$, 70, $-2 \le m \le 10$, $-4 \le n \le 14$, and 247 respectively
hint: section 3.1

(2) $-1.5cm \le x \le 4cm$ and $-3cm \le y \le 6.6cm$ and $-0.75cm \le x \le 2cm$ and $-1.5cm \le y \le 3.3cm$ respectively hint: section 3.1

(3) $$X = \begin{bmatrix} -0.5 & -0.2 & 0.1 & 0.4 & 0.7 \\ -0.5 & -0.2 & 0.1 & 0.4 & 0.7 \\ -0.5 & -0.2 & 0.1 & 0.4 & 0.7 \\ -0.5 & -0.2 & 0.1 & 0.4 & 0.7 \\ -0.5 & -0.2 & 0.1 & 0.4 & 0.7 \end{bmatrix} \text{ and } Y = \begin{bmatrix} -1 & -1 & -1 & -1 & -1 \\ -0.5 & -0.5 & -0.5 & -0.5 & -0.5 \\ 0 & 0 & 0 & 0 & 0 \\ 0.5 & 0.5 & 0.5 & 0.5 & 0.5 \\ 1 & 1 & 1 & 1 & 1 \end{bmatrix}$$

$f(X,Y) = 3XY^3 - X^3$

$$f(x,y) \text{ samples: } \begin{bmatrix} 1.6250 & 0.6080 & -0.3010 & -1.2640 & -2.4430 \\ 0.3125 & 0.0830 & -0.0385 & -0.2140 & -0.6055 \\ 0.1250 & 0.0080 & -0.0010 & -0.0640 & -0.3430 \\ -0.0625 & -0.0670 & 0.0365 & 0.0860 & -0.0805 \\ -1.3750 & -0.5920 & 0.2990 & 1.1360 & 1.7570 \end{bmatrix}$$

hint: section 3.2

(4) f_{min} =–2.443, f_{max} =1.757, Δf =1.4, and $$f[m,n] = \begin{bmatrix} 3 & 2 & 2 & 1 & 0 \\ 2 & 2 & 2 & 2 & 1 \\ 2 & 2 & 2 & 2 & 2 \\ 2 & 2 & 2 & 2 & 2 \\ 1 & 1 & 2 & 3 & 3 \end{bmatrix}$$

$$\hat{f}(x,y) = \begin{bmatrix} 1.7570 & 0.3570 & 0.3570 & -1.0430 & -2.4430 \\ 0.3570 & 0.3570 & 0.3570 & 0.3570 & -1.0430 \\ 0.3570 & 0.3570 & 0.3570 & 0.3570 & 0.3570 \\ 0.3570 & 0.3570 & 0.3570 & 0.3570 & 0.3570 \\ -1.0430 & -1.0430 & 0.3570 & 1.7570 & 1.7570 \end{bmatrix}$$

mse=0.1484

$$\hat{f}(x,y) = \begin{bmatrix} -1.0430 & -1.0430 & 0.3570 & 1.7570 & 1.7570 \\ 0.3570 & 0.3570 & 0.3570 & 0.3570 & 0.3570 \\ 0.3570 & 0.3570 & 0.3570 & 0.3570 & 0.3570 \\ 0.3570 & 0.3570 & 0.3570 & 0.3570 & -1.0430 \\ 1.7570 & 0.3570 & 0.3570 & -1.0430 & -2.4430 \end{bmatrix}$$

hint: section 3.2

(5) f_{min} =0.6, f_{max} =1.2, Δf =0.2, and $$f[m,n] = \begin{bmatrix} 3 & 3 & 0 & 2 & 2 \\ 2 & 0 & 0 & 0 & 2 \\ 2 & 1 & 2 & 1 & 2 \\ 2 & 1 & 3 & 2 & 2 \\ 3 & 3 & 2 & 1 & 2 \\ 2 & 1 & 2 & 1 & 2 \\ 1 & 2 & 1 & 1 & 2 \\ 1 & 1 & 2 & 1 & 1 \end{bmatrix}$$

$$\hat{f}(x,y) = \begin{bmatrix} 1.2 & 1.2 & 0.6 & 1 & 1 \\ 1 & 0.6 & 0.6 & 0.6 & 1 \\ 1 & 0.8 & 1 & 0.8 & 1 \\ 1 & 0.8 & 1.2 & 1 & 1 \\ 1.2 & 1.2 & 1 & 0.8 & 1 \\ 1 & 0.8 & 1 & 0.8 & 1 \\ 0.8 & 1 & 0.8 & 0.8 & 1 \\ 0.8 & 0.8 & 1 & 0.8 & 0.8 \end{bmatrix}$$

mse=0.0019, $0 \le x \le 1.6$ and $0 \le y \le 4.2$ assuming 0 start of x and y

(6) $f_{\min}$ =–6, $f_{\max}$ =12, Δf =6, and $f[m,n] = \begin{bmatrix} 3 & 2 & 1 & 2 \\ 0 & 1 & 3 & 1 \\ 2 & 2 & 2 & 1 \\ 2 & 1 & 3 & 3 \\ 3 & 1 & 3 & 2 \end{bmatrix}$

$$\hat{f}(x,y) = \begin{bmatrix} 12 & 6 & 0 & 6 \\ -6 & 0 & 12 & 0 \\ 6 & 6 & 6 & 0 \\ 6 & 0 & 12 & 12 \\ 12 & 0 & 12 & 6 \end{bmatrix}$$

mse=2.402, $0 \le x \le 0.9$ and $0 \le y \le 2$ assuming 0 start of x and y

(7) $f_{\min}$, $f_{\max}$, Δf, $f[m,n]$, and $\hat{f}(x,y)$ are the same as those in question (6) just domain interval is different which is $0 \le x \le 4.5$ and $0 \le y \le 4$ with Δx =1.5 and Δy =1. Also get all data by executing first D=xlsread('Data6.xls'); and then f=D(:,1:4); for the $f(x,y)$ samples where D is a user-chosen variable.

(8) For randomness we are not going to get unique values. Codes: M=8/0.2+1; N=6/0.3+1; f=22*rand(N,M)-7; df=(15-(-7))/(12-1); fmn=round((f-(-7))/df); f_hat=fmn*df+min(f(:)); mse(f-f_hat) where the symbols have their usual meanings and assuming level variation between given minimum and maximum.

(9) (a)

$$P = \begin{bmatrix} -2 & -1 & 0 & 1 & 2 & 3 & 4 \\ -2 & -1 & 0 & 1 & 2 & 3 & 4 \\ -2 & -1 & 0 & 1 & 2 & 3 & 4 \\ -2 & -1 & 0 & 1 & 2 & 3 & 4 \\ -2 & -1 & 0 & 1 & 2 & 3 & 4 \end{bmatrix}$$

$$Q = \begin{bmatrix} -1 & -1 & -1 & -1 & -1 & -1 & -1 \\ 0 & 0 & 0 & 0 & 0 & 0 & 0 \\ 1 & 1 & 1 & 1 & 1 & 1 & 1 \\ 2 & 2 & 2 & 2 & 2 & 2 & 2 \\ 3 & 3 & 3 & 3 & 3 & 3 & 3 \end{bmatrix}$$

175

(b) –175 (c) 0.9599 (d) 243.6 (e) –499.8 hint: section 3.4

(10) (a) 1048 (b) 0.0251 (c) 2.852 (d) –542.1622 and –0.4004%
hint: section 3.5

(11) (a) $G_m = \begin{bmatrix} -24 & -2 & 16 \\ -22 & 3 & 21 \\ -77 & -1 & 63 \\ -59 & 1 & 25 \\ -11 & 7 & 58 \end{bmatrix}$ and $G_n = \begin{bmatrix} -5 & -3 & 2 & 7 \\ 54 & -1 & -5 & 37 \\ -11 & 7 & 9 & -29 \\ -56 & -8 & -2 & 31 \end{bmatrix}$

(b) $G_m = \begin{bmatrix} -24 & -2 & 16 & 16 \\ -22 & 3 & 21 & 21 \\ -77 & -1 & 63 & 63 \\ -59 & 1 & 25 & 25 \\ -11 & 7 & 58 & 58 \end{bmatrix}$ and $G_n = \begin{bmatrix} -5 & -3 & 2 & 7 \\ 54 & -1 & -5 & 37 \\ -11 & 7 & 9 & -29 \\ -56 & -8 & -2 & 31 \\ -56 & -8 & -2 & 31 \end{bmatrix}$

(c) $G_m = \begin{bmatrix} -24 & -2 & 16 & -19 \\ -22 & 3 & 21 & -26 \\ -77 & -1 & 63 & -63 \\ -59 & 1 & 25 & -34 \\ -11 & 7 & 58 & -65 \end{bmatrix}$ and $G_n = \begin{bmatrix} -5 & -3 & 2 & 7 \\ 54 & -1 & -5 & 37 \\ -11 & 7 & 9 & -29 \\ -56 & -8 & -2 & 31 \\ -11 & 0 & -7 & -65 \end{bmatrix}$

(d) for (b) $G = \begin{bmatrix} 24.5153 & 3.6056 & 16.1245 & 17.4642 \\ 58.3095 & 3.1623 & 21.5870 & 42.5441 \\ 77.7817 & 7.0711 & 63.6396 & 69.3542 \\ 81.3449 & 8.0623 & 25.0799 & 39.8246 \\ 57.0701 & 10.6301 & 58.0345 & 65.7647 \end{bmatrix}$

for (c) $G = \begin{bmatrix} 24.5153 & 3.6056 & 16.1245 & 20.2485 \\ 58.3095 & 3.1623 & 21.5870 & 45.2217 \\ 77.7817 & 7.0711 & 63.6396 & 69.3542 \\ 81.3449 & 8.0623 & 25.0799 & 46.0109 \\ 15.5563 & 7.0000 & 58.4209 & 91.9239 \end{bmatrix}$

(e) $G_{2m} = \begin{bmatrix} 22 & 18 \\ 25 & 18 \\ 76 & 64 \\ 60 & 24 \\ 18 & 51 \end{bmatrix}$ and $G_{2n} = \begin{bmatrix} 59 & 2 & -7 & 30 \\ -65 & 8 & 14 & -66 \\ -45 & -15 & -11 & 60 \end{bmatrix}$

hint: section 3.6

(12) (a) $G_x = \begin{bmatrix} 0 & 0 & 0 & 0 \\ -2.5 & -2.5 & -2.5 & -2.5 \\ -5 & -5 & -5 & -5 \\ -7.5 & -7.5 & -7.5 & -7.5 \\ -10 & -10 & -10 & -10 \end{bmatrix}$ and $G_y = \begin{bmatrix} 0.5 & -0.75 & -2 & -3.25 & -4.5 \\ 1.5 & 0.25 & -1 & -2.25 & -3.5 \\ 2.5 & 1.25 & 0 & -1.25 & -2.5 \\ 3.5 & 2.25 & 1 & -0.25 & -1.5 \end{bmatrix}$

(b)

$$G_x = \begin{bmatrix} 0 & 0 & 0 & 0 & 0 \\ -2.5 & -2.5 & -2.5 & -2.5 & -2.5 \\ -5 & -5 & -5 & -5 & -5 \\ -7.5 & -7.5 & -7.5 & -7.5 & -7.5 \\ -10 & -10 & -10 & -10 & -10 \end{bmatrix}$$

$$G_y = \begin{bmatrix} 0.5 & -0.75 & -2 & -3.25 & -4.5 \\ 1.5 & 0.25 & -1 & -2.25 & -3.5 \\ 2.5 & 1.25 & 0 & -1.25 & -2.5 \\ 3.5 & 2.25 & 1 & -0.25 & -1.5 \\ 3.5 & 2.25 & 1 & -0.25 & -1.5 \end{bmatrix}$$

(c)

$$G_x = \begin{bmatrix} 0 & 0 & 0 & 0 & 0 \\ -2.5 & -2.5 & -2.5 & -2.5 & 9 \\ -5 & -5 & -5 & -5 & 16 \\ -7.5 & -7.5 & -7.5 & -7.5 & 21 \\ -10 & -10 & -10 & -10 & 24 \end{bmatrix}$$

$$G_y = \begin{bmatrix} 0.5 & -0.75 & -2 & -3.25 & -4.5 \\ 1.5 & 0.25 & -1 & -2.25 & -3.5 \\ 2.5 & 1.25 & 0 & -1.25 & -2.5 \\ 3.5 & 2.25 & 1 & -0.25 & -1.5 \\ -8 & -3 & 2 & 7 & 12 \end{bmatrix}$$

(d) for (b) $G = \begin{bmatrix} 0.5 & 0.75 & 2 & 3.25 & 4.5 \\ 2.9155 & 2.5125 & 2.6926 & 3.3634 & 4.3012 \\ 5.5902 & 5.1539 & 5 & 5.1539 & 5.5902 \\ 8.2765 & 7.8302 & 7.5664 & 7.5042 & 7.6485 \\ 10.5948 & 10.25 & 10.0499 & 10.0031 & 10.1119 \end{bmatrix}$

for (c) $G = \begin{bmatrix} 0.5 & 0.75 & 2 & 3.25 & 4.5 \\ 2.9155 & 2.5125 & 2.6926 & 3.3634 & 9.6566 \\ 5.5902 & 5.1539 & 5 & 5.1539 & 16.1941 \\ 8.2765 & 7.8302 & 7.5664 & 7.5042 & 21.0535 \\ 12.8062 & 10.4403 & 10.1980 & 12.2066 & 26.8328 \end{bmatrix}$

(e) $G_{2x} = \begin{bmatrix} 0 & 0 & 0 \\ 0 & 0 & 0 \\ 0 & 0 & 0 \\ 0 & 0 & 0 \\ 0 & 0 & 0 \end{bmatrix}$ and $G_{2y} = \begin{bmatrix} 2 & 2 & 2 & 2 & 2 \\ 2 & 2 & 2 & 2 & 2 \\ 2 & 2 & 2 & 2 & 2 \end{bmatrix}$ hint: section 3.6

(13)

$$G = \begin{bmatrix} 24.5153 & 13.3417 & 7.2801 & 17.4642 \\ 32.9280 & 9.7082 & 12.0934 & 30.4138 \\ 79.9453 & 39.1152 & 31.0644 & 63.1269 \\ 67.8473 & 29.0043 & 13.4629 & 25.02 \\ 57.0701 & 8.2462 & 32.5615 & 65.7647 \end{bmatrix}$$

hint: section 3.6

(14)

$$G = \begin{bmatrix} 0.5 & 0.75 & 2 & 3.25 & 4.5 \\ 2.6926 & 2.5125 & 2.9155 & 3.7165 & 4.717 \\ 5.3852 & 5.0559 & 5.0249 & 5.2974 & 5.831 \\ 8.0777 & 7.7015 & 7.5166 & 7.5374 & 7.7621 \\ 10.5948 & 10.25 & 10.0499 & 10.0031 & 10.1119 \end{bmatrix}$$

hint: section 3.6 but here you need to enter the Δx and Δy information with syntax gradient(f, Δx , Δy) hence execute [Gx,Gy]=gradient(f,0.25, 0.5); upon finding f.

(15) (a) $f[m',n']$=63 (b) $f[m',n']$=40.58 (c) $f[m',n']$=63, 34, and 34 respectively (d) $f[m',n']$=40.58, 39.7, and 39.06 respectively (e) $f[m',n']$= $\begin{bmatrix} 21.3 \\ 23.4 \\ 25.5 \\ 27.6 \\ 29.7 \\ 31.8 \end{bmatrix}$ (f) $f[m',n']$=[3.7 3.8 3.9 4 4.1 4.2]

$$(g)\ f[m',n'] = \begin{bmatrix} 1.7 & 1.8 & 1.9 & 2 & 2.1 & 2.2 & 2.3 & 2.4 & 2.5 \\ 1.52 & 1.58 & 1.64 & 1.7 & 1.76 & 1.82 & 1.88 & 1.94 & 2 \\ 1.34 & 1.36 & 1.38 & 1.4 & 1.42 & 1.44 & 1.46 & 1.48 & 1.5 \\ 1.16 & 1.14 & 1.12 & 1.1 & 1.08 & 1.06 & 1.04 & 1.02 & 1 \\ 0.98 & 0.92 & 0.86 & 0.8 & 0.74 & 0.68 & 0.62 & 0.56 & 0.5 \\ 0.8 & 0.7 & 0.6 & 0.5 & 0.4 & 0.3 & 0.2 & 0.1 & 0 \end{bmatrix}$$

$$(h)\ f[m',n'] = \begin{bmatrix} 1 & 1 & 1 & 0 & 0 & 0 & 0 & 0 & 0 \\ 1 & 1 & 1 & 0 & 0 & 0 & 0 & 0 & 0 \\ 1 & 1 & 1 & 0 & 0 & 0 & 0 & 0 & 0 \\ 1 & 1 & 1 & 0 & 0 & 0 & 0 & 0 & 0 \\ 1 & 1 & 1 & 0 & 0 & 0 & 0 & 0 & 0 \\ 1 & 1 & 1 & 0 & 0 & 0 & 0 & 0 & 0 \end{bmatrix}$$

hint: section 3.7

(16) (a) $f(x',y')$=–8.9933 (b) $f(x',y')$=–6.8911 (c) $f(x',y')$=–8.9933, –5.9975, and –5.9975 respectively (d) $f(x',y')$=–6.8911, –6.4938, and –6.3956 respectively (e) $f(x',y')$= $\begin{bmatrix} 1.6562 \\ 1.9417 \\ 2.2273 \\ 2.5129 \\ 2.7984 \\ 3.0840 \end{bmatrix}$ (f) $f(x',y')$=[–5.5438 –6.0583 –6.5727 –7.0871 –7.6016 –8.1160]

$$(g)\ f(x',y') = \begin{bmatrix} -3.3579 & -4.3675 & -5.3740 & -6.3775 & -7.3810 \\ -2.7675 & -3.7748 & -4.7799 & -5.7826 & -6.7853 \\ -2.1740 & -3.1799 & -4.1839 & -5.1861 & -6.1883 \\ -1.5775 & -2.5826 & -3.5861 & -4.5880 & -5.5898 \\ -0.9810 & -1.9853 & -2.9883 & -3.9898 & -4.9914 \end{bmatrix}$$

$$(h)\ f(x',y') = \begin{bmatrix} -3.9817 & -3.9817 & -3.9817 & -3.9817 & -8.9933 \\ -3.9817 & -3.9817 & -3.9817 & -3.9817 & -8.9933 \\ -3.9817 & -3.9817 & -3.9817 & -3.9817 & -8.9933 \\ -3.9817 & -3.9817 & -3.9817 & -3.9817 & -8.9933 \\ -0.9933 & -0.9933 & -0.9933 & -0.9933 & -5.9975 \end{bmatrix}$$

hint: section 3.7

(17) (a) Figure E.3(d) (b) Figure E.3(e) (c) Figure E.3(f) (d) Figure E.3(g) (e) Figure E.3(h) (f) Figure E.3(i) hint: section 3.8

Figure E.3(d) Contour plot of $e^{-x-y} - 5x + 3y$ – right side figure

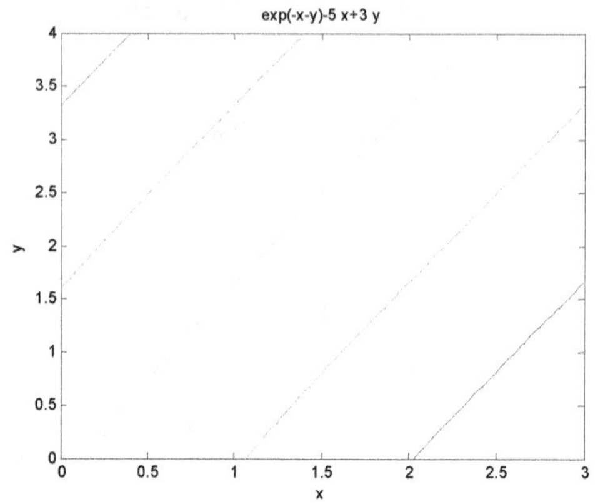

Figure E.3(e) Surface plot of $e^{-x-y} - 5x + 3y$ – right side figure

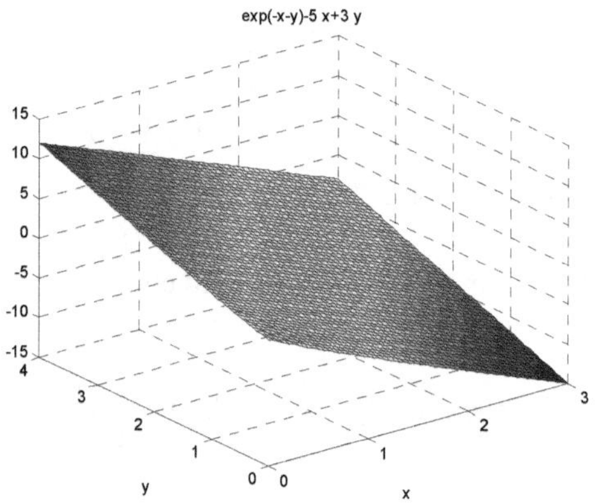

Figure E.3(f) Surface plot of $x = \sin(u + v)$, $y = u^2$, and $z = uv$ – right side figure

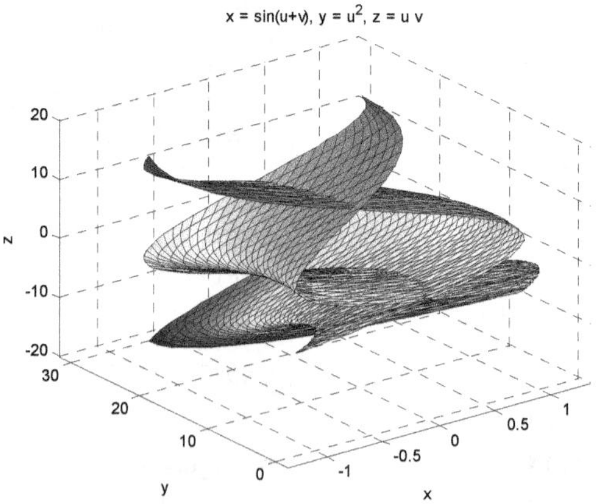

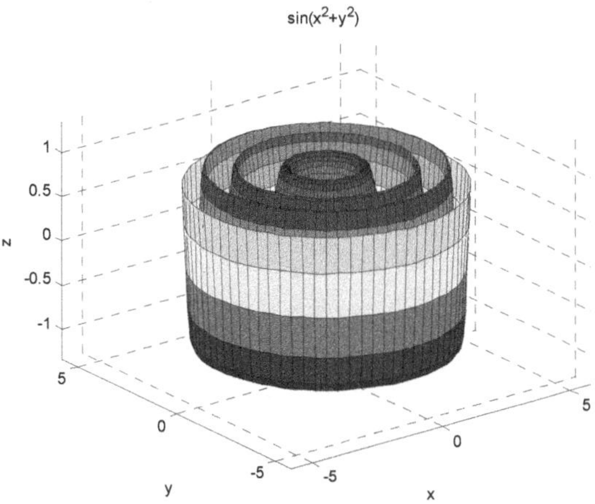

Figure E.3(g) Surface plot on a circular base – right side figure

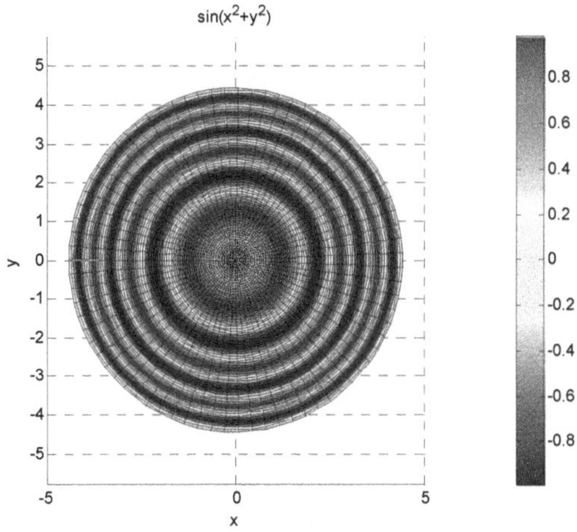

Figure E.3(h) Top view of the surface plot on a circular base – right side figure

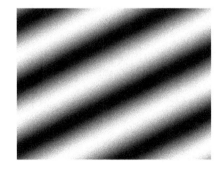

Figure E.3(i) Intensity image plot of $-12\sin(x+y)$ – right side figure

(18) (a) Figure E.3(j) (b) Figure E.3(k) hint: section 3.8

Figure E.3(j) Contour plot of sampled data – right side figure

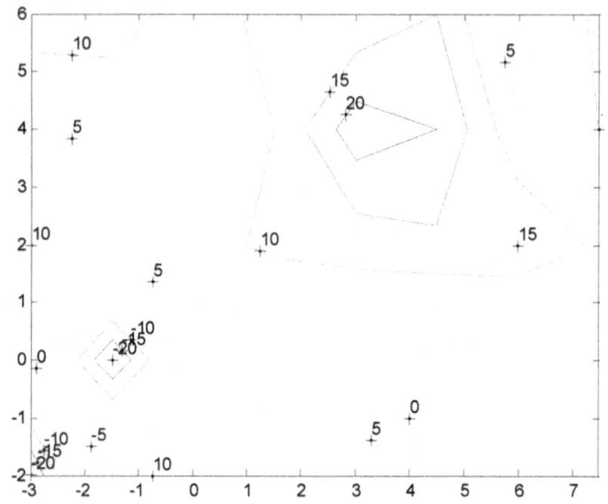

Figure E.3(k) Surface plot of sampled data – right side figure

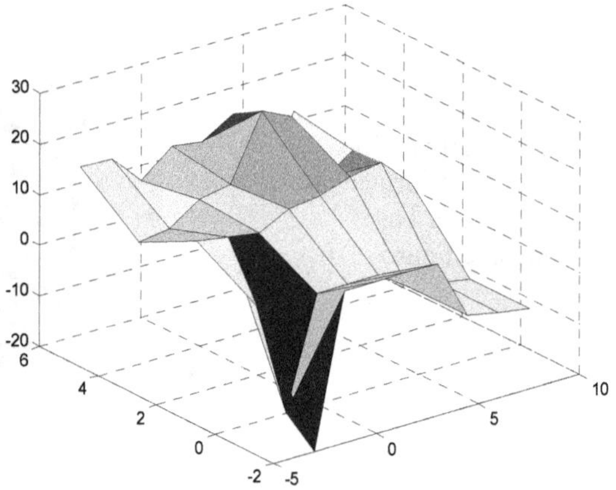

Figure E.3(l) Two dimensional plot on fixed y – right side figure

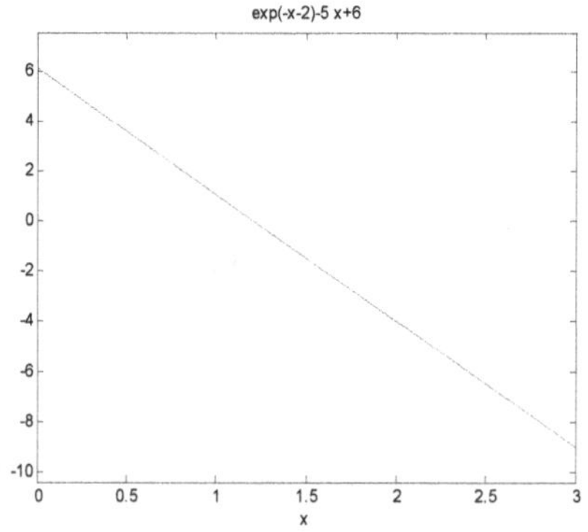

(19) (a) Figure E.3(l): can use ezplot('exp(-x-2)-5*x+6',[0 3]) (b) Figure E.3(m): can use ezplot('exp(-1-y)-5+3*y',[0 4]) (c) Figure E.3(n): can use y=0:0.1:15; f=-12*sin(5+y); plot(y,f) (d) Figure E.3(o): can use x=0:0.05:10; f=-12*sin(x+10); plot(x,f) hint: section 3.8

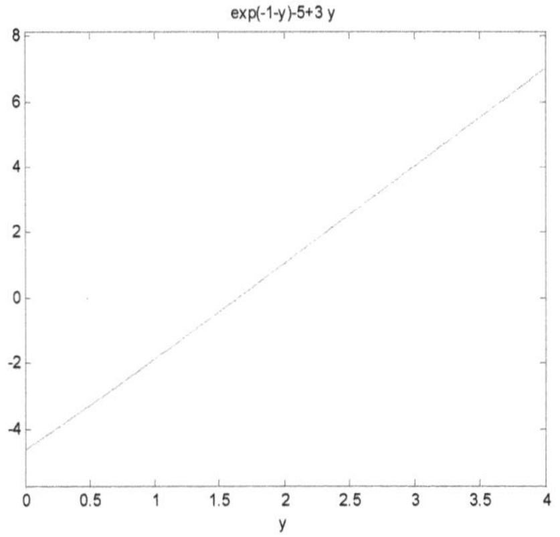

Figure E.3(m) Two dimensional plot on fixed x – right side figure

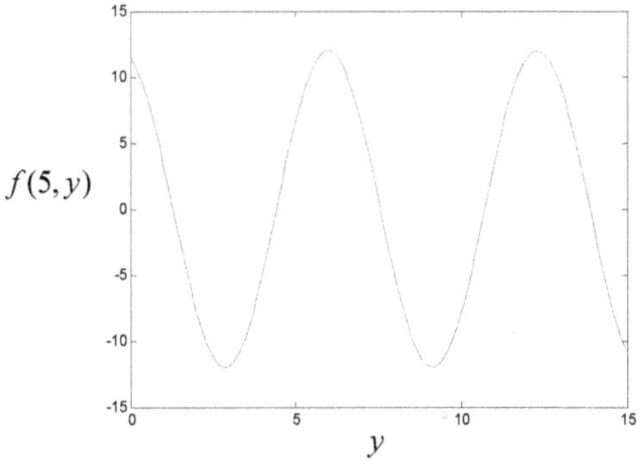

Figure E.3(n) $f(5,y)$ versus y plot – right side figure

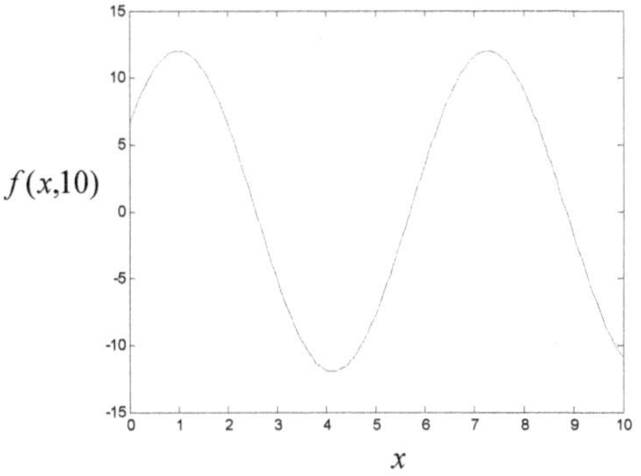

Figure E.3(o) $f(x,10)$ versus x plot – right side figure

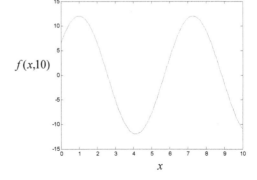

Chapter 4

Finite Difference in Ordinary Differential Equations

This chapter focuses implementation of ordinary differential equations which relate to finite difference (FD) techniques. Very often differential equations come into view in mathematical models that endeavor to describe real-life problems in science and engineering. Not only that differential equations are put into practice even in business fields. When differential equations are systemized, available tools make the solution finding amazingly comfortable which we have tried to demonstrate. However the chapter underlines the following:

- Introductory discussion on ordinary differential equations
- Transforming an ordinary differential equation to its finite difference counterpart
- Embedded FD function to solve ordinary differential equation
- Plotting tools for FD derived differential equation solutions

4.1 What is an ordinary differential equation?

To forecast the behavior or to study the response undergoing some excitation on a physical system, we construct mathematical models. We know that continuous derivatives measure a system rate change of response. Frequently derivatives constitute mathematical model of the system. The mathematical models or equations involving the derivatives are called differential equations. When we have one dependent and one independent variables, the differential equation is termed as the ordinary differential equation abbreviatedly ODE.

For instance $\frac{dy}{dx}+y=9$ and $\frac{d^4y}{dx^4}+y=9$ are the ordinary differential equations where y is the dependent and x is the independent variables.

Order of a differential equation is the highest order of derivatives present in the equation. Thus

a first order ordinary differential equation has the form $f\left(x,y,\frac{dy}{dx}\right)=0$,

a second order ordinary differential equation has the form $f\left(x,y,\frac{dy}{dx},\frac{d^2y}{dx^2}\right)=0$, and so forth.

The solution of a differential equation is a function that satisfies the differential equation over some interval of the independent variable. Method of finding the solution of a differential equation can be analytical or numerical. Since FD always relates to numerical, our discussion follows so. Numeric nature of FD compels us to choose initial value or boundary value of the ODE.

Broadly we may view the ODE problems as applying elementary programming method and readymade tools available in MATLAB.

4.2 How to express an ODE by FD terms?

In section 2.4 we have introduced the definitions of four theoretical numerical derivatives. Out of the four, the central difference with the divided term is likely to be the most accurate. ODE solving by FD technique requires some preliminary steps which we elucidate in the following.

(1) Numerical difference replaces the derivative terms of ODE.
(2) From the initial or boundary value we form a set of linear equations.
(3) We solve the linear equation set by **solve** function (appendix D) of MATLAB.

This sort of computing is applicable only for class discussed problems. Robust ODE solving does not apply this approach.

In symbolic form we write the central numerical derivatives as follows:

First order: $\frac{dy}{dx}\approx\frac{\Delta y}{\Delta x}=\frac{y[m+1]-y[m-1]}{2\Delta x}$

Second order: $\frac{d^2y}{dx^2}\approx\frac{y[m+1]-2y[m]+y[m-1]}{(\Delta x)^2}$

Third order: $\frac{d^3y}{dx^3} \approx \frac{y[m+2]-2y[m+1]+2y[m-1]-y[m-2]}{2(\Delta x)^3}$

Fourth order: $\frac{d^4y}{dx^4} \approx \frac{y[m+2]-4y[m+1]+6y[m]-4y[m-1]+y[m-2]}{(\Delta x)^4}$

The Δx and $y[m]$ have the chapter 2 mentioned meanings. All the above derivative definitions are at the m -th sample both in x and y. The samples that are associated with definitions are as follows:

first order: ($m-1$), m, and ($m+1$)-th i.e. 3 consecutive samples,
second order: ($m-1$), m, and ($m+1$)-th i.e. 3 consecutive samples,
third order: ($m-2$), ($m-1$), m, ($m+1$), and ($m+2$)-th i.e. 5 consecutive samples, and
fourth order: ($m-2$), ($m-1$), m, ($m+1$), and ($m+2$)-th i.e. 5 consecutive samples.

Note that every derivative definition is symmetric about the index m. Suppose there are five samples in y then the maximum number of linear equations we can have is 3 for the first and second order derivatives which are illustrated by the following:

m=0 1 2 3 4
$\leftarrow Eqn\ 1 \rightarrow$
$\leftarrow Eqn\ 2 \rightarrow$
$\leftarrow Eqn\ 3 \rightarrow$

As a general strategy the probable number of linear equations is

number of samples in y − number of consecutive samples in the highest order derivative+1.

◆ Developing linear equations from FD approximation

In order to develop linear equations from an ODE by using FD approximations we observe the following steps:

(a) replace x by $x[m]$,
(b) replace y by $y[m]$,
(c) find the lowest index and customarily that lowest index is assumed to be 0; if the lowest index is m, we choose m as 0 onwards, if the lowest index is $m-1$, we choose m as 1 onwards, and so on,
(d) from given Δx and interval we determine how many sample points are there in x or y,
(e) from the derivative order we decide how many sample points are required to write each linear equation, and

(f) finally we make sure that the number of unknowns in the equation is equal to the number of equations in order to get the solution.

Let us see an example in this regard.

Suppose we have to solve $\frac{d^2y}{dx^2}=5x+6y$ by FD employing Δx =0.25 over $0 \le x \le 1$ where the boundary conditions are $y(0)=0$ and $y(1)=2$.

There are five samples of $y[m]$ at $x[m]$=0, 0.25, 0.5, 0.75, and 1 customarily for m=0, 1, 2, 3, and 4 respectively. Employing FD approximation and replacing x by $x[m]$ and y by $y[m]$, the given equation is written as

$$\frac{y[m+1]-2y[m]+y[m-1]}{(\Delta x)^2}=5x[m]+6y[m].$$

The lowest index in the equation is $m-1$ so choose m=1. For the five samples the linear equation set is developed as

for m=1: $$\frac{y[2]-2y[1]+0}{0.25^2}=5\times 0.25+6\times y[1],$$

for m=2: $$\frac{y[3]-2y[2]+y[1]}{0.25^2}=5\times 0.5+6y[2], \text{ and}$$

for m=3: $$\frac{2-2y[3]+y[2]}{0.25^2}=5\times 0.75+6y[3].$$

For the second order derivative the equation number we should have is 5–3+1 or 3 which is the case in above.

There are three unknowns ($y[1]$, $y[2]$, and $y[3]$) and three equations so after solving the three linear equations one obtains $y[1]$= 0.1194, $y[2]$=0.3616, and $y[3]$=0.8957 which is what we expect from MATLAB.

♦ Solving the linear equation set in MATLAB

Having formed the linear equations, one needs to call the solver of MATLAB for the solution. The symbology we apply is the following: y1⇔ $y[1]$, y2⇔ $y[2]$, y3⇔ $y[3]$ and so on where y1, y2, ... are user-chosen. We may assign the equations to intermediate variables e.g. to e1, e2, etc. The variables e1, e2, ... are also user-chosen.

On concept and symbology so introduced, above numerical example is implemented as follows:

```
>>e1='(y2-2*y1+0)/0.25^2=5*0.25+6*y1'; ↵ ← First equation assigned to e1
>>e2='(y3-2*y2+y1)/0.25^2=5*0.5+6*y2'; ↵ ← Second equation assigned to e2
>>e3='(2-2*y3+y2)/0.25^2=5*0.75+6*y3'; ↵ ← Third equation assigned to e3
```

```
>>s=solve(e1,e2,e3); ↵      ← Calling the solver, s holds symbolic solution where
                                s is user-chosen
>>double([s.y1 s.y2 s.y3]) ↵      ← For viewing the decimal solution

ans =
      0.1194   0.3616   0.8957
        ↑        ↑        ↑
       y[1]     y[2]     y[3]
```

In last executions the first equation $\frac{y[2]-2y[1]+0}{0.25^2}=5\times0.25+6\times y[1]$ has the code (y2-2*y1+0)/0.25^2=5*0.25+6*y1 which we assigned to **e1**, so does the other equations.

Let us see another example on a second order equation.

Example:

Solve $x\frac{d^2y}{dx^2}+2\frac{dy}{dx}=x$ by FD using Δx =0.2 over $0\le x\le 1$ where the initial conditions are $y(0)=1$ and $y'(0)=0$.

Related $x[m]$s are 0, 0.2, 0.4, 0.6, 0.8, and 1 which correspond to $y[0]$, $y[1]$, $y[2]$, $y[3]$, $y[4]$, and $y[5]$ respectively, out of which $y[0]$ is known and the rest five are to be calculated.

The FD equation is $x[m]\frac{y[m+1]-2y[m]+y[m-1]}{(\Delta x)^2}+$ $2\times\frac{y[m+1]-y[m-1]}{2\Delta x}=x[m]$. Given interval says there are six samples and expect 6–3+1 or 4 equations. Let us write them:

for m =1: $0.2\frac{y[2]-2y[1]+y[0]}{0.2^2}+2\times\frac{y[2]-y[0]}{2\times0.2}=0.2$,

for m =2: $0.4\frac{y[3]-2y[2]+y[1]}{0.2^2}+2\times\frac{y[3]-y[1]}{2\times0.2}=0.4$,

for m =3: $0.6\frac{y[4]-2y[3]+y[2]}{0.2^2}+2\times\frac{y[4]-y[2]}{2\times0.2}=0.6$, and

for m =4: $0.8\frac{y[5]-2y[4]+y[3]}{0.2^2}+2\times\frac{y[5]-y[3]}{2\times0.2}=0.8$.

As you see there are five unknowns ($\because$ $y[0]=1$) but 4 FD equations. Another equation we get from the $y'(0)=0$ i.e. $\frac{y[m+1]-y[m-1]}{2\Delta x}=0$ for m =1 or $\frac{y[2]-y[0]}{2\times0.2}=0$. With $y[0]=1$, call the solver as follows:

```
>>e1='0.2*(y2-2*y1+1)/0.2^2+2*(y2-1)/2/0.2=0.2'; ↵      ← for m =1
>>e2='0.4*(y3-2*y2+y1)/0.2^2+2*(y3-y1)/2/0.2=0.4'; ↵     ← for m =2
>>e3='0.6*(y4-2*y3+y2)/0.2^2+2*(y4-y2)/2/0.2=0.6'; ↵     ← for m =3
>>e4='0.8*(y5-2*y4+y3)/0.2^2+2*(y5-y3)/2/0.2=0.8'; ↵     ← for m =4
>>e5='(y2-1)/2/0.2=0'; ↵                       ← from the initial condition
```

```
>>s=solve(e1,e2,e3,e4,e5); ↵                    ← calling the solver
>>double([s.y1 s.y2 s.y3 s.y4 s.y5]) ↵          ← for the decimal solution

ans =
        0.9800    1.0000    1.0333    1.0800    1.1400
          ↑         ↑         ↑         ↑         ↑
         y[1]      y[2]      y[3]      y[4]      y[5]
```

Above result shows the solution. Last two numerical demonstration is just for understanding the concept hidden in FD approach to solve ODE. Embedded functions help us bypass all these hassle of computing which will be addressed in next section.

4.3 ODE solution in FD sense by embedded function

MATLAB is rich in having differential equation solvers. There are many embedded functions which solve variety of differential equations. Following steps should be exercised before executing an ODE solver.

Essential steps for embedded ODE solver

Step A

How an M-file as well as function file is opened and executed (see chapter 1 and appendix F regarding this),

Step B

A function file by name **f** (as we follow in subsequent discussions) must contain the differential equation (s),

Step C

Differential equation (s) must be expressible in highest order

$$\left[\text{ for example } \frac{dy}{dx} = f(x, y) \text{ or } \frac{d^2y}{dx^2} = f\left(x, y, \frac{dy}{dx}\right) \right],$$

Step D

User's working path and the path containing the function file **f** must be identical,

Step E

An ODE solver is often chosen based on the approximation order, stiffness of dependent variable, and accuracy required,

Step F

Relative and absolute errors must be considered if it is necessary,

Step G

Initial values of the dependent variable (s) and the derivative (s) must be known $\left[\text{ for instance } y \text{ or } \frac{dy}{dx} \text{ at } x=0 \right]$,

Step H

In general arguments of the function file f are column vectors, and

Step I

Most ODE solvers operate in terms of a system of differential equations which will be explained later.

The acronyms and elaborations of some ODE solvers are provided in table 4.A.

Table 4.A Acronyms and descriptions of some ODE solvers

Name of ODE solver	Description of the solver
ode23	Can solve nonstiff differential equations using low order method [uses Runge-Kutta (2,3) formula]
ode45	Can solve nonstiff differential equations using medium order method [uses Runge-Kutta (4,5) formula]
ode113	Can solve nonstiff differential equations using variable order method
ode23s	Can solve stiff differential equations using low order method
ode15s	Can solve stiff differential equations using variable order method
ode23t	Can solve moderately stiff differential equations using trapezoidal rule
ode23tb	Can solve stiff differential equations using low order method

Linearization of higher order ODEs

When an ODE is of first order, rearranging the equation is easy. For higher order ODE it is mandatory that we express the higher order ones in terms of the first order derivatives. A substitution technique is applied as follows:

for the second order derivative $\frac{d^2y}{dx^2}$:

$$y = y_1,\ \frac{dy}{dx} = y_2,\ \text{and}\ \frac{d^2y}{dx^2} = \frac{dy_2}{dx},$$

for the third order derivative $\frac{d^3y}{dx^3}$:

$$y = y_1,\ \frac{dy}{dx} = y_2,\ \frac{d^2y}{dx^2} = y_3,\ \text{and}\ \frac{d^3y}{dx^3} = \frac{dy_3}{dx},$$

for the fourth order derivative $\frac{d^4y}{dx^4}$:

$$y = y_1,\ \frac{dy}{dx} = y_2,\ \frac{d^2y}{dx^2} = y_3,\ \frac{d^3y}{dx^3} = y_4,\ \text{and}\ \frac{d^4y}{dx^4} = \frac{dy_4}{dx},$$

and so on.

Systemization of higher order ODEs

Having expressed in first order terms, higher order derivatives also form an ODE system as follows:

for the second order derivative $\frac{d^2y}{dx^2} = f(x,y)$:

$$\begin{Bmatrix} \frac{dy}{dx} = y_2 \\ \frac{d^2y}{dx^2} = f(x,y) \end{Bmatrix} \text{ or } \begin{Bmatrix} \frac{dy_1}{dx} = y_2 \\ \frac{dy_2}{dx} = f(x,y) \end{Bmatrix},$$

for the third order derivative $\frac{d^3y}{dx^3} = f(x,y)$:

$$\begin{Bmatrix} \frac{dy}{dx} = y_2 \\ \frac{d^2y}{dx^2} = y_3 \\ \frac{d^3y}{dx^3} = f(x,y) \end{Bmatrix} \text{ or } \begin{Bmatrix} \frac{dy_1}{dx} = y_2 \\ \frac{dy_2}{dx} = y_3 \\ \frac{dy_3}{dx} = f(x,y) \end{Bmatrix},$$

for the fourth order derivative $\frac{d^4y}{dx^4} = f(x,y)$:

$$\begin{Bmatrix} \frac{dy}{dx} = y_2 \\ \frac{d^2y}{dx^2} = y_3 \\ \frac{d^3y}{dx^3} = y_4 \\ \frac{d^4y}{dx^4} = f(x,y) \end{Bmatrix} \text{ or } \begin{Bmatrix} \frac{dy_1}{dx} = y_2 \\ \frac{dy_2}{dx} = y_3 \\ \frac{dy_3}{dx} = y_4 \\ \frac{dy_4}{dx} = f(x,y) \end{Bmatrix},$$

and so forth.

Example of ODE systemization

Before coding we rearrange the given ODE such that the highest order is on the left side and the right side should hold the rest of the equation. Some examples are included in the sequel:

Example 1:

The ODE $\frac{1}{y^2}\frac{dy}{dx} = 4x^4$ is written as $\frac{dy}{dx} = 4x^4y^2$.

Example 2:

The ODE $(x^2 + y^3)\frac{dy}{dx} = x + \sinh y$ is written as $\frac{dy}{dx} = \frac{x + \sinh y}{x^2 + y^3}$.

Example 3:

The ODE $2\frac{d^2y}{dx^2}-5\frac{dy}{dx}+2y=x$ is first written as $\frac{d^2y}{dx^2}=\frac{5}{2}\frac{dy}{dx}-y+\frac{x}{2}$ and then systemized as $\left\{\begin{matrix}\frac{dy_1}{dx}=y_2\\ \frac{dy_2}{dx}=f(x,y)\end{matrix}\right\}$ where $f(x,y)=\frac{5}{2}\frac{dy}{dx}-y+\frac{x}{2}=\frac{5}{2}y_2-y_1+\frac{x}{2}$ with $y=y_1$ and $\frac{dy}{dx}=y_2$.

Example 4:

The ODE $6x\frac{d^3y}{dx^3}-7xy\frac{d^2y}{dx^2}+(9x+y)\frac{dy}{dx}-4y=3x$ is first written as $\frac{d^3y}{dx^3}=\frac{1}{2}+\frac{7y}{6}\frac{d^2y}{dx^2}-\frac{(9x+y)}{6x}\frac{dy}{dx}+\frac{2y}{3x}$ and then systemized as $\left\{\begin{matrix}\frac{dy_1}{dx}=y_2\\ \frac{dy_2}{dx}=y_3\\ \frac{dy_3}{dx}=f(x,y)\end{matrix}\right\}$ where $f(x,y)=\frac{1}{2}+\frac{7y}{6}\frac{d^2y}{dx^2}-\frac{(9x+y)}{6x}\frac{dy}{dx}+\frac{2y}{3x}=$ $\frac{1}{2}+\frac{7y_1y_3}{6}-\frac{(9x+y_1)}{6x}y_2+\frac{2y_1}{3x}$ with $y=y_1$, $\frac{dy}{dx}=y_2$, and $\frac{d^2y}{dx^2}=y_3$.

Example 5:

The ODE $x^4\frac{d^4y}{dx^4}-x^2\frac{d^2y}{dx^2}-4y=3\sin x$ is first written as $\frac{d^4y}{dx^4}=\frac{3\sin x}{x^4}+\frac{1}{x^2}\frac{d^2y}{dx^2}+\frac{4y}{x^4}$ and then systemized as $\left\{\begin{matrix}\frac{dy_1}{dx}=y_2\\ \frac{dy_2}{dx}=y_3\\ \frac{dy_3}{dx}=y_4\\ \frac{dy_4}{dx}=f(x,y)\end{matrix}\right\}$ where $f(x,y)=\frac{3\sin x}{x^4}+\frac{1}{x^2}\frac{d^2y}{dx^2}+\frac{4y}{x^4}=\frac{3\sin x}{x^4}+\frac{y_3}{x^2}+\frac{4y_1}{x^4}$ with $y=y_1$, $\frac{dy}{dx}=y_2$, $\frac{d^2y}{dx^2}=y_3$, and $\frac{d^3y}{dx^3}=y_4$.

Example 6:

The set $\left\{\begin{matrix}\frac{dx}{dt}=31x-21y-e^{-3t}\\ \frac{dy}{dt}=44x-30y+2t\end{matrix}\right\}$ is same as $\left\{\begin{matrix}\frac{dy_1}{dt}=31y_1-21y_2-e^{-3t}\\ \frac{dy_2}{dt}=44y_1-30y_2+2t\end{matrix}\right\}$ because the given set is already systemized of coarse considering $y_1=x$ and $y_2=y$.

Coding an ODE for embedded solver

First step of solving an ODE is to systemize the given ODE as pointed out. Next we code the ODE as a function file. Following points are important while coding an ODE:

(a) A column matrix holds all derivatives in order. Suppose dy is a column matrix, then first element or dy(1) means $\frac{dy}{dx}$, second element or dy(2) means $\frac{d^2y}{dx^2}$, third element or dy(3) means $\frac{d^3y}{dx^3}$, and so on. The dy is a user-chosen variable.

(b) Another column matrix y holds all systemized dependent variables i.e. first element or y(1) means y_1, second element or y(2) means y_2, third element or y(3) means y_3, and so on. The y is a user-chosen variable.

(c) The ODE function file name is user-chosen (say f). The left assignee or return variable of the function file is dy.

(d) The function file has two input arguments – x and y where x is the independent variable and y is the systemized dependent variable (s).

(e) If we write dy(1), automatically machine understands first element of row matrix dy. For this reason at the end we turn the row dy to column one by writing dy=dy'; in the function file.

In systemization discussion we quoted six examples now we are going to provide their function file code.

Example 1:

The ODE $\frac{1}{y^2}\frac{dy}{dx} = 4x^4$ has the following function file code:

```
function dy=f(x,y)
dy=4*x^4*y^2;
```

Variable equivalence:

y⇔ y, x⇔ x, and dy⇔ $\frac{dy}{dx}$

Example 2:

For the ODE $(x^2 + y^3)\frac{dy}{dx} = x + \sinh y$:

```
function dy=f(x,y)
dy=(x+sinh(y))/(x^2+y^3);
```

Variable equivalence:

y⇔ y, x⇔ x, and dy⇔ $\frac{dy}{dx}$

Example 3:

For the ODE $2\frac{d^2y}{dx^2} - 5\frac{dy}{dx} + 2y = x$:

```
function dy=f(x,y)
dy(1)=y(2);
dy(2)=5/2*y(2)-y(1)+x/2;
dy=dy';
```

Variable equivalence:
y(1)⇔ y_1 , y(2)⇔ y_2 , x⇔ x , dy(1) ⇔ $\frac{dy}{dx}$, and dy(2)⇔ $\frac{d^2y}{dx^2}$

Example 4:

For the ODE $6x\frac{d^3y}{dx^3} - 7xy\frac{d^2y}{dx^2} + (9x+y)\frac{dy}{dx} - 4y = 3x$:

```
function dy=f(x,y)
dy(1)=y(2);
dy(2)=y(3);
dy(3)=1/2+7*y(1)*y(3)/6-(9*x+y(1))*y(2)/6/x+2*y(1)/3/x;
dy=dy';
```

Variable equivalence:

y(1)⇔ y_1 , y(2)⇔ y_2 , y(3)⇔ y_3 , x⇔ x , dy(1)⇔ $\frac{dy}{dx}$, dy(2)⇔ $\frac{d^2y}{dx^2}$, and dy(3)⇔ $\frac{d^3y}{dx^3}$

Example 5:

For the ODE $x^4\frac{d^4y}{dx^4} - x^2\frac{d^2y}{dx^2} - 4y = 3\sin x$:

```
function dy=f(x,y)
dy(1)=y(2);
dy(2)=y(3);
dy(3)=y(4);
dy(4)=3*sin(x)/x^4+y(3)/x^2+4*y(1)/x^4;
dy=dy';
```

Variable equivalence:

y(1)⇔ y_1 , y(2)⇔ y_2 , y(3)⇔ y_3 , y(4)⇔ y_4 , x⇔ x , dy(1)⇔ $\frac{dy}{dx}$, dy(2)⇔ $\frac{d^2y}{dx^2}$, dy(3)⇔ $\frac{d^3y}{dx^3}$, and dy(4)⇔ $\frac{d^4y}{dx^4}$

Example 6:

For the ODE system $\left\{\begin{aligned}\frac{dx}{dt} &= 31x - 21y - e^{-3t}\\ \frac{dy}{dt} &= 44x - 30y + 2t\end{aligned}\right\}$:

```
function dy=f(t,y)
dy(1)=31*y(1)-21*y(2)-exp(-3*t);
dy(2)=44*y(1)-30*y(2)+2*t;
dy=dy';
```

Variable equivalence:
y(1)⇔ x , y(2)⇔ y , t⇔ t , dy(1)⇔ $\frac{dx}{dt}$, and dy(2)⇔ $\frac{dy}{dt}$

As the function input argument now we have independent variable t so write f(t,y) instead of f(x,y).

Executing an ODE for the solution

It is given that the solution of $\frac{dy}{dx}=4x^4y^2$ with the initial condition $y(0)=2$ is y=2, 2, 2.001, 2.0078, 2.0333, and 2.1053 for x=0, 0.1, 0.2, 0.3, 0.4 and 0.5 respectively which we intend to compute.

As a first step write the function file code of the ODE which is as follows:

```
function dy=f(x,y)
dy=4*x^4*y^2;
```

Save the file in your working path of MATLAB by the name f. This sort of differential equation is usually solved by the ode23 of table 4.A. The ODE file f has to be called from MATLAB command prompt but through ode23. The ode23 has two output arguments, x and y respectively. There are three input arguments of ode23 which are function file name under quote, wanted sample points of x as a row matrix, and initial value of y at the first element of row matrix respectively. Knowing the syntax one may call the ODE solver as follows:

```
>>[x y]=ode23('f',[0:0.1:0.5],2); ↵
```

Above execution indicates that the solution is found and the results are returned to x and y. The x and y are also user-chosen. To view the result side by side we may call:

```
>>[x y] ↵

ans =

         0    2.0000
    0.1000    2.0000
    0.2000    2.0010
    0.3000    2.0078
    0.4000    2.0333
    0.5000    2.1052
      ↑         ↑
      x         y
```

As you see, wanted values are returned as a column matrix. Should the reader need to access each element, y(1), y(2), y(3), etc can be called for example call y(5) for y=2.0333.

More examples are included in the following.

Example 1:

It is given that solution of the first order differential equation $\frac{du}{dt}=\frac{-t^2+e^t}{u}$ using FD from $t=1$ to $t=1.5$ with step size 0.1 subject to $u(1)=-3$ is the following tabular data which we wish to obtain.

t	1	1.1	1.2	1.3	1.4	1.5
u	-3	-3.058	-3.1174	-3.1787	-3.2421	-3.3081

The equation is already arranged so the function file as well as its command prompt calling is presented below:

Function file: function du=f(t,u) du=(-t^2+exp(t))/u;	>>[t u]=ode23('f',[1:0.1:1.5],-3); ↵ >>[t u] ↵ ans =
Variable equivalence: u⇔u , du⇔$\frac{du}{dt}$, and t⇔t	1.0000 -3.0000 1.1000 -3.0580 1.2000 -3.1174 1.3000 -3.1787 1.4000 -3.2421 1.5000 -3.3081 ↑ ↑ t u

Example 2:

The first order ODE $(x^2+y^3)\frac{dy}{dx}=x+\sinh y$ using FD from $x=0$ to $x=0.3$ with step size 0.05 subject to $y(0)=5$ has the following tabular data solution which we wish to obtain.

x	0	0.05	0.1	0.15	0.2	0.25	0.3
y	5	5.0299	5.0601	5.0908	5.1218	5.1533	5.1852

Like example 1 its straightforward execution is as follows:

Function file: function dy=f(x,y) dy=(x+sinh(y))/(x^2+y^3);	>>[x y]=ode23('f',[0:.05:0.3],5); ↵ >>[x y] ↵ ans =
Variable equivalence: y⇔y , x⇔x , and dy⇔$\frac{dy}{dx}$	0 5.0000 0.0500 5.0299 0.1000 5.0601 0.1500 5.0908 0.2000 5.1218 0.2500 5.1533 0.3000 5.1852 ↑ ↑ x y

Example 3:

Employing FD technique the second order ODE $2\frac{d^2y}{dx^2}-5\frac{dy}{dx}+2y=x$ subject to initial condition $\begin{Bmatrix} y(0)=2 \\ y'(0)=-3 \end{Bmatrix}$ has the following tabular data solution with Δx =0.1 over $0\le x\le 0.5$.

x	0	0.1	0.2	0.3	0.4	0.5
y	2	1.649	1.1801	0.5657	-0.2278	-1.2419
$\frac{dy}{dx}$	-3	-4.0584	-5.3657	-6.9777	-8.9626	-11.4039

We wish to obtain above solution.

Involvement of the second order ODE requires us find the systemized representation of the ODE like earlier discussion hence we get $\begin{Bmatrix} \frac{dy_1}{dx} = y_2 \\ \frac{dy_2}{dx} = \frac{5}{2}y_2 - y_1 + \frac{x}{2} \end{Bmatrix}$ where $y_1 = y$, $y_2 = \frac{dy}{dx}$, and $\frac{dy_2}{dx} = \frac{d^2y}{dx^2} = \frac{5}{2}\frac{dy}{dx} - y + \frac{x}{2} = \frac{5}{2}y_2 - y_1 + \frac{x}{2}$. The functional code and the calling are shown below:

Function file:	

`function dy=f(x,y)`
`dy(1)=y(2);`
`dy(2)=5/2*y(2)-y(1)+x/2;`
`dy=dy';`
	`>>[x y]=ode23('f',[0:0.1:0.5],[2 -3]);` ↵
	`>>[x y]` ↵
	
	`ans =`
	`0 2.0000 -3.0000`
	`0.1000 1.6490 -4.0584`
	`0.2000 1.1801 -5.3657`
	`0.3000 0.5657 -6.9777`
	`0.4000 -0.2278 -8.9626`
	`0.5000 -1.2419 -11.4039`
	↑ ↑ ↑
	x y $\frac{dy}{dx}$

Variable equivalence: y(1)⇔ y_1, y(2)⇔ y_2, x⇔ x, dy(1)⇔ $\frac{dy}{dx}$, and dy(2) ⇔ $\frac{d^2y}{dx^2}$	

Since there are two initial conditions, the third input argument of the ode23 is a row matrix whose elements are $y(0)$ and $y'(0)$ respectively. Unlike example 1 now the returns to y are two column matrices; one for y and the other for $\frac{dy}{dx}$. Should the reader wish the two data sets to be separated, the commands y(:,1) and y(:,2) are exercised for y and $\frac{dy}{dx}$ respectively. Once again the initial values of y and $\frac{dy}{dx}$ must correspond to the first element of the second input argument which is [0:0.1:0.5] inside the ode23.

Example 4:

The third order Euler differential equation $6t^3\frac{d^3u}{dt^3}-7t^2\frac{d^2u}{dt^2}+9t\frac{du}{dt}-4u=3t-3$ under the initial conditions $\begin{Bmatrix} u''(1)=1 \\ u'(1)=3 \\ u(1)=0 \end{Bmatrix}$ with Δt=0.05 over $1\le t\le 1.25$ has the following tabular solution:

t	1	1.05	1.1	1.15	1.2	1.25
u	0	0.1512	0.3045	0.4595	0.6159	0.7733
$\frac{du}{dt}$	3	3.0459	3.0841	3.115	3.1391	3.1568
$\frac{d^2u}{dt^2}$	1	0.8392	0.6892	0.5486	0.4163	0.2913

Our objective is to obtain above solution.

Now the dependent variable is u. As mentioned before the rearranged equation is $\frac{d^3u}{dt^3}=\frac{3t-3+7t^2\frac{d^2u}{dt^2}-9t\frac{du}{dt}+4u}{6\,t^3}=$ $\frac{3t-3+7t^2u_3-9tu_2+4u_1}{6\,t^3}$ subject to substitutions $u_1=u$, $u_2=\frac{du}{dt}$, and $u_3=\frac{d^2u}{dt^2}$ thereby providing the system of differential equations $\begin{Bmatrix} \frac{du_1}{dt}=u_2 \\ \frac{du_2}{dt}=u_3 \\ \frac{du_3}{dt}=\frac{3t-3+7t^2u_3-9tu_2+4u_1}{6\,t^3} \end{Bmatrix}$ on that the relevant codes and calling are the following:

Function file:

```
function du=f(t,u)
du(1)=u(2);
du(2)=u(3);
du(3)=(3*t-3+7*t^2*u(3)-9*t*u(2)+4*u(1))/t^3/6;
du=du';
```

Variable equivalence:

u(1)⇔u_1, u(2)⇔u_2, u(3)⇔u_3, t⇔t, du(1)⇔$\frac{du}{dt}$, du(2)⇔$\frac{d^2u}{dt^2}$, and du(3)⇔$\frac{d^3u}{dt^3}$

Calling for the solution:
```
>>[t u]=ode23('f',[1:0.05:1.25],[0 3 1]); ↵
>>[t u] ↵

ans =
    1.0000         0    3.0000    1.0000
    1.0500    0.1512    3.0459    0.8392
    1.1000    0.3045    3.0841    0.6892
    1.1500    0.4595    3.1150    0.5486
    1.2000    0.6159    3.1391    0.4163
    1.2500    0.7733    3.1568    0.2913
      ↑         ↑         ↑         ↑
```
t $\quad u \quad \frac{du}{dt} \quad \frac{d^2u}{dt^2}$

In order to get hand on the u, $\frac{du}{dt}$, and $\frac{d^2u}{dt^2}$ data, one can call u(:,1), u(:,2), and u(:,3) respectively.

Example 5:

The ODE system $\begin{Bmatrix} \frac{dx}{dt} = 3x - 2y - e^{-3t} \\ \frac{dy}{dt} = 4x - 5y + 2t \end{Bmatrix}$ under the initial conditions $\begin{Bmatrix} x(1) = 1 \\ y(1) = 3 \end{Bmatrix}$ with Δt=0.05 over $1 \le t \le 1.25$ has the following tabular solution:

t	1	1.05	1.1	1.15	1.2	1.25
x	1	0.8579	0.7334	0.6223	0.5211	0.4266
y	3	2.5907	2.253	1.9736	1.7418	1.5484

We intend to determine above numerical solution.

The system is provided in arranged form. All we need is code the system with earlier defined variable equivalence and call the solver as follows:

Function file:
```
function dy=f(t,y)
dy(1)=3*y(1)-2*y(2)-exp(-3*t);
dy(2)=4*y(1)-5*y(2)+2*t;
dy=dy';
```
Variable equivalence:

y(1)⇔x, y(2)⇔y, t⇔t, dy(1)⇔$\frac{dx}{dt}$, and dy(2)⇔$\frac{dy}{dt}$

```
Calling for the solution:
>>[t y]=ode23('f',[1:0.05:1.25],[1 3]); ↵
>>[t y] ↵

ans =
         1.0000   1.0000   3.0000
         1.0500   0.8579   2.5907
         1.1000   0.7334   2.2530
         1.1500   0.6223   1.9736
         1.2000   0.5211   1.7418
         1.2500   0.4266   1.5484
           ↑        ↑        ↑
           t        x        y
```

One obtains the x and y data by calling y(:,1) and y(:,2) respectively.

Factors to be considered for the solution

Correct or at least close to exact solution employing FD depends on several factors, some of which are addressed in the following.

Order of the approximation:

Inserting inputs and obtaining outputs for all ODE solvers presented in table 4.A operate in the same way as we did for the ode23. Of coarse higher order approximation of the dependent variable would return improved result. We know that the Runge-Kutta 4-5 order (whose MATLAB counterpart is the ode45) is more accurate than the Runge-Kutta 2-3 (ode23). Computationally we wish to demonstrate that.

Referring to the example 3, the ODE $2\frac{d^2y}{dx^2} - 5\frac{dy}{dx} + 2y = x$ has the analytical solution $y(x) = -\frac{31e^{2x}}{12} + \frac{10e^{\frac{x}{2}}}{3} + \frac{5}{4} + \frac{x}{2}$ from which one obtains the exact solution by inserting different x samples.

x	0	0.1	0.2	0.3	0.4	0.5
y (exact)	2	1.6489	1.18	0.5656	-0.228	-1.2421
y (by ode23)	2	1.649	1.1801	0.5657	-0.2278	-1.2419

Above table shows the y values from the exact expression as well as the ode23. What if we call the ode45 to solve the same equation (i.e. higher order approximation)?

```
>>[x y]=ode45('f',[0:0.1:0.5],[2 -3]); ↵
>>[x y] ↵
```

```
ans =
         0    2.0000    -3.0000
    0.1000    1.6489    -4.0585
    0.2000    1.1800    -5.3658
    0.3000    0.5656    -6.9779
    0.4000   -0.2280    -8.9630
    0.5000   -1.2421   -11.4044
      ↑         ↑          ↑
```

$x \qquad y \qquad \frac{dy}{dx}$

Last execution indicates that the solution becomes precise with the increased order approximation.

Relative error in the computing:

Although higher order solver provides better result, this might not be true always because the selection of relative or absolute error is a factor of accuracy too.

The default relative error of the **ode23** is 10^{-3}. What if one tries to find the solution with the relative error 10^{-6}. To argument the relative error, another built-in function **odeset** is exercised. The relative error is a property of the differential equation solver, which is notified by RelTol (abbreviation for Relative Tolerance) but under a quote. Execute the following:

```
>>O=odeset('RelTol',1e-6); ↵
```

Above command says that you defined the relative error as 10^{-6} (i.e. 1e-6) and assigned the property to O where O is a user-chosen variable. In order to inject this property to ode23 we need another input argument (appended as the fourth). Consider the last example with less order and call the solver with the added input argument as follows:

```
>>[x y]=ode23('f',[0:0.1:0.5],[2 -3],O); ↵
>>[x y] ↵

ans =
         0    2.0000    -3.0000
    0.1000    1.6489    -4.0585
    0.2000    1.1800    -5.3658
    0.3000    0.5656    -6.9779
    0.4000   -0.2280    -8.9630
    0.5000   -1.2421   -11.4044
      ↑         ↑          ↑
```

$x \qquad y \qquad \frac{dy}{dx}$

Compare above return to the tabular data. Reducing the relative error from 10^{-3} to 10^{-6} makes the solution exact. Either increasing the approximation order or reducing the relative error may yield better solution.

When does the FD method fail?

There are instances when the FD numerical method would fail. Earlier we solved the ODE $\frac{dy}{dx}=4x^4y^2$ from $x=0$ to $x=0.5$. Try to solve the equation from $x=0$ to $x=1.5$ with the same step size:

```
>>[x y]=ode23('f',[0:0.1:1.5],2); ↵

Warning: Failure at t=9.105613e-001. Unable to meet integration
tolerances without reducing the step size below the smallest value
allowed (1.776357e-015) at time t.
In ode23 at 346
```

What went wrong? Why is the machine printing some warning message? Make no mistake if some ODE does not have analytical solution, the embedded function can not solve that too.

The ODE has analytical solution $y=\frac{-10}{8x^5-5}$. Setting the denominator $8x^5-5$ to 0 provides $x=\sqrt[5]{\frac{5}{8}}$ =0.9103. At $x=\sqrt[5]{\frac{5}{8}}$, the y becomes infinity or undefined that is why the above warning message is appearing. It becomes clearer when we look at the graph of y versus x which is presented in figure 4.1(a). Machine never handles any number which is infinity.

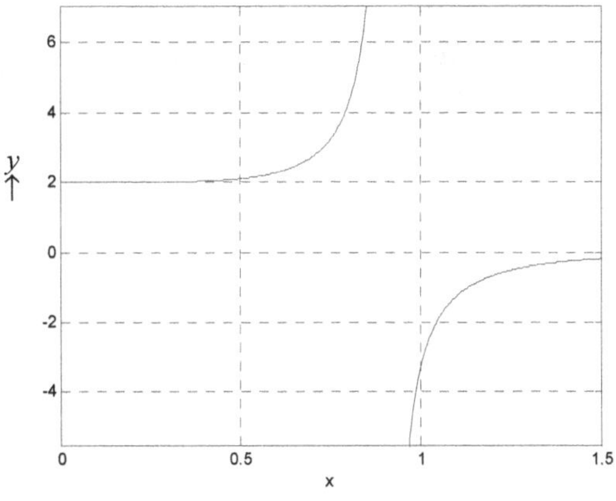

Figure 4.1(a) Plot of y versus x

What is the solution? Truly speaking there is no complete solution. One option can be detect the point of singularity and obtain the values before the singularity. The **ode23** has the default independent variable **t** so any message will be in terms of **t**.

According to the warning message the failure or singularity point is at **t=9.105613e-001** or 9.105613×10^{-1} i.e. x=0.9105613.

The **ode23** already returned the solution for x <0.9105613. We may view that by calling:

```
>>[x y] ↵

ans =

         0    2.0000
    0.1000    2.0000
    0.2000    2.0009
    0.3000    2.0075
    0.4000    2.0329
    0.5000    2.1048
    0.6000    2.2833
    0.7000    2.7338
    0.8000    4.1971
    0.9000   35.3044
      ↑         ↑
      x         y
```

The inference we make out of this demonstration is over the required interval of x, there must not be any x at which the y is undefined.

4.4 Graphing ODE solution after FD computing

Having found the ODE numerical solution by FD technique, one might be interested to graph the solution. In this regard the **plot** of appendix E is helpful. While graphing the solution, step size should be as small as possible in order to obtain smooth curve. The reader might be interested in the following.

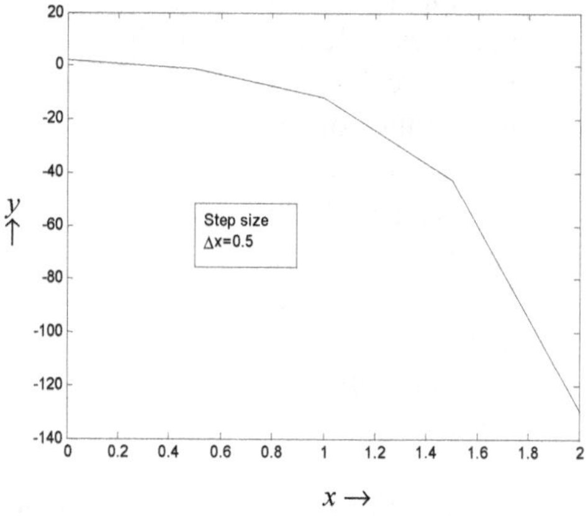

Figure 4.1(b) Plot of y versus x for step size 0.5 – right side figure

Just the solution of ODE

In last section we solved the ODE $2\frac{d^2y}{dx^2} - 5\frac{dy}{dx} + 2y = x$ by **ode23** (example 3). We wish to plot the y versus x on Δx =0.5 over $0 \le x \le 2$.

Assuming the ODE describing function file is in your workspace, call the following:

```
>>[x y]=ode23('f',[0:0.5:2],[2 -3]); ↵
```

The solution is found and the y data is stored in y(:,1) so execute the **plot** as follows:

```
>>plot(x,y(:,1)) ↵
```

The last command results the figure 4.1(b) which shows nonsmooth variation of the curve because of wide step size. Let us reduce the step size to 0.05 and call the solver and plotter again:

```
>>[x y]=ode23('f',[0:0.05:2],[2 -3]); ↵
>>plot(x,y(:,1)) ↵
```

MATLAB returns the graph of figure 4.1(c) which indicates smooth variation.

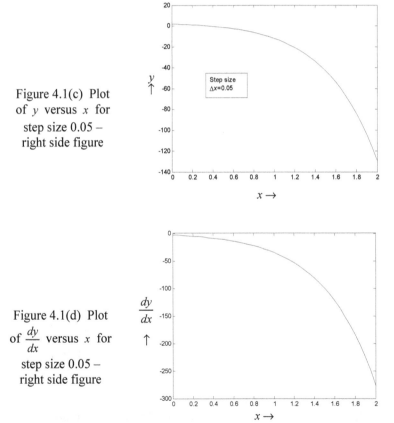

Figure 4.1(c) Plot of y versus x for step size 0.05 – right side figure

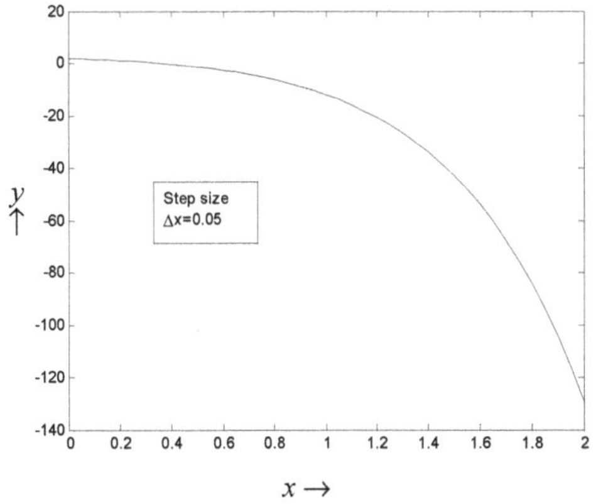

Figure 4.1(d) Plot of $\frac{dy}{dx}$ versus x for step size 0.05 – right side figure

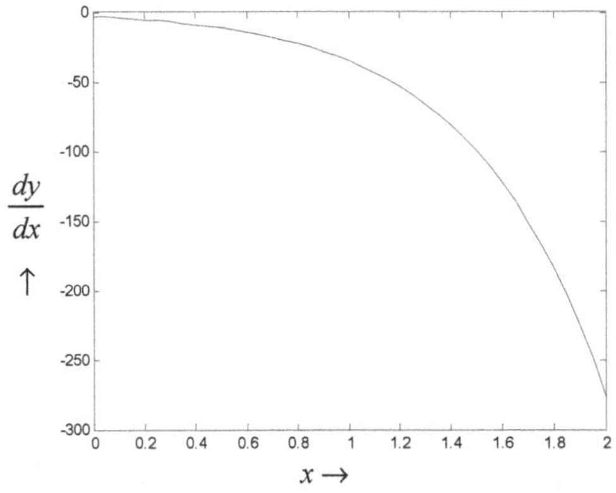

Derivative plotting

Usually the ranges of y and $\frac{dy}{dx}$ data are different so it is suggested we plot the two curves in two different traces. In ongoing example suppose we wish to plot $\frac{dy}{dx}$ versus x. We know that the $\frac{dy}{dx}$ data is available in y(:,2) so graph the derivative by the following:

```
>>plot(x,y(:,2)) ↵
```

Figure 4.1(d) depicts the graph.

Solutions of y and $\frac{dy}{dx}$ together

If the reader persists in plotting the two traces together, appendix E mentioned **subplot** can be exercised. For the last y and $\frac{dy}{dx}$ we call the window splitter (assuming that the y data is available in workspace from previous execution) as follows:

```
>>subplot(211), plot(x,y(:,1)) ↵
>>subplot(212), plot(x,y(:,2)) ↵
```

MATLAB responds with the figure 4.1(e) in which you find the y and $\frac{dy}{dx}$ graphs together.

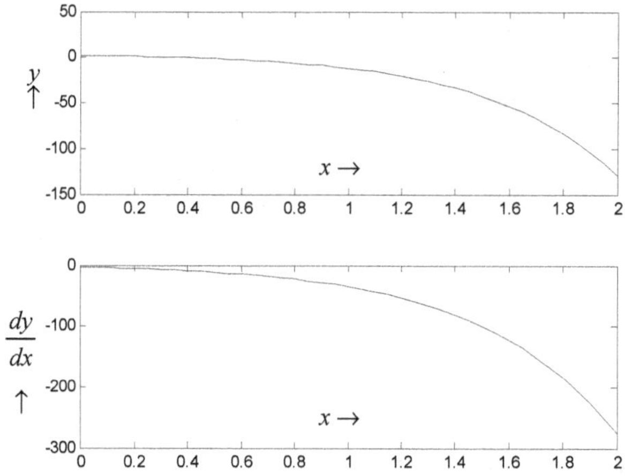

Figure 4.1(e) Plots of y and $\frac{dy}{dx}$ versus x for step size 0.05

Comparison on solutions

Sometimes we need to compare the FD solution with analytical one. Analytical solution usually has close form expression. Independent sample points are inserted to these expressions to obtain actual solution. Consider the example 1 of last section which has the analytical solution $u(t) = -\frac{1}{3}\sqrt{-6t^3+18e^t+87-18e}$. Insert the t sample points to get the exact solution as –3, –3.058, –3.1174, –3.1787, –3.2421, and –3.3081 respectively. In this regard we may use the built-in function **eval** with two input arguments which has the syntax **eval**(expression scalar code according to appendix B, wanted independent variable sample points as a row or column matrix). The t sample points we generate by:

```
>>t=1:0.1:1.5; ↵
```

The $u(t)$ expression has the scalar code:

```
>>ue='-1/3*sqrt(-6*t.^3+18*exp(t)+87-18*exp(1))'; ↵
```

The ue and t are user-chosen variables. Call the evaluator as:

```
>>eval(ue,t) ↵

ans =
        -3.0000  -3.0580  -3.1174  -3.1787  -3.2421  -3.3081
```

Had we written ua=eval(ue,t), the return would have been assigned to the ua where ua is a user-chosen variable. The ode23 return is in column matrix form so we can turn the ua to a column one by writing ua=eval(ue,t)'.

We introduced the mean square error computing in section 2.2 which can be a deviance measure of numerical solution from the analytical one. Let us see that for the ongoing example. The error between the exact and FD computed one we obtain by ua-u (reexecute the example 1 of last section to make u available) so just call the following:

```
>>mse(ua-u) ↵

ans =
          1.4348e-014
```

As the execution returns, the mean square error is 1.4348×10^{-14} – negligible indeed. On comparison of the exact with numerical solution, precision of numerical computation is appreciated to a great extent.

What about graphical comparison?

One might say I wish to plot both the analytical and FD derived solutions together. Take the example 3 of last section which has the analytical solution $y(x) = -\frac{31}{12}e^{2x} + \frac{10}{3}e^{\frac{x}{2}} + \frac{x}{2} + \frac{5}{4}$. In this sort of problem we graph the expression without calculation by **ezplot** of appendix E but the functional code should be in vector form as regards to appendix B and let us do so:

```
>>yx='-31/12*exp(2*x)+10/3*exp(x/2)+5/4+x/2'; ↵
```

The code of $y(x)$ is assigned to yx where yx is a user-chosen variable. The grapher is called then:

```
>>ezplot(yx,[0 2]) ↵
```

Above command results a figure window in which you find the smooth graph of $y(x)$ and can hold the graph by:

```
>>hold ↵
```

Call the **ode23** to make the FD solution available in workspace (assuming that the ODE function file is in the working path):

```
>>[x y]=ode23('f',[0:0.5:2],[2 -3]); ↵
```

The $y(x)$ data is in y(:,1) so call the **plot** like we did before:

```
>>plot(x,y(:,1)) ↵
```

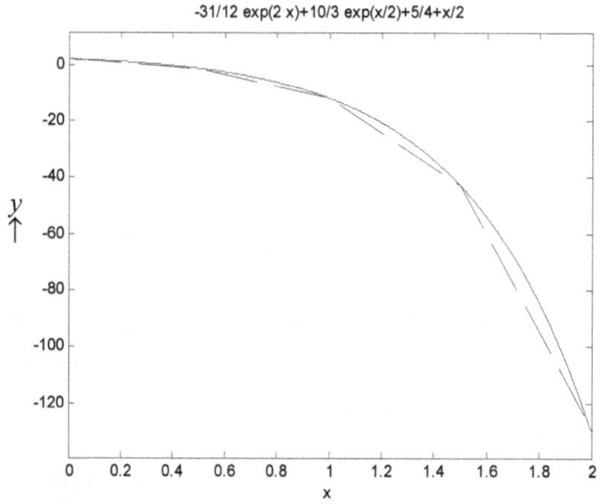

Figure 4.1(f) Analytical and FD solutions together

Figure 4.1(f) presents outcome from the last command. The solid and broken lines stand for analytical and FD method respectively. By inspection one gains some insight on the accuracy of FD. However you need extra processing to turn the plot like the figure. Click the Edit plot icon (chapter 1), bring the mouse pointer on the curve, rightclick the mouse, and select available line style for the curve.

We hope exemplified simple differential equations will pave the way for an understanding of more complicated and practical ODE systems that it would follow.

Anyhow we bring to an end of the chapter with this example.

Exercises

1. Systemize the following ODEs such that they can be fed to embedded solver of MATLAB: (a) $xy+(x+3)\frac{dy}{dx}=3x^2$ (b) $(1+y^3)\frac{dy}{dx}=2x+\cosh y$ (c) $8\frac{d^2y}{dx^2}-5xy\frac{dy}{dx}+2y=\sin x$ (d) $(5x+y)\frac{d^3y}{dx^3}+xy\frac{d^2y}{dx^2}-\sin x\frac{dy}{dx}+2y=3\cos x$ (e) $x^3\frac{d^4y}{dx^4}+(x^2+y)\frac{d^2y}{dx^2}+4y=3(x+e^{-3x})$.
2. In question (1) provide the MATLAB function file code for each of the ODEs.
3. Employing FD approximation for each of the following ODEs determine: the number of samples in independent or dependent variable and the number of FD equations and develop the FD equations: (a) $3\frac{d^2y}{dx^2}=5(y+x)$ with Δx =0.3 over $0\le x\le 0.9$ where $y(0)=2$ and $y'(0)=5$ (b) $4\frac{d^2y}{dx^2}+5\frac{dy}{dx}=6y$ with Δx =0.1 over $0\le x\le 0.5$ where $y(0)=0$ and $y'(0)=-2$ (c) $\frac{d^2y}{dx^2}+y\left(\frac{dy}{dx}\right)^2=x$ with Δx =0.2 over $1\le x\le 2$ where $y(1)=0$ and $y'(1)=0$.
4. Apply embedded Runge-Kutta 2-3 order solver of MATLAB to determine the solution of following differential equations:

   (a) $5\frac{dy}{dx}=6x$ with Δx =0.3 over $0\le x\le 0.9$ where $y(0)=2$

   (b) $\frac{dy}{dx}=x+y$ with Δx =0.2 over $1\le x\le 2$ where $y(1)=2$

   (c) $4\frac{d^2y}{dx^2}+5\frac{dy}{dx}=6y$ with Δx =0.1 over $0\le x\le 0.5$ where $y(0)=0$ and $y'(0)=-2$

   (d) $3t^3\frac{d^3u}{dt^3}+4t^2\frac{d^2u}{dt^2}-2t\frac{du}{dt}+6u=2t+1$ under the initial conditions $\begin{Bmatrix} u''(0.5)=-1 \\ u'(0.5)=2 \\ u(0.5)=3 \end{Bmatrix}$ with Δt =0.05 over $0.5\le t\le 0.75$

   (e) $(x+y)\frac{d^3y}{dx^3}+2x\frac{d^2y}{dx^2}+y\frac{dy}{dx}+3y=3x+2y$ with Δx =0.1 over $0.5\le x\le 1$ where $y(0.5)=0$, $y'(0.5)=3$, and $y''(0.5)=-3$

   (f) $(0.5+x^3)\frac{d^4y}{dx^4}-x\frac{d^2y}{dx^2}-4xy=3x+2$ with Δx =0.02 over $0\le x\le 0.1$ where $y(0)=0$, $y'(0)=0$, $y''(0)=-3$, and $y'''(0)=2$

(g) $\left\{\begin{aligned}\frac{dx}{dt} &= 5x-2y-3t \\ \frac{dy}{dt} &= 6x-7y+(2+t)e^{-2t}\end{aligned}\right\}$ subject to $x(0)=1$ and $y(0)=3$ with Δt =0.05 over $0 \le t \le 0.25$

(h) in part (d) determine the $\frac{du}{dt}$ and $\frac{d^2u}{dt^2}$ data

(i) in part (f) determine the $\frac{dy}{dx}$, $\frac{d^2y}{dx^2}$, and $\frac{d^3y}{dx^3}$ data.

5. (a) in question 4(e) choose Δx =0.001 over $0.5 \le x \le 1$ and graph the y versus x solution
   (b) in question 4(d) choose Δt =0.0001 over $0.5 \le t \le 0.75$ and graph the u versus t solution
   (c) in question 4(c) choose Δx =0.0001 over $0 \le x \le 0.5$ and graph the y versus x and $\frac{dy}{dx}$ versus x solutions as a single figure
   (d) in question 4(f) choose Δx =0.0001 over $0 \le x \le 1$ and graph the y versus x, $\frac{dy}{dx}$ versus x, and $\frac{d^2y}{dx^2}$ versus x solutions as a single figure.

6. (a) The ODE $4\frac{d^2y}{dx^2}+5\frac{dy}{dx}=6y$ has the exact solution $y(x)=\frac{8}{11}e^{-2x}-\frac{8}{11}e^{\frac{3}{4}x}$ subject to $y(0)=0$ and $y'(0)=-2$. Calculate the exact solution on Δx = 0.5 over $0 \le x \le 2$ up to 4 decimal accuracy. Compare the exact solution to those from the Runge-Kutta 2-3 and 4-5 orders as embedded in MATLAB. What do you infer from the comparison?

   (b) In part (a) do the same for the ODE $\frac{d^3u}{dt^3}+3\frac{d^2u}{dt^2}+3\frac{du}{dt}+u=3t$ with Δt =1 over $0 \le t \le 4$ which has the exact solution $u(t)=-9+3t+12e^{-t}+11te^{-t}+\frac{9}{2}t^2e^{-t}$ subject to $\left\{\begin{aligned}u''(0)&=-1 \\ u'(0)&=2 \\ u(0)&=3\end{aligned}\right\}$.

7. In question 6(a) choose the order of the solver as Runge-Kutta 2-3 and apply the `ode23` to determine the solution on relative error (a) 0.1 (b) 0.01 (c) 0.0001 (d) 10^{-6}. Compare the obtained solutions to the exact one. Do the same for the question 6(b). What do you infer from these two computing?

8. (a) In question 6(a) graph the exact solution along with the FD one which is derived from Runge-Kutta 2-3 order subject to relative error 0.01. Compute the mean square error due to the FD computing (b) Do the same for the question 6(b) quoted ODE.

9. Try to solve the ODE $3\frac{dy}{dx}=8x^2y^2$ employing Runge-Kutta 2-3 order subject to initial condition $y(0)=4$ on Δx =0.1 over $0 \le x \le 1$. Is the solution achieved? If not, what went wrong? Find the solution.

Answers:

(1) (a) $\dfrac{dy}{dx}=\dfrac{3x^2-xy}{x+3}$ (b) $\dfrac{dy}{dx}=\dfrac{2x+\cosh y}{1+y^3}$ (c) $\begin{Bmatrix} \dfrac{dy_1}{dx}=y_2 \\ \dfrac{dy_2}{dx}=f(x,y) \end{Bmatrix}$ where $f(x,y)=$

$\dfrac{5xy}{8}\dfrac{dy}{dx}-\dfrac{y}{4}+\dfrac{\sin x}{8}=\dfrac{5xy_1y_2}{8}-\dfrac{y_1}{4}+\dfrac{\sin x}{8}$ with $y=y_1$ and $\dfrac{dy}{dx}=y_2$ (d)

$\begin{Bmatrix} \dfrac{dy_1}{dx}=y_2 \\ \dfrac{dy_2}{dx}=y_3 \\ \dfrac{dy_3}{dx}=f(x,y) \end{Bmatrix}$ where $f(x,y)=-\dfrac{xy}{5x+y}\dfrac{d^2y}{dx^2}+\dfrac{\sin x}{5x+y}\dfrac{dy}{dx}+\dfrac{3\cos x-2y}{5x+y}=$

$\dfrac{-xy_1y_3+y_2\sin x+3\cos x-2y_1}{5x+y_1}$ with $y=y_1$, $\dfrac{dy}{dx}=y_2$, and $\dfrac{d^2y}{dx^2}=y_3$ (e)

$\begin{Bmatrix} \dfrac{dy_1}{dx}=y_2 \\ \dfrac{dy_2}{dx}=y_3 \\ \dfrac{dy_3}{dx}=y_4 \\ \dfrac{dy_4}{dx}=f(x,y) \end{Bmatrix}$ where $f(x,y)=\dfrac{3(x+e^{-3x})}{x^3}-\dfrac{x^2+y}{x^3}\dfrac{d^2y}{dx^2}-\dfrac{4y}{x^3}=$

$\dfrac{3(x+e^{-3x})-(x^2+y_1)y_3-4y_1}{x^3}$ with $y=y_1$, $\dfrac{dy}{dx}=y_2$, $\dfrac{d^2y}{dx^2}=y_3$, and $\dfrac{d^3y}{dx^3}=y_4$

hint: section 4.3

(2) (a)
```
function dy=f(x,y)
  dy=(3*x^2-x*y)/(x+3);
```
(b)
```
function dy=f(x,y)
  dy=(2*x+cosh(y))/(1+y^3);
```
(c)
```
function dy=f(x,y)
  dy(1)=y(2);
  dy(2)=5*x*y(1)*y(2)/8-y(1)/4+sin(x)/8;
  dy=dy';
```
(d)
```
function dy=f(x,y)
  dy(1)=y(2);
  dy(2)=y(3);
  dy(3)=(-x*y(1)*y(3)+sin(x)*y(2)+3*cos(x)-2*y(1))/(5*x+y(1));
  dy=dy';
```
(e)
```
function dy=f(x,y)
  dy(1)=y(2);
  dy(2)=y(3);
  dy(3)=y(4);
  dy(4)=(3*(x+exp(-3*x))-(x^2+y(1))*y(3)-4*y(1))/x^3;
  dy=dy';
```
hint: section 4.3

(3) (a) sample number: 4 and number of FD equations: 2

FD equation: $3\dfrac{y[m+1]-2y[m]+y[m-1]}{(\Delta x)^2}=5(y[m]+x[m])$ where $x[m]$ =0, 0.3, 0.6, and 0.9

Linear equations:

for m =1: $3\dfrac{y[2]-2y[1]+y[0]}{0.3^2}=5(y[1]+0.3)$ and

for m =2: $3\dfrac{y[3]-2y[2]+y[1]}{0.3^2}=5(y[2]+0.6)$

Equations from initial values: $y[0]$ =2 and $\dfrac{y[2]-y[0]}{2\times 0.3}$ =5

Solution: $y[1]$ =3.2349, $y[2]$ =5, and $y[3]$ =7.6051

(b) sample number: 6 and number of FD equations: 4

FD equation: $4\dfrac{y[m+1]-2y[m]+y[m-1]}{(\Delta x)^2}+5\dfrac{y[m+1]-y[m-1]}{2\Delta x}=6y[m]$ where $x[m]$ =0, 0.1, 0.2, 0.3, 0.4, and 0.5

Linear equations:

for m =1: $4\dfrac{y[2]-2y[1]+y[0]}{0.1^2}+5\dfrac{y[2]-y[0]}{2\times 0.1}=6y[1]$

for m =2: $4\dfrac{y[3]-2y[2]+y[1]}{0.1^2}+5\dfrac{y[3]-y[1]}{2\times 0.1}=6y[2]$

for m =3: $4\dfrac{y[4]-2y[3]+y[2]}{0.1^2}+5\dfrac{y[4]-y[2]}{2\times 0.1}=6y[3]$

for m =4: $4\dfrac{y[5]-2y[4]+y[3]}{0.1^2}+5\dfrac{y[5]-y[3]}{2\times 0.1}=6y[4]$

Equations from initial values: $y[0]$ =0 and $\dfrac{y[2]-y[0]}{2\times 0.1}$ =–2

Solution: $y[1]$ =–0.2109, $y[2]$ =–0.4, $y[3]$ =–0.5725, $y[4]$ =–0.7328, and $y[5]$ =–0.8845

(c) sample number: 6 and number of FD equations: 4

FD equation: $\dfrac{y[m+1]-2y[m]+y[m-1]}{(\Delta x)^2}+y[m]\left(\dfrac{y[m+1]-y[m-1]}{2\Delta x}\right)^2=x[m]$

where $x[m]$ =1, 1.2, 1.4, 1.6, 1.8, and 2

Linear equations:

for m =1: $\dfrac{y[2]-2y[1]+y[0]}{0.2^2}+y[1]\left(\dfrac{y[2]-y[0]}{2\times 0.2}\right)^2$ =1.2

for m =2: $\dfrac{y[3]-2y[2]+y[1]}{0.2^2}+y[2]\left(\dfrac{y[3]-y[1]}{2\times 0.2}\right)^2$ =1.4

for m =3: $\dfrac{y[4]-2y[3]+y[2]}{0.2^2}+y[3]\left(\dfrac{y[4]-y[2]}{2\times 0.2}\right)^2$ =1.6

for m =4: $\dfrac{y[5]-2y[4]+y[3]}{0.2^2}+y[4]\left(\dfrac{y[5]-y[3]}{2\times 0.2}\right)^2$ =1.8

Equations from initial values: $y[0]=0$ and $\frac{y[2]-y[0]}{2\times 0.2}=0$

In this problem: $y[0]=y(1)$, $y[1]=y(1.2)$, $y[2]=y(1.4)$, $y[3]=y(1.6)$, $y[4]=y(1.8)$, and $y[5]=y(2)$

The ODE is nonlinear so multiple solutions exist which are presented in the following table:

For the ODE in part (c)				
x	y	y	y	y
1	0	0	0	0
1.2	–0.024	–0.024	–0.024	–0.024
1.4	0	0	0	0
1.6	0.08	0.08	0.08	0.08
1.8	–50.223	–50.223	0.223	0.223
2	–2.7101	2.9498	–18.2079	0.4311

hint: section 4.2

(4) Following tables present the solutions:

For the ODE in part (a)	
x	y
0	2
0.3	2.054
0.6	2.216
0.9	2.486

For the ODE in part (b)	
x	y
1	2
1.2	2.6856
1.4	3.5672
1.6	4.6883
1.8	6.1019
2	7.8727

For the ODE in part (c)	
x	y
0	0
0.1	-0.1885
0.2	-0.3575
0.3	-0.5117
0.4	-0.6549
0.5	-0.7906

For the ODE in part (d)	
t	u
0.5	3
0.55	3.0981
0.6	3.1902
0.65	3.274
0.7	3.3479
0.75	3.4107

For the ODE in part (e)	
x	y
0.5	0
0.6	0.2862
0.7	0.5482
0.8	0.7892
0.9	1.0115
1	1.2164

For the ODE in part (f)	
x	y
0	0
0.02	-0.0006
0.04	-0.0024
0.06	-0.0053
0.08	-0.0094
0.1	-0.0147

For the ODE in part (g)		
t	x	y
0	1	3
0.05	0.9711	2.4435
0.1	0.9797	2.0433
0.15	1.0210	1.7624
0.2	1.0922	1.5738
0.25	1.1923	1.4580

For the ODE in part (h)		
t	$\frac{du}{dt}$	$\frac{d^2u}{dt^2}$
0.5	2	-1
0.55	1.9121	-2.4186
0.6	1.7660	-3.3643
0.65	1.5808	-4
0.7	1.3695	-4.4259
0.75	1.1407	-4.7067

For the ODE in part (i)			
x	$\frac{dy}{dx}$	$\frac{d^2y}{dx^2}$	$\frac{d^3y}{dx^3}$
0	0	-3	2
0.02	-0.0596	-2.9592	2.08
0.04	-0.1184	-2.9168	2.1601
0.06	-0.1763	-2.8728	2.2402
0.08	-0.2333	-2.8272	2.3205
0.1	-0.2893	-2.7800	2.4009

hint: section 4.3

(5) (a) Figure E.4(a) (b) Figure E.4(b) (c) Figure E.4(c) (d) Figure E.4(d)
hint: section 4.4

Figure E.4(a) y versus x solution of ODE – right side figure

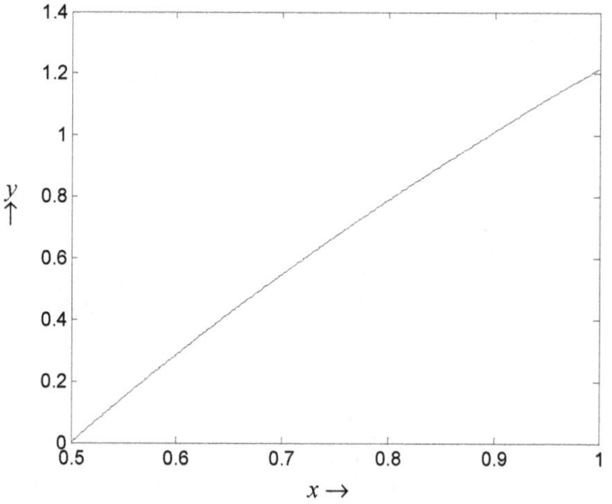

Figure E.4(b) u versus t solution – right side figure

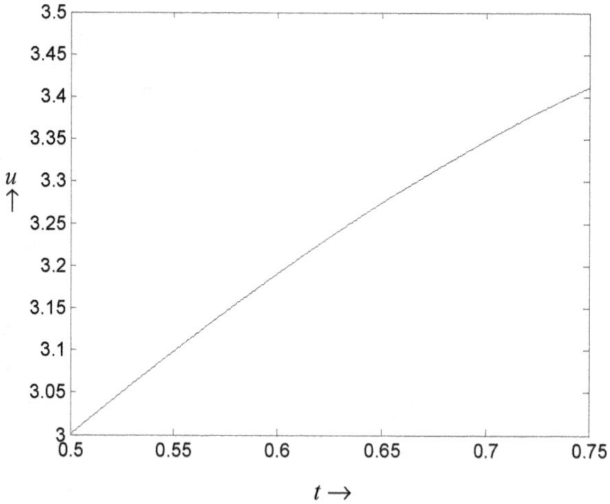

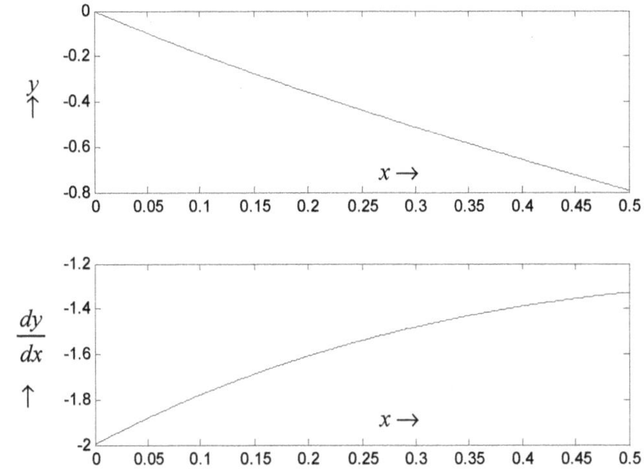

Figure E.4(c) Plots of y and $\frac{dy}{dx}$ solutions versus x

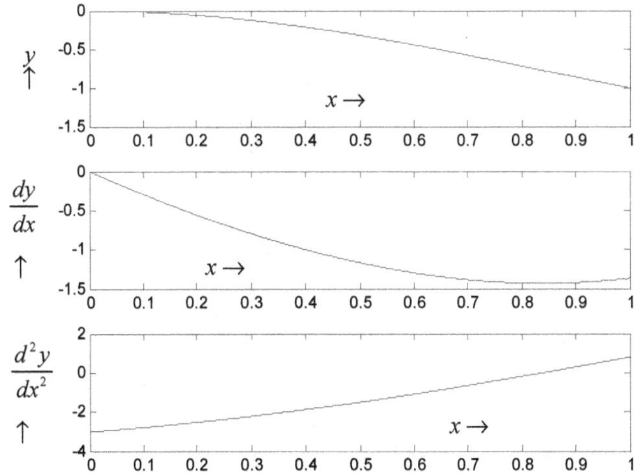

Figure E.4(d) Plots of y, $\frac{dy}{dx}$, and $\frac{d^2y}{dx^2}$ solutions versus x

(6) (a) Table 4.B (b) Table 4.C
Inference: Higher order approximation improves the FD solution.
hint: section 4.3

Table 4.B Comparison on exact and FD solutions of different orders

x	y_{exact}	$y_{\text{Runge-Kutta 2-3 order}}$	$y_{\text{Runge-Kutta 4-5 order}}$
0	0	0	0
0.5	-0.7906	-0.7908	-0.7906
1	-1.4412	-1.4416	-1.4412
1.5	-2.2039	-2.2040	-2.2039
2	-3.2461	-3.2458	-3.2461

Table 4.C Comparison on exact and FD solutions of different orders

t	u_{exact}	$u_{\text{Runge-Kutta 2-3 order}}$	$u_{\text{Runge-Kutta 4-5 order}}$
0	3	3	3
1	4.1167	4.1165	4.1167
2	4.0374	4.0378	4.0375
3	4.2568	4.2571	4.2568
4	5.3444	5.3448	5.3444

(7) Table 4.D for question 6(a) and Table 4.E for question 6(b)

Table 4.D Comparison of exact and FD solutions on different relative errors

x	y_{exact}	y on relative error 0.1	y on relative error 0.01	y on relative error 0.001	y on relative error 10^{-6}
0	0	0	0	0	0
0.5	-0.7906	-0.7913	-0.7913	-0.7908	-0.7906
1	-1.4412	-1.4417	-1.4417	-1.4416	-1.4412
1.5	-2.2039	-2.2040	-2.2040	-2.2040	-2.2039
2	-3.2461	-3.2457	-3.2457	-3.2458	-3.2461

Table 4.E Comparison of exact and FD solutions on different relative errors

t	u_{exact}	u on relative error 0.1	u on relative error 0.01	u on relative error 0.001	u on relative error 10^{-6}
0	3	3	3	3	3
1	4.1167	4.1102	4.1134	4.1165	4.1167
2	4.0374	4.0440	4.0404	4.0378	4.0374
3	4.2568	4.2634	4.2598	4.2571	4.2568
4	5.3444	5.3468	5.3457	5.3448	5.3444

Inference: Reducing the relative error of FD computing improves the ODE solution.

hint: section 4.3

(8) (a) Figure E.4(e) for 6(a) and mse=1.7999×10^{-7} only for the 5 samples
(b) Figure E.4(f) for 6(b) and mse=5.9974×10^{-6} only for the 5 samples
hint: section 4.4

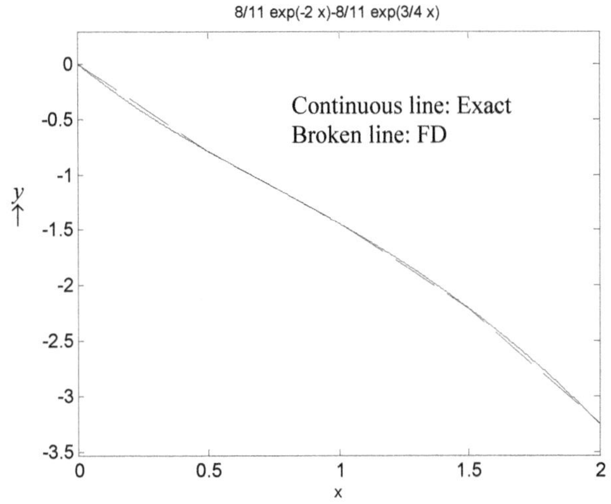

Figure E.4(e) Graph of exact and FD solutions

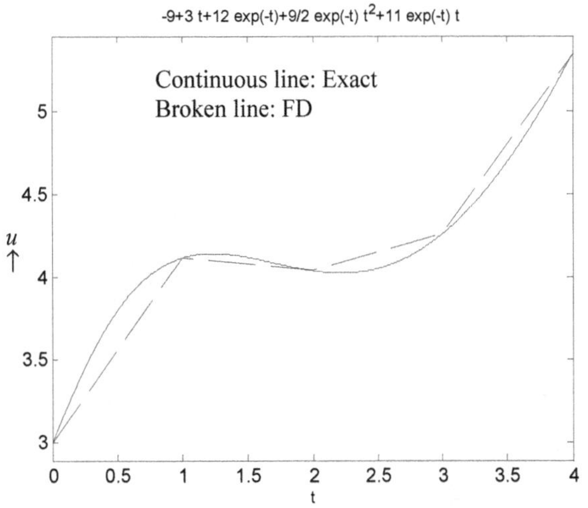

Figure E.4(f) Graph of exact and FD solutions

(9) Partial solution is achieved. A singularity occurs at x =0.6554905. Table 4.F presents the partial solution of the ODE.
hint: section 4.3

Table 4.F Partial solution of the ODE

x	y
0	4.0000
0.1	4.0143
0.2	4.1170
0.3	4.4243
0.4	5.1763
0.5	7.1937
0.6	17.1675

Chapter 5

Finite Difference in Partial Differential Equations

In this chapter we concentrate on implementation of partial differential equations which are abbreviated as PDE. A PDE involves more than one independent variable for this reason its finite difference implementation has to go through more complexity. An ODE solution evolves as a row or column matrix whereas the PDE counterpart results two or there dimensional array. Our approach is to demonstrate how a PDE transforms to multiple algebraic equations through finite difference operators. Having found the algebraic equations, MATLAB solver easily determines the solution in academic context for which the discourses are on the following:

- Elementary discussion on partial differential equations
- Way to express a PDE by finite difference terms
- Solving PDEs employing algebraic equation solver
- Comparing and plotting tools of PDE solutions

5.1 Why partial differential equation?

In ordinary differential equations the independent variable is just one. There are some physical processes and laws whose differential equations need to involve two or more independent variables. For instance an electromagnetic wave is the function of distance and time as well. Likewise the dependent variable has more than one derivative thereby requiring partial derivatives. Realistic systems always involve multiple parameters or factors hence the partial differential equation is more appropriate to describe a multi-parameter system dynamics than ordinary differential equation.

Any differential equation containing partial derivatives is termed as the partial differential equation (PDE). According to the PDE notation if z is a function of two independent variables that is $z = f(x, y)$, its different partial derivatives are denoted by

$\frac{\partial z}{\partial x}$ or z_x indicates the first order partial derivative with respect to x

$\frac{\partial z}{\partial y}$ or z_y indicates the first order partial derivative with respect to y

$\frac{\partial^2 z}{\partial x^2}$ or z_{xx} indicates the second order partial derivative with respect to x

$\frac{\partial^2 z}{\partial y^2}$ or z_{yy} indicates the second order partial derivative with respect to y

$\frac{\partial^2 z}{\partial y \partial x}$ or z_{yx} indicates the second order partial derivative with respect to first y and then x, $\cdots$ etc.

In each of the above, the f could replace z i.e. $\frac{\partial z}{\partial x}$ or $\frac{\partial f}{\partial x}$ bears the same meaning.

By resemblance with the theory of ordinary differential equation, the order of a partial differential equation is the highest order partial differential coefficient occurring in it. Thus

$4y^2 \frac{\partial z}{\partial x} + \frac{\partial z}{\partial y} = x + y$ is a first order partial differential equation when z is a function of x and y,

$4v^2 \frac{\partial^2 f}{\partial u^2} + \frac{\partial f}{\partial v} + \frac{\partial f}{\partial w} = u \frac{\partial^2 f}{\partial v \partial u}$ is a second order partial differential equation when f is a function of u, v, and w, and

$\frac{\partial^3 g}{\partial p^3} = \left(\frac{\partial g}{\partial q}\right)^2 + p + q$ is a third order partial differential equation when g is a function of p and q.

Solutions of partial differential equations encounter much more difficult problem than the solutions of ordinary differential equations do except certain linear or nonlinear partial differential equations. In MATLAB the provision for solving partial differential equations has been accounted for but to certain extent. A great variety of partial differential equations occurring in physics, chemistry, or engineering can be solved analytically following the symbolism of MATLAB which is not our objective. Our focus is on the application of FD technique to solve PDEs which will be explained in the following sections.

5.2 How to express a PDE by FD terms?

Expressing a PDE to its equivalent FD form is somewhat clumsy. In section 3.6 we have introduced the definitions of two dimensional numerical derivatives. The coordinate convention introduced in section 3.1 will be observed here too. Only the central difference derivative is addressed because of its accuracy than the others. We wish to address two variable PDE up to the second order.

In symbolic form we write the central numerical partial derivatives as follows:

first order f with respect to x: $\frac{\partial f}{\partial x}=f_x \approx \frac{\Delta f}{\Delta x}=\frac{f[m+1,n]-y[m-1,n]}{2\Delta x}$,

first order f with respect to y: $\frac{\partial f}{\partial y}=f_y \approx \frac{\Delta f}{\Delta y}=\frac{f[m,n+1]-y[m,n-1]}{2\Delta y}$,

second order f with respect to only x: $\frac{\partial^2 f}{\partial x^2}=f_{xx} \approx \frac{f[m+1,n]-2f[m,n]+f[m-1,n]}{(\Delta x)^2}$,

second order f with respect to only y: $\frac{\partial^2 f}{\partial y^2}=f_{yy} \approx \frac{f[m,n+1]-2f[m,n]+f[m,n-1]}{(\Delta y)^2}$, and

second order f with respect to first x and then y: $\frac{\partial^2 f}{\partial x \partial y}=f_{xy} \approx \frac{f[m+1,n+1]-f[m+1,n-1]-f[m-1,n+1]+f[m-1,n-1]}{4\Delta x\Delta y}$.

With the grid point convention of section 3.1 the surrounding 8 grid points of center point p have the following integer coordinates:

$\bullet\,(m-1,n-1)$	$\bullet\,(m,n-1)$	$\bullet\,(m+1,n-1)$
$\bullet\,(m-1,n)$	$p\bullet\,(m,n)$	$\bullet\,(m+1,n)$
$\bullet\,(m-1,n+1)$	$\bullet\,(m,n+1)$	$\bullet\,(m+1,n+1)$

If we consider relative locations of above grid points with respect to the center point p, we may write the positions as presented in the following:

• Upper left	• Up	• Upper right
• Left	p • Center	• Right
• Lower left	• Down	• Lower right

If one introduces the relative grid points, various partial derivatives are written as follows:

first order f with respect to x: $\dfrac{\partial f}{\partial x} \approx \dfrac{right - left}{2\Delta x}$,

first order f with respect to y: $\dfrac{\partial f}{\partial y} \approx \dfrac{down - up}{2\Delta y}$,

second order f with respect to only x: $\dfrac{\partial^2 f}{\partial x^2} \approx \dfrac{right - 2\times center + left}{(\Delta x)^2}$,

second order f with respect to only y: $\dfrac{\partial^2 f}{\partial y^2} \approx \dfrac{down - 2\times center + up}{(\Delta y)^2}$,

and

second order f with respect to first x and then y: $\dfrac{\partial^2 f}{\partial x \partial y} = f_{xy} \approx$

$$\frac{Upper\ left + Lower\ right - Upper\ right - Lower\ left}{4\Delta x \Delta y}.$$

Essential grid points for FD equations:

Having gone through FD approximation on partial derivatives, particular grid point structure must be present in given PDE domain.

For the $\dfrac{\partial f}{\partial x}$ we must have $[\bullet \quad p \quad \bullet]$ grid points available. If the given grid point evolves as e.g. $\begin{bmatrix} \bullet & \\ p & \bullet \end{bmatrix}$, we can not write the FD equation for the $\dfrac{\partial f}{\partial x}$. Similarly

for the $\dfrac{\partial f}{\partial y}$, grid points $\begin{bmatrix} \bullet \\ p \\ \bullet \end{bmatrix}$ must be available,

for the $\dfrac{\partial^2 f}{\partial x^2}$, grid points $[\bullet \quad p \quad \bullet]$ must be available,

for the $\dfrac{\partial^2 f}{\partial y^2}$, grid points $\begin{bmatrix} \bullet \\ p \\ \bullet \end{bmatrix}$ must be available, and

for the $\dfrac{\partial^2 f}{\partial x \partial y}$, grid points $\begin{bmatrix} \bullet & & \bullet \\ & p & \\ \bullet & & \bullet \end{bmatrix}$ must be available.

Unequal spacing of the grid points:

Previous discussions so far consider equal spacing of grids i.e. Δx or Δy is the same for all points. When a PDE domain is other than rectangular e.g. circular or triangular, one encounters unequal spacing. The FD definitions of various partial derivatives are modified as follows:

$\frac{\partial f}{\partial x} \approx \frac{right - left}{\Delta x_1 + \Delta x_2}$ where the unequally spaced grid points are $\begin{bmatrix} \bullet & p & \bullet \\ \leftarrow \Delta x_1 \rightarrow & \leftarrow \Delta x_2 \rightarrow & \end{bmatrix}$,

$\frac{\partial f}{\partial y} \approx \frac{down - up}{\Delta y_1 + \Delta y_2}$ where the unequally spaced grid points are $\begin{bmatrix} \bullet \\ \uparrow \\ \Delta y_1 \\ \downarrow \\ p \\ \uparrow \\ \Delta y_2 \\ \downarrow \\ \bullet \end{bmatrix}$,

$\frac{\partial^2 f}{\partial x^2} \approx \frac{4(right - 2 \times center + left)}{(\Delta x_1 + \Delta x_2)^2}$ where the unequally spaced grid points are $\begin{bmatrix} \bullet & p & \bullet \\ \leftarrow \Delta x_1 \rightarrow & \leftarrow \Delta x_2 \rightarrow & \end{bmatrix}$,

$\frac{\partial^2 f}{\partial y^2} \approx \frac{4(down - 2 \times center + up)}{(\Delta y_1 + \Delta y_2)^2}$ where the unequally spaced grid points are $\begin{bmatrix} \bullet \\ \uparrow \\ \Delta y_1 \\ \downarrow \\ p \\ \uparrow \\ \Delta y_2 \\ \downarrow \\ \bullet \end{bmatrix}$, and

$\frac{\partial^2 f}{\partial x \partial y} \approx \frac{Upper\ left + Lower\ right - Upper\ right - Lower\ left}{(\Delta x_1 + \Delta x_2)(\Delta y_1 + \Delta y_2)}$ where the unequally spaced grid points are $\begin{bmatrix} \bullet & & \bullet \\ & \uparrow & \\ & \Delta y_1 & \\ & \downarrow & \\ \leftarrow \Delta x_1 \rightarrow & p & \leftarrow \Delta x_2 \rightarrow \\ & \uparrow & \\ & \Delta y_2 & \\ & \downarrow & \\ \bullet & & \bullet \end{bmatrix}$.

In FD literature essential grid points of a partial derivative are often termed as a FD molecule.

◆ Describing a solution domain

A PDE is solved on certain domain while applying FD approach. The domain can be two, three, or higher dimensional. Two dimensional means involvement of two independent variables, three dimensional means involvement of three independent variables, and so on.

We confine ourselves only up to two dimensions which stretch to some rectangular area in regular FD computing. Truly speaking any area may fall in the solution domain but rectangular basis is better for equation writing. If some domain is not rectangular, we approximate that to a closest rectangular one. Let us see the following examples.

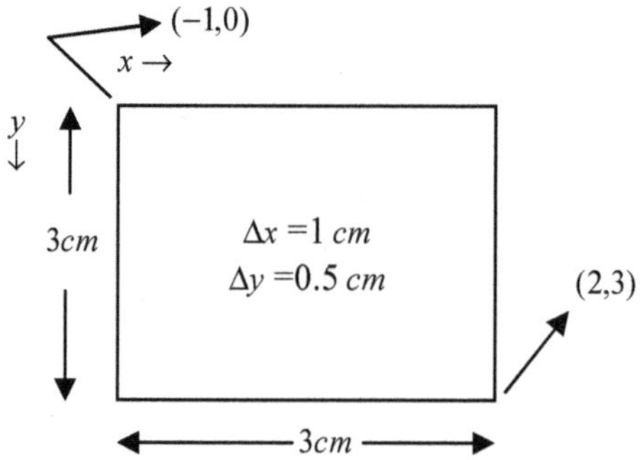

Figure 5.1(a) A rectangular domain is chosen for PDE solution

Example 1:

A solution domain of PDE is described by $-1 \le x \le 2$ and $0 \le y \le 3$. Analyze the grid points with $\Delta x = 1$ and $\Delta y = 0.5$.

The domain is a rectangular area which is the ideal situation. The grid points are located like in figure 3.1(a). In the x and y directions we have 4 and 7 grid points (chapters 2 and 3) respectively so there are 4×7=28 grid points in the domain. The number 4 comes from $\frac{x_2 - x_1}{\Delta x} + 1$ or (2-(-1))/1+1. Similar explanation goes for the y directed grid points. The grid points are equally spaced in each direction but $\Delta x \neq \Delta y$.

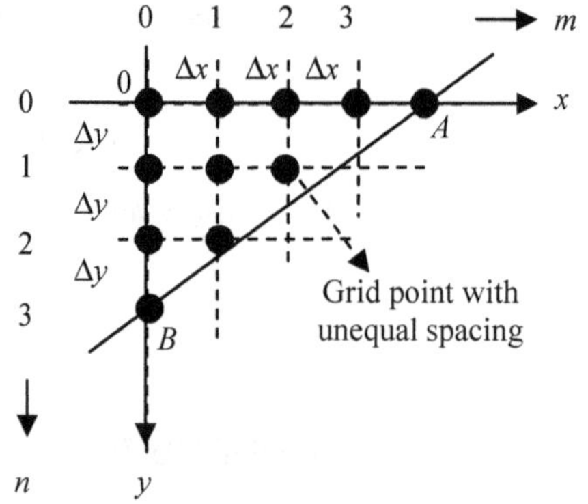

Figure 5.1(b) A triangular area is discretized for FD analysis

Example 2:

Figure 5.1(a) shows a rectangular

domain for PDE solution. How do we quantify the domain? This is exactly the one in example 1. The upper left grid point has the coordinate (−1,0), so is the (2,3) for the lower right grid point (indicated by arrow in figure 5.1(a)). Note that the coordinate convention of section 3.1 is maintained throughout this chapter.

Example 3:

Figure 5.1(b) shows a triangular domain OAB for PDE solution where equation of line AB is $y=9(1-x/8)$ and both the x and y are in cm. Analyze the domain subject to $\Delta x=2\,cm$ and $\Delta y=3\,cm$.

All grid points in the triangular domain are shown by a bold dot in figure 5.1(b). There are eleven regular grid points in the figure. Grid points on or next to the line AB need extra treatment depending on the partial derivative. In the figure a grid point with unequal spacing is indicated by a dotted arrow. Exact coordinate of this grid point is $(2\,\Delta x, \Delta y)$ or $(4\,cm, 3\,cm)$. The intersection of $y=\Delta y=3$ and $y=9(1-x/8)$ provides x=16/3, so is y=9/2 from the intersection of $x=2\,\Delta x=4$ and $y=9(1-x/8)$ hence the dotted arrow indicated grid point evolves as $\begin{bmatrix} & \bullet & \\ & \uparrow & \\ & 3cm & \\ & \downarrow & \\ \bullet \leftarrow 2cm \rightarrow & p & \leftarrow 16/3cm \rightarrow \bullet \\ & \uparrow & \\ & 9/2cm & \\ & \downarrow & \\ & \bullet & \end{bmatrix}$.

❖ Developing algebraic equations from FD approximation

In order to develop equations by using FD approximations on a PDE we observe the following steps:

(a) from given Δx and Δy information, determine the grid points in x and y directions,

(b) replace x of PDE by $x[m,n]$ if there is any,

(c) replace y of PDE by $y[m,n]$ if there is any,

(d) label the grid points by some variable (e.g. f_1, f_2, f_3, etc),

(e) from the given PDE, determine which FD molecule is required at every single grid point,

(f) write FD equation for every grid point including the boundary condition,

(g) make sure that the number of unknown variables in the written equations is equal to the number of equations, and

(h) finally call the solver to determine the solution.

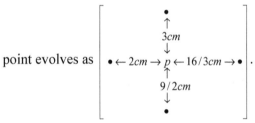

PDE solving means finding the dependant variable solution. All equation writing must be within the given domain. The solution so obtained is unique. Linear PDE results single solution whereas the nonlinear counterpart causes multiple solutions.

◆ Example on FD equation writing for a PDE

Solve the PDE $x\frac{\partial z}{\partial x}+y\frac{\partial z}{\partial y}=2(x+y)z$ employing FD technique subject to the boundary conditions $z(0,y)=2\ V$, $z(2,y)=4\ V$, $z(0<x<2cm,0)=0\ V$, and $z(0<x<2cm,1.8cm)=0\ V$ on Δx =0.5 cm and Δy =0.6 cm over $0\le x\le 2cm$ and $0\le y\le 1.8cm$.

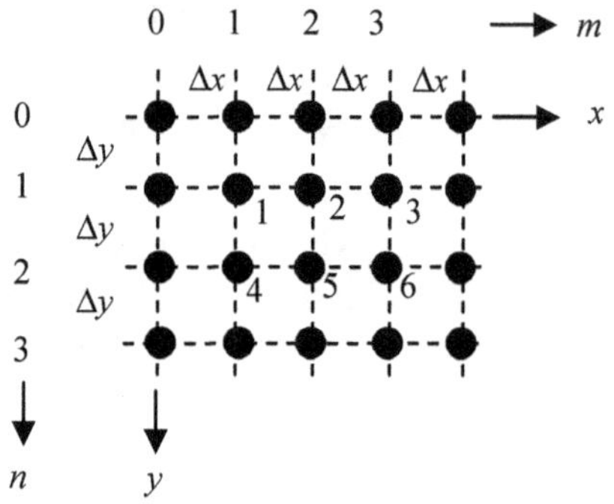

Figure 5.1(c) Discretizing the domain of example PDE

From the specification of Δx and Δy, the grid points in the domain evolve as shown in figure 5.1(c). There are 20 grid points in the figure. We labeled the unknown z values by 1 through 6 at inside grid points. You could have chosen other symbols like a, b, c, etc. At grid point 1, the unknown value is z_1. Similar explanation goes for the other grid points. From the given boundary conditions the dependent variable values at different grid points become $\begin{bmatrix} 2 & 0 & 0 & 0 & 4 \\ 2 & z_1 & z_2 & z_3 & 4 \\ 2 & z_4 & z_5 & z_6 & 4 \\ 2 & 0 & 0 & 0 & 4 \end{bmatrix}$.

Applying earlier definitions we obtain FD approximated equation of the PDE as follows:

$$x[m,n]\frac{right-left}{2\Delta x}+y[m,n]\frac{down-up}{2\Delta y}=2(x[m,n]+y[m,n])z[m,n].$$

The $x[m,n]$, $y[m,n]$, or $z[m,n]$ is merely a symbolism. Important point is relative connectedness among FD molecules. The $z[m,n]$ is the value of z at any continuous (x , y) or discrete (m , n). Let us write the FD equations for the six unknown grid points:

at grid point 1:

$$0.5\times\frac{z_2-2}{2\times 0.5}+0.6\times\frac{z_4-0}{2\times 0.6}=2(0.5+0.6)z_1,$$

at grid point 2:

$$1\times\frac{z_3-z_1}{2\times0.5}+0.6\times\frac{z_5-0}{2\times0.6}=2(1+0.6)z_2,$$

at grid point 3:

$$1.5\times\frac{4-z_2}{2\times0.5}+0.6\times\frac{z_6-0}{2\times0.6}=2(1.5+0.6)z_3,$$

at grid point 4:

$$0.5\times\frac{z_5-2}{2\times0.5}+1.2\times\frac{0-z_1}{2\times0.6}=2(0.5+1.2)z_4,$$

at grid point 5:

$$1\times\frac{z_6-z_4}{2\times0.5}+1.2\times\frac{0-z_2}{2\times0.6}=2(1+1.2)z_5,\text{ and}$$

at grid point 6:

$$1.5\times\frac{4-z_5}{2\times0.5}+1.2\times\frac{0-z_3}{2\times0.6}=2(1.5+1.2)z_6.$$

Solving the six equations one obtains the solution as:

z_1=–0.3687 V, z_2=0.5479 V, z_3=1.3324 V, z_4=–0.1704 V, z_5= 0.1041 V, and z_6=0.8355 V.

Principally this is what we intend to attain by solving a PDE on FD approximation.

5.3 Solving PDE in MATLAB

There is one dedicated toolbox in MATLAB which solves PDE problems. The reader is referred to [12] for the toolbox. But the problem is the toolbox is for professional use and solves specific type of PDEs. Our objective is to provide academic flavor in the computing that is why we do not wish to address the toolbox.

In the last section we elaborately explained how to solve a PDE employing FD approximation. In this section we are going to solve some PDEs by using the MATLAB algebraic equation solver (appendix D).

What is the bottomline? – the user has to write FD equations and MATLAB just solves those. The symbology of section 4.2 is equally applicable here.

◆ Example 1

In last section we developed six FD equations for one PDE. We wish to solve those equations.

The symbology we apply is the following: z1⇔z_1, z2⇔z_2, z3⇔z_3, and so on where z1, z2, ... are user-chosen. Assigning equations to intermediate variables (e.g. to e1, e2, etc) reduces the hassle where e1, e2, ... are also user-chosen. Let us enter the six equations of last section as follows:

```
>>e1='0.5*(z2-2)/2/0.5+0.6*z4/2/0.6=2*(0.5+0.6)*z1'; ↵
```

```
>>e2='1*(z3-z1)/2/0.5+0.6*z5/2/0.6=2*(1+0.6)*z2'; ↵
>>e3='1.5*(4-z2)/2/0.5+0.6*z6/2/0.6=2*(1.5+0.6)*z3'; ↵
>>e4='0.5*(z5-2)/2/0.5+1.2*(0-z1)/2/0.6=2*(0.5+1.2)*z4'; ↵
>>e5='1*(z6-z4)/2/0.5+1.2*(0-z2)/2/0.6=2*(1+1.2)*z5'; ↵
>>e6='1.5*(4-z5)/2/0.5+1.2*(0-z3)/2/0.6=2*(1.5+1.2)*z6'; ↵
```

For instance the first grid point equation $0.5\times\frac{z_2-2}{2\times0.5}+0.6\times\frac{z_4-0}{2\times0.6}=2(0.5+0.6)z_1$ has the code `0.5*(z2-2)/2/0.5+0.6*z4/2/0.6=2*(0.5+0.6)*z1` which we assigned to `e1`. Equation entering is finished, the next is to call the solver:

```
>>s=solve(e1,e2,e3,e4,e5,e6); ↵
```

Above workspace `s` (`s` is user-chosen) holds the solution as a symbolic structured array whose decimal form is seen by:

```
>>z=double([s.z1 s.z2 s.z3 s.z4 s.z5 s.z6]) ↵

z =

   -0.3687    0.5479    1.3324   -0.1704    0.1041    0.8355
      ↑          ↑         ↑         ↑         ↑         ↑
      z1         z2        z3        z4        z5        z6
```

The decimal solution is assigned to `z` where `z` is a user-chosen variable. Making the solution sequentially available, one accesses to each solution by calling specific `z` for example `z(1)` for z_1, `z(2)` for z_2, and so forth.

♦ Example 2

Solve the PDE $x\frac{\partial z}{\partial x}+y=z\sin(x+y)$ employing FD technique over the triangular domain of figure 5.1(b) on the same Δx and Δy specifications. Along the line AB, the boundary condition is $z_{AB}(x,y)=2x+y$ where x and y are in cm, also is $z_{OB}(0,0\le y<9cm)=0$ on the line OB.

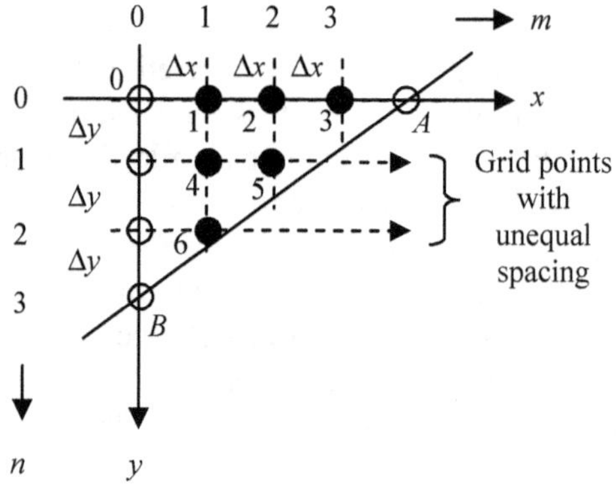

Figure 5.2(a) Triangular area of figure 5.1(b) is marked for PDE solving

Since $\frac{\partial z}{\partial x}$ is involved in the PDE, we have to deal with the FD molecule which takes the pattern [• p •]. Figure 5.1(b) is labeled with grid numbers which is seen in figure 5.2(a). The black bold grid points are unknowns and are numbered 1 through 6. The grid points at which the z values are known from the boundary conditions are indicated by round circles. Two grid points evolve with unequal spacing which are numbered as 5 and 6.

For the regular grid points, the FD equation on given PDE is

$$x[m,n]\,\frac{right-left}{2\Delta x}+y[m,n]=z[m,n]\sin(x[m,n]+y[m,n])\,.$$

Let us write the FD equation at every labeled grid point.

At grid point 1:

$$2\times\frac{z_2-0}{2\times 2}+0=z_1\sin(2+0)\,.$$

At grid point 2:

$$4\times\frac{z_3-z_1}{2\times 2}+0=z_2\sin(4+0)\,.$$

At grid point 3:

At this grid point $z_{AB}(x,y)=2x+y$ must be used which makes functional value of $z_{AB}(8cm,0cm)=16$ available and that is the value of the z too thereby providing:

$$6\times\frac{16-z_2}{2\times 2}+0=z_3\sin(6+0)\,.$$

At grid point 4:

$$2\times\frac{z_5-0}{2\times 2}+3=z_4\sin(2+3)\,.$$

At grid point 5:

Intersection of $y=9(1-x/8)$ and y=3 provides x=16/3 so the grid point 5 evolves as $[\bullet\leftarrow 2cm\rightarrow p\leftarrow 4/3cm\rightarrow\bullet]$ which needs the unequal spacing FD approximation $\frac{right-left}{2\Delta x}=\frac{right-left}{\Delta x_1+\Delta x_2}$. From the boundary condition $z_{AB}(x,y)$, the value of z at the intersection is 2×16/3+3=41/3 so the FD equation is

$$x[m,n]\,\frac{right-left}{\Delta x_1+\Delta x_2}+y[m,n]=z[m,n]\sin(x[m,n]+y[m,n])$$ or

$$4\times\frac{41/3-z_4}{2+4/3}+3=z_5\sin(4+3)\,.$$

At grid point 6:

Like point 5 evolution of the grid from intersection of $y=9(1-x/8)$ and y=6 is $[\bullet\leftarrow 2cm\rightarrow p\leftarrow 2/3cm\rightarrow\bullet]$ hence the boundary functional value is 2×8/3+6=34/3. The FD equation is then:

$$2\times\frac{34/3-0}{2+2/3}+6=z_6\sin(2+6)\,.$$

Knowing all six equations and maintaining symbology of the example 1, we execute the following:

```
>>e1='2*(z2-0)/2/2+0=z1*sin(2+0)'; ↵            ← FD equation 1
>>e2='4*(z3-z1)/2/2+0=z2*sin(4+0)'; ↵           ← FD equation 2
>>e3='6*(16-z2)/2/2+0=z3*sin(6+0)'; ↵           ← FD equation 3
>>e4='2*(z5-0)/2/2+3=z4*sin(2+3)'; ↵            ← FD equation 4
>>e5='4*(41/3-z4)/(2+4/3)+3=z5*sin(4+3)'; ↵ ← FD equation 5
>>e6='2*(34/3-0)/(2+2/3)+6=z6*sin(2+6)'; ↵  ← FD equation 6
```

Let us call the solver and assign the solution to **s**:

```
>>s=solve(e1,e2,e3,e4,e5,e6); ↵
```

Extract symbolic solution from structure array and assign that to **z** as a row matrix:

```
>>z=[s.z1 s.z2 s.z3 s.z4 s.z5 s.z6]; ↵
```

Exercise **double** to view the decimal solution:

```
>>double(z) ↵

ans =

         8.4715   15.4062   -3.1880 -389.0268  740.0946   14.6560
```

Hence one easily reads out the solution as: z_1=8.4715, z_2=15.4062, z_3= –3.188, z_4=–389.0268, z_5=740.0946, and z_6 =14.656.

♦ Example 3

Solve the Laplace equation $\frac{\partial^2 z}{\partial x^2}+\frac{\partial^2 z}{\partial y^2}$=0 employing FD technique on the same boundary and Δx and Δy spacing information over the domain of figure 5.1(c).

Second order FD approximation of the PDE provides the molecular equation as: $\frac{right-2\times center+left}{(\Delta x)^2}+\frac{down-2\times center+up}{(\Delta y)^2}$=0.

Given the PDE structure, essential molecular patterns are discovered as $\begin{bmatrix} & 0 & \\ & \uparrow & \\ 2\leftarrow & z_1 & \rightarrow z_2 \\ & \downarrow & \\ & z_4 & \end{bmatrix}$, $\begin{bmatrix} & 0 & \\ & \uparrow & \\ z_1\leftarrow & z_2 & \rightarrow z_3 \\ & \downarrow & \\ & z_5 & \end{bmatrix}$, $\begin{bmatrix} & 0 & \\ & \uparrow & \\ z_2\leftarrow & z_3 & \rightarrow 4 \\ & \downarrow & \\ & z_6 & \end{bmatrix}$, $\begin{bmatrix} & z_1 & \\ & \uparrow & \\ 2\leftarrow & z_4 & \rightarrow z_5 \\ & \downarrow & \\ & 0 & \end{bmatrix}$, $\begin{bmatrix} & z_2 & \\ & \uparrow & \\ z_4\leftarrow & z_5 & \rightarrow z_6 \\ & \downarrow & \\ & 0 & \end{bmatrix}$, and $\begin{bmatrix} & z_3 & \\ & \uparrow & \\ z_5\leftarrow & z_6 & \rightarrow 4 \\ & \downarrow & \\ & 0 & \end{bmatrix}$ for the six grid points respectively therefore the FD equations are written as follows:

at grid point 1:

$$\frac{z_2-2z_1+2}{0.5^2}+\frac{z_4-2z_1+0}{0.6^2}=0,$$

at grid point 2:

$$\frac{z_3-2z_2+z_1}{0.5^2}+\frac{z_5-2z_2+0}{0.6^2}=0,$$

at grid point 3:

$$\frac{4-2z_3+z_2}{0.5^2}+\frac{z_6-2z_3+0}{0.6^2}=0,$$

at grid point 4:

$$\frac{z_5-2z_4+2}{0.5^2}+\frac{0-2z_4+z_1}{0.6^2}=0,$$

at grid point 5:

$$\frac{z_6-2z_5+z_4}{0.5^2}+\frac{0-2z_5+z_2}{0.6^2}=0, \text{ and}$$

at grid point 6:

$$\frac{4-2z_6+z_5}{0.5^2}+\frac{0-2z_6+z_3}{0.6^2}=0.$$

Having known the FD equations, coding with ongoing symbology happens by:

```
>>e1='(z2-2*z1+2)/0.5^2+(z4-2*z1+0)/0.6^2=0'; ↵
>>e2='(z3-2*z2+z1)/0.5^2+(z5-2*z2+0)/0.6^2=0'; ↵
>>e3='(4-2*z3+z2)/0.5^2+(z6-2*z3+0)/0.6^2=0'; ↵
>>e4='(z5-2*z4+2)/0.5^2+(0-2*z4+z1)/0.6^2=0'; ↵
>>e5='(z6-2*z5+z4)/0.5^2+(0-2*z5+z2)/0.6^2=0'; ↵
>>e6='(4-2*z6+z5)/0.5^2+(0-2*z6+z3)/0.6^2=0'; ↵
>>s=solve(e1,e2,e3,e4,e5,e6); ↵
>>z=[s.z1 s.z2 s.z3 s.z4 s.z5 s.z6]; ↵
>>double(z) ↵

ans =
          1.1656    1.1407    1.9079    1.1656    1.1407    1.9079
```

Reading out the solution, one obtains z_1=1.1656 V, z_2=1.1407 V, z_3= 1.9079 V, z_4=1.1656 V, z_5=1.1407 V, and z_6=1.9079 V.

◆ Example 4

In example 3 now the PDE is $3\frac{\partial^2 z}{\partial x^2}+2\frac{\partial^2 z}{\partial y^2}+5\frac{\partial z}{\partial x}+7\frac{\partial z}{\partial y}-3z=4\sin x$ which is also known as elliptic PDE in the literature.

FD approximation on various partial derivatives provides the molecular equation as: $3\frac{right-2\times center+left}{(\Delta x)^2}+2\frac{down-2\times center+up}{(\Delta y)^2}+5\frac{right-left}{2\Delta x}+7\frac{down-up}{2\Delta y}-3z[m,n]=4\sin(x[m,n])$.

FD molecular structure of example 3 applies here too. For the first grid point the pattern is $\begin{bmatrix} & 0 & \\ & \uparrow & \\ 2\leftarrow & z_1 & \rightarrow z_2 \\ & \downarrow & \\ & z_4 & \end{bmatrix}$ so the FD equation is the following:

$$3\frac{z_2-2z_1+2}{0.5^2}+2\frac{z_4-2z_1+0}{0.6^2}+5\frac{z_2-2}{2\times0.5}+7\frac{z_4-0}{2\times0.6}-3z_1=4\sin0.5.$$

Similar equation writing for the other grids provides:

grid 2: $3\frac{z_3-2z_2+z_1}{0.5^2}+2\frac{z_5-2z_2+0}{0.6^2}+5\frac{z_3-z_1}{2\times0.5}+7\frac{z_5-0}{2\times0.6}-3z_2=4\sin1$,

grid 3: $3\frac{4-2z_3+z_2}{0.5^2}+2\frac{z_6-2z_3+0}{0.6^2}+5\frac{4-z_2}{2\times0.5}+7\frac{z_6-0}{2\times0.6}-3z_3=4\sin1.5$,

grid 4: $3\frac{z_5-2z_4+2}{0.5^2}+2\frac{0-2z_4+z_1}{0.6^2}+5\frac{z_5-2}{2\times0.5}+7\frac{0-z_1}{2\times0.6}-3z_4=4\sin0.5$,

grid 5: $3\frac{z_6-2z_5+z_4}{0.5^2}+2\frac{0-2z_5+z_2}{0.6^2}+5\frac{z_6-z_4}{2\times0.5}+7\frac{0-z_2}{2\times0.6}-3z_5=4\sin1$, and

grid 6: $3\frac{4-2z_6+z_5}{0.5^2}+2\frac{0-2z_6+z_3}{0.6^2}+5\frac{4-z_5}{2\times0.5}+7\frac{0-z_3}{2\times0.6}-3z_6=4\sin1.5$.

Coding above equations like the other examples we have:

```
e1='3*(z2-2*z1+2)/0.5^2+2*(z4-2*z1+0)/0.6^2+5*(z2-2)/2/0.5+7*(z4-0)/2/0.6-3*z1=4*sin(0.5)';
e2='3*(z3-2*z2+z1)/0.5^2+2*(z5-2*z2+0)/0.6^2+5*(z3-z1)/2/0.5+7*(z5-0)/2/0.6-3*z2=4*sin(1)';
e3='3*(4-2*z3+z2)/0.5^2+2*(z6-2*z3+0)/0.6^2+5*(4-z2)/2/0.5+7*(z6-0)/2/0.6-3*z3=4*sin(1.5)';
e4='3*(z5-2*z4+2)/0.5^2+2*(0-2*z4+z1)/0.6^2+5*(z5-2)/2/0.5+7*(0-z1)/2/0.6-3*z4=4*sin(0.5)';
e5='3*(z6-2*z5+z4)/0.5^2+2*(0-2*z5+z2)/0.6^2+5*(z6-z4)/2/0.5+7*(0-z2)/2/0.6-3*z5=4*sin(1)';
e6='3*(4-2*z6+z5)/0.5^2+2*(0-2*z6+z3)/0.6^2+5*(4-z5)/2/0.5+7*(0-z3)/2/0.6-3*z6=4*sin(1.5)';
s=solve(e1,e2,e3,e4,e5,e6);
z=[s.z1 s.z2 s.z3 s.z4 s.z5 s.z6];
double(z)
```

whose execution results z_1=1.1864V, z_2=1.4926V, z_3=2.496V, z_4= 0.681V, z_5=0.8354V, and z_6=1.8148V.

❖ Example 5

Solve the PDE $\frac{\partial^2 z}{\partial x^2}+\frac{\partial z}{\partial x}+\frac{\partial z}{\partial y}-3z=e^{-x-y}$ subject to Δx = 1 and Δy =1 over the area $x^2+y^2\le4$. The boundary condition is described as follows:

$z_B(x,y)=20^0C$ when $x^2+y^2=4$ and $y\le0$ and

$z_B(x,y)=0^0C$ when $x^2+y^2=4$ and $y>0$.

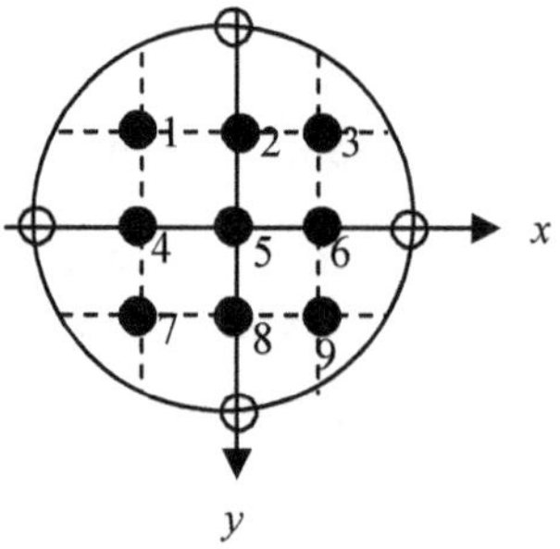

Figure 5.2(b) Circular area is marked for PDE solving

The $x^2+y^2\le4$ is a circular area with radius 2 and center origin. Based on the spacing specification the grid structure is shown in figure 5.2(b). Grids on the periphery are indicated by round circles whose values are known from the boundary conditions. The black bold dots are unknown temperatures and labeled by 1 through 9.

Unequal spacing arises at the grids 1, 3, 9, and 7. Intersection of $y=1$ or $x=1$ with $x^2+y^2=4$ provides coordinates $(-\sqrt{3},-1)$ and $(-1,-\sqrt{3})$ near grid 1, $(1,-\sqrt{3})$ and $(\sqrt{3},-1)$ near grid 3, $(\sqrt{3},1)$ and $(1,\sqrt{3})$ near grid 9, and $(-1,\sqrt{3})$ and $(-\sqrt{3},1)$ near grid 7. Only x directed spacings are $[\bullet \leftarrow \sqrt{3}-1 \rightarrow p \leftarrow 1 \rightarrow \bullet]$, $[\bullet \leftarrow 1 \rightarrow p \leftarrow \sqrt{3}-1 \rightarrow \bullet]$, $[\bullet \leftarrow 1 \rightarrow p \leftarrow \sqrt{3}-1 \rightarrow \bullet]$, and $[\bullet \leftarrow \sqrt{3}-1 \rightarrow p \leftarrow 1 \rightarrow \bullet]$ for the grids 1, 3, 9, and 7 respectively. Again only y directed spacings are $\begin{bmatrix} \bullet \\ \uparrow \\ \sqrt{3}-1 \\ \downarrow \\ p \\ \uparrow \\ 1 \\ \downarrow \\ \bullet \end{bmatrix}$, $\begin{bmatrix} \bullet \\ \uparrow \\ \sqrt{3}-1 \\ \downarrow \\ p \\ \uparrow \\ 1 \\ \downarrow \\ \bullet \end{bmatrix}$, $\begin{bmatrix} \bullet \\ \uparrow \\ 1 \\ \downarrow \\ p \\ \uparrow \\ \sqrt{3}-1 \\ \downarrow \\ \bullet \end{bmatrix}$, and $\begin{bmatrix} \bullet \\ \uparrow \\ 1 \\ \downarrow \\ p \\ \uparrow \\ \sqrt{3}-1 \\ \downarrow \\ \bullet \end{bmatrix}$ for the same four grids respectively.

The nine grid points evolve as $\begin{bmatrix} & 20 & \\ & \uparrow & \\ 20 \leftarrow & z_1 & \rightarrow z_2 \\ & \downarrow & \\ & z_4 & \end{bmatrix}$, $\begin{bmatrix} & 20 & \\ & \uparrow & \\ z_1 \leftarrow & z_2 & \rightarrow z_3 \\ & \downarrow & \\ & z_5 & \end{bmatrix}$, $\begin{bmatrix} & 20 & \\ & \uparrow & \\ z_2 \leftarrow & z_3 & \rightarrow 20 \\ & \downarrow & \\ & z_6 & \end{bmatrix}$, $\begin{bmatrix} & z_1 & \\ & \uparrow & \\ 20 \leftarrow & z_4 & \rightarrow z_5 \\ & \downarrow & \\ & z_7 & \end{bmatrix}$, $\begin{bmatrix} & z_2 & \\ & \uparrow & \\ z_4 \leftarrow & z_5 & \rightarrow z_6 \\ & \downarrow & \\ & z_8 & \end{bmatrix}$, $\begin{bmatrix} & z_3 & \\ & \uparrow & \\ z_5 \leftarrow & z_6 & \rightarrow 20 \\ & \downarrow & \\ & z_9 & \end{bmatrix}$, $\begin{bmatrix} & z_4 & \\ & \uparrow & \\ 0 \leftarrow & z_7 & \rightarrow z_8 \\ & \downarrow & \\ & 0 & \end{bmatrix}$, $\begin{bmatrix} & z_5 & \\ & \uparrow & \\ z_7 \leftarrow & z_8 & \rightarrow z_9 \\ & \downarrow & \\ & 0 & \end{bmatrix}$, and $\begin{bmatrix} & z_6 & \\ & \uparrow & \\ z_8 \leftarrow & z_9 & \rightarrow 0 \\ & \downarrow & \\ & 0 & \end{bmatrix}$ for grids 1 through 9 respectively. Coordinates i.e. $(x[m,n], y[m,n])$ of the nine unknown grids are (–1,–1), (0,–1), (1,–1), (–1,0), (0,0), (1,0), (–1,1), (0,1), and (1,1) for numbers 1 through 9 respectively.

Associated partial derivatives result the FD molecular equation as: $\frac{right-2\times center+left}{(\Delta x)^2}+\frac{right-left}{2\Delta x}+\frac{down-up}{2\Delta y}-3z[m,n]=e^{-x[m,n]-y[m,n]}$ obviously considering equal spacing. Let us write the FD equations for the regular grids:

grid 2: $\frac{z_3-2z_2+z_1}{1^2}+\frac{z_3-z_1}{2\times 1}+\frac{z_5-20}{2\times 1}-3z_2=e^{0+1}$,

grid 4: $\frac{z_5-2z_4+20}{1^2}+\frac{z_5-20}{2\times 1}+\frac{z_7-z_1}{2\times 1}-3z_4=e^{1+0}$, grid 5: $\frac{z_6-2z_5+z_4}{1^2}+\frac{z_6-z_4}{2\times1}+\frac{z_8-z_2}{2\times1}-3z_5=e^{0+0}$,

grid 6: $\frac{20-2z_6+z_5}{1^2}+\frac{20-z_5}{2\times1}+\frac{z_9-z_3}{2\times1}-3z_6=e^{-1+0}$, and

grid 8: $\frac{z_9-2z_8+z_7}{1^2}+\frac{z_9-z_7}{2\times1}+\frac{0-z_5}{2\times1}-3z_8=e^{0-1}$.

Because of unequal spacing, the FD equation for the other grid has to be modified which is

$$4\frac{right-2\times center+left}{(\Delta x_1+\Delta x_2)^2}+\frac{right-left}{\Delta x_1+\Delta x_2}+\frac{down-up}{\Delta y_1+\Delta y_2}-3z[m,n]=e^{-x[m,n]-y[m,n]}.$$

Knowing so the FD molecular equations of unequally spaced grids are the following:

for grid 1: $4\frac{z_2-2z_1+20}{(\sqrt{3}-1+1)^2}+\frac{z_2-20}{\sqrt{3}-1+1}+\frac{z_4-20}{\sqrt{3}-1+1}-3z_1=e^{1+1}$,

for grid 3: $4\frac{20-2z_3+z_2}{(1+\sqrt{3}-1)^2}+\frac{20-z_2}{1+\sqrt{3}-1}+\frac{z_6-20}{\sqrt{3}-1+1}-3z_3=e^{-1+1}$,

for grid 9: $4\frac{0-2z_9+z_8}{(1+\sqrt{3}-1)^2}+\frac{0-z_8}{1+\sqrt{3}-1}+\frac{0-z_6}{1+\sqrt{3}-1}-3z_9=e^{-1-1}$, and

for grid 7: $4\frac{z_8-2z_7+0}{(\sqrt{3}-1+1)^2}+\frac{z_8-0}{\sqrt{3}-1+1}+\frac{0-z_4}{1+\sqrt{3}-1}-3z_7=e^{1-1}$.

We are in a state of code writing and do so by (equal and unequal spacings respectively):

```
e2='z3-2*z2+z1+(z3-z1)/2+(z5-20)/2-3*z2=exp(0+1)';
e4='z5-2*z4+20+(z5-20)/2+(z7-z1)/2-3*z4=exp(1+0)';
e5='z6-2*z5+z4+(z6-z4)/2+(z8-z2)/2-3*z5=exp(0+0)';
e6='20-2*z6+z5+(20-z5)/2+(z9-z3)/2-3*z6=exp(-1+0)';
e8='z9-2*z8+z7+(z9-z7)/2+(0-z5)/2-3*z8=exp(0-1)';

e1='4*(z2-2*z1+20)/3+(z2-20)/sqrt(3)+(z4-20)/sqrt(3)-3*z1=exp(1+1)';
e3='4*(20-2*z3+z2)/3+(20-z2)/sqrt(3)+(z6-20)/sqrt(3)-3*z3=exp(-1+1)';
e9='4*(0-2*z9+z8)/3+(0-z8)/sqrt(3)+(0-z6)/sqrt(3)-3*z9=exp(-1-1)';
e7='4*(z8-2*z7+0)/3+(z8-0)/sqrt(3)+(0-z4)/sqrt(3)-3*z7=exp(1-1)';
```

Then solver calling takes place by:

```
s=solve(e1,e2,e3,e4,e5,e6,e7,e8,e9);
```

The solution is found and the symbolic result is stored in the variable **s** from which each solution as a row matrix **z** we get by:

```
z=[s.z1 s.z2 s.z3 s.z4 s.z5 s.z6 s.z7 s.z8 s.z9];
```

Just to see the decimal solution:

```
double(z)

ans =
```

```
-0.7951 -0.9630 4.9649 1.9932 1.7067 5.5352 -0.5465 -0.4951 -0.6539
```

Clearly we write the solution as z_1=–0.7951 ^0C, z_2=–0.963 ^0C, z_3= 4.9649 ^0C, z_4=1.9932 ^0C, z_5=1.7067 ^0C, z_6=5.5352 ^0C, z_7=–0.5465 ^0C, z_8= –0.4951 ^0C, and z_9=–0.6539 ^0C.

5.4 Comparison of PDE solutions in MATLAB

In multi-variable problems it is a common practice that we apply the FD technique to get the PDE solution and compare the solution with standard result. It paves the way for FD applications which can not be solved in conventional technique. We wish to present one example in this regard.

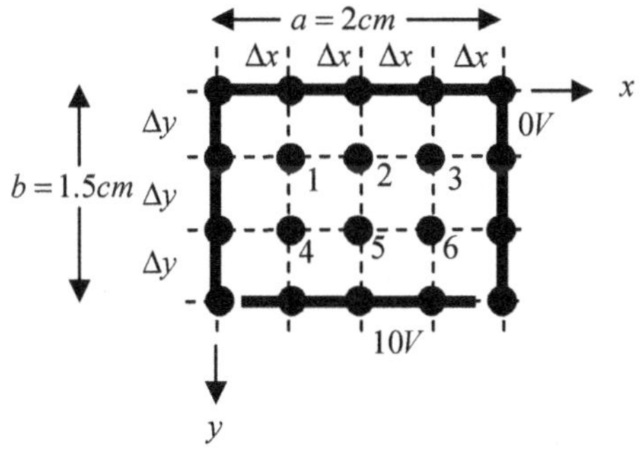

Figure 5.3(a) Discretizing the domain of example PDE

Figure 5.3(a) depicts a rectangular domain formed by $0 \le x \le 2cm$ and $0 \le y \le 1.5cm$ over which Laplace equation $\frac{\partial^2 z}{\partial x^2} + \frac{\partial^2 z}{\partial y^2} = 0$ has to be solved by choosing step sizes Δx =0.5 cm and Δy =0.5 cm. The boundary condition is stated as follows: $z(0, 0 \le y \le 1.5) = 0V$, $z(0 \le x \le 2, 0) = 0V$, $z(2, 0 \le y \le 1.5) = 0V$, and $z(0 < x < 2, 1.5) = 10V$ where coordinate dimensions are in cm. We present the conventional solution followed by the FD one.

Solution by variable separation:

The harmonic analytical solution by variable separation is given by $z(x, y) = \sum_{k=1}^{\infty} c_k \sin a_k x \sinh a_k y$ where $a_k = \frac{k\pi}{a}$ and $c_k = \frac{40}{\pi k \sinh\left(\frac{b}{a}\pi k\right)}$ and k is odd.

It is not feasible that we compute the solution until $k = \infty$. Let us say $k = 15$ and the computed solution in accordance with the coordinate of figure 5.3(a) is

$$z(x, y) = \begin{bmatrix} 0 & 0 & 0 & 0 & 0 \\ 0 & 1.5219 & 2.0788 & 1.5219 & 0 \\ 0 & 4.2077 & 5.2462 & 4.2077 & 0 \\ 0 & 9.4435 & 9.6036 & 9.4435 & 0 \end{bmatrix}.$$

In order to obtain the harmonic solution one needs to apply programming tactic. Sections 3.2 and 3.3 are the prerequisite for this coding. The k variation is conducted by a for-loop (appendix C.4). The odd number from 1 to 15 needs us to exercise 1:2:15. The x only and y only grid points we generate by the **meshgrid**. Scalar code (appendix B) with regard to $c_k \sin a_k x \sinh a_k y$ is written to compute the harmonic solution for every k. Before entering to the for-loop we initialize some user-chosen variable **Z** to 0. Every harmonic solution is found as a rectangular matrix and added to the preceding one until $k=15$. However the whole programming codes are in the sequel:

```
Z=0;
[X,Y]=meshgrid(0:0.5:2,0:0.5:1.5);
for k=1:2:15
        ak=k*pi/2;
        ck=40/pi/k/sinh(1.5/2*pi*k);
        Z=Z+ck*sin(ak*X).*sinh(ak*Y);
end
```

In above codes we have the equivalences k$\Leftrightarrow k$, ak$\Leftrightarrow a_k$, ck$\Leftrightarrow c_k$, and Z$\Leftrightarrow z$. Input arguments of **meshgrid** evolve from $0 \le x \le 2cm$ and $0 \le y \le 1.5cm$ with given step sizes (i.e. Δx and Δy). You may execute the commands line by line at the command prompt or in an M file. Having executed, the workspace variable **Z** holds the solution as a rectangular matrix. Just call it by:

```
>>Z ↵

Z =
     0         0         0         0         0
     0    1.5219    2.0788    1.5219    0.0000
     0    4.2077    5.2462    4.2077    0.0000
     0    9.4435    9.6036    9.4435    0.0000
```

This is the solution we presented before. All variable names are user-chosen. Obviously increased k would make the solution more exact.

Solution by the finite difference technique:

Sections 5.2 and 5.3 are the prerequisite for this discussion. Since the two step sizes are equal, finite difference Laplace equation reduces to

$right - 2\times center + left + down - 2\times center + up = 0$ in relative grid points.

With the grid point labeling of figure 5.3(a), the six FD equations are the following:

at grid 1: $z_2 - 2z_1 + 0 + z_4 - 2z_1 + 0 = 0$,

at grid 2: $z_3 - 2z_2 + z_1 + z_5 - 2z_2 + 0 = 0$,

at grid 3: $0-2z_3+z_2+z_6-2z_3+0=0$,

at grid 4: $z_5-2z_4+0+10-2z_4+z_1=0$,

at grid 5: $z_6-2z_5+z_4+10-2z_5+z_2=0$, and

at grid 6: $0-2z_6+z_5+10-2z_6+z_3=0$.

Exercising earlier symbology, we implement the following in MATLAB:

```
e1='z2-2*z1+0+z4-2*z1+0=0';
e2='z3-2*z2+z1+z5-2*z2+0=0';
e3='0-2*z3+z2+z6-2*z3+0=0';
e4='z5-2*z4+0+10-2*z4+z1=0';
e5='z6-2*z5+z4+10-2*z5+z2=0';
e6='0-2*z6+z5+10-2*z6+z3=0';
s=solve(e1,e2,e3,e4,e5,e6);
z=double([s.z1 s.z2 s.z3 s.z4 s.z5 s.z6]);
```

Hence the z values at the six grid points of figure 5.3(a) are stored in the workspace **z**. If we wish to form a matrix like the analytical solution, row by row entering of z samples helps us obtain that:

```
zd=[zeros(1,5);0 z(1) z(2) z(3) 0;0 z(4) z(5) z(6) 0; 0 10 10 10 0]

zd =
     0         0         0         0    0
     0    1.5528    2.0497    1.5528    0
     0    4.1615    5.0932    4.1615    0
     0   10.0000   10.0000   10.0000    0
```

where above **zd** is a user-chosen workspace variable. Harmonic solution is not even exact due to Fourier ringing phenomenon. Clearly there is some difference between the analytical (stored in **Z**) and finite difference (stored in **zd**) solutions. For instance the solutions are 2.0788 V and 2.0497 V at (x,y) $=(1cm,0.5cm)$ respectively. By inspection the reader easily draws a level of comparison.

5.5 Handling finer FD grids for PDE

Having found the solution of PDE it is often desired that we improve the resolution i.e. decrease the step sizes Δx and Δy. This causes solving enormous number of equations which is a drawback of FD. One way to solve the problem is interpolate which we elaborately addressed in section 3.7.

Just to provide one example, consider the last section mentioned FD solution which is stored in the workspace variable **zd**. In the problem we had $\Delta x=\Delta y=0.5cm$. Say we wish to find the solution employing bilinear interpolation on $\Delta x=\Delta y=0.25cm$.

On the found solution the grid points are obtained by:

```
>>[X,Y]=meshgrid(0:0.5:2,0:0.5:1.5); ↵
```

We need to regenerate the grid points for the new step sizes which are conducted by the following:

```
>>[Xn,Yn]=meshgrid(0:0.25:2,0:0.25:1.5); ↵
```

In the last execution the Xn and Yn are user-chosen variables which hold the x only and y only grid points for the new step sizes respectively. Immediately we may call the interpolator in order to see the new solution assuming that the previous one is available in zd:

```
>>zn=interp2(X,Y,zd,Xn,Yn) ↵

zn =
     0         0         0         0         0         0         0         0    0
     0    0.3882    0.7764    0.9006    1.0248    0.9006    0.7764    0.3882    0
     0    0.7764    1.5528    1.8012    2.0497    1.8012    1.5528    0.7764    0
     0    1.4286    2.8571    3.2143    3.5714    3.2143    2.8571    1.4286    0
     0    2.0807    4.1615    4.6273    5.0932    4.6273    4.1615    2.0807    0
     0    3.5404    7.0807    7.3137    7.5466    7.3137    7.0807    3.5404    0
     0    5.0000   10.0000   10.0000   10.0000   10.0000   10.0000    5.0000    0
```

The zn is a user-chosen variable which keeps the samples of $z(x, y)$ at the new grid points.

We reduced the step sizes to half that is not the case for graphical problems instead the Δx or Δy is awfully fine say 0.01 cm for each, which you can also generate in a similar fashion.

5.6 Graphing PDE solution in MATLAB

Graphing PDE solution is just like graphing a two dimensional data what we addressed in sections 3.8. Let us see the following examples.

♦ Example 1

In section 5.4 we described the harmonic solution of Laplace PDE over a rectangular domain. We wish to view the surface plot on the solution.

For the surface plot finer resolution is required so let us say $\Delta x = \Delta y =$ $0.05cm$ based on that reexecute the commands:

```
Z=0;
[X,Y]=meshgrid(0:0.05:2,0:0.05:1.5);
for k=1:2:15
        ak=k*pi/2;
        ck=40/pi/k/sinh(1.5/2*pi*k);
        Z=Z+ck*sin(ak*X).*sinh(ak*Y);
end
```

Surface plotter requires x and y directed variations as a row matrix which we generate by:

```
x=0:0.05:2; y=0:0.05:1.5;
```

Then call the surface grapher as:

```
surf(x,y,Z)
```

Include axes labeling as we did before:

```
xlabel('x spacing in cm')
ylabel('y spacing in cm')
zlabel('Voltage value in volt')
```

Successful execution of above results the figure 5.3(b). Harmonic theory says that there is ringing phenomenon about the final value which is lucid from the figure 5.3(b). About the $10\,V$ we see swinging on $y = 1.5cm$ plane.

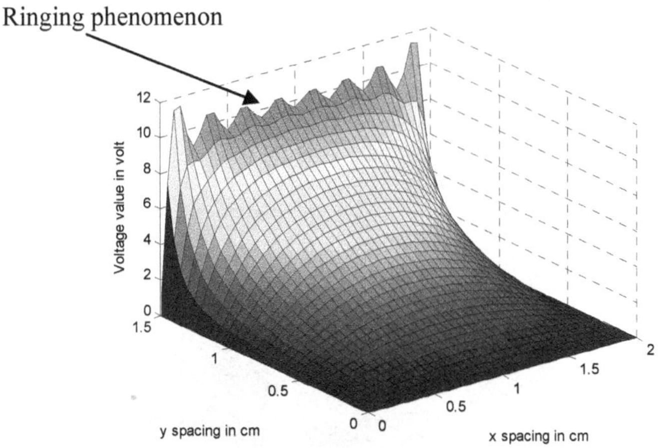

Figure 5.3(b) Surface graph of analytical solution on Laplace equation

♦ Example 2

In example 1 we graphed only the analytical solution. Now we wish to surface graph the FD solution.

Reexecute the finite difference related commands of section 5.4. The FD solution is available in the workspace variable **zd** where $\Delta x = \Delta y = 0.5cm$ and for which the x only and y only grid points are obtained by:

```
[X,Y]=meshgrid(0:0.5:2,0:0.5:1.5);
```

In section 5.5 two dimensional bilinear interpolation is also explained. For the surface graph finer resolution is required so let us choose $\Delta x = \Delta y = 0.05cm$ based on that the new x only and y only grid points are obtained by:

```
[Xn,Yn]=meshgrid(0:0.05:2,0:0.05:1.5);
```

Then we call the interpolator by:

```
zn=interp2(X,Y,zd,Xn,Yn);
```

Therefore the last `zn` keeps the interpolated samples of $z(x,y)$ on account of fine resolution. For the grapher input argument we need x and y directed variations as a row matrix i.e.

```
x=0:0.05:2; y=0:0.05:1.5;
```

After that call the surface grapher as:

```
surf(x,y,zn)
```

Axis label inclusion takes place by:

```
xlabel('x spacing in cm')
ylabel('y spacing in cm')
zlabel('Voltage value in volt')
```

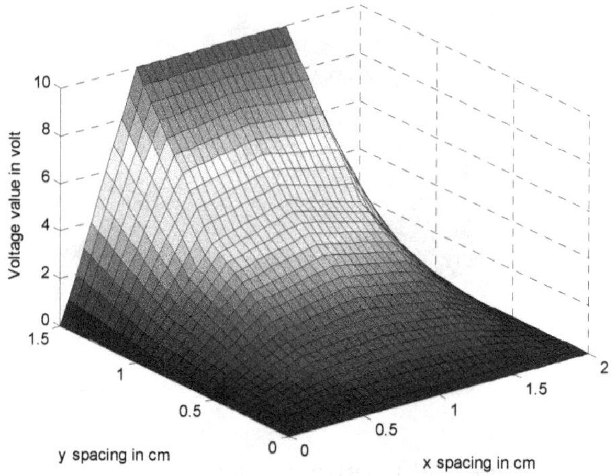

Figure 5.3(c) Surface graph of finite difference solution on Laplace equation

Implementation of all above brings about the figure 5.3(c) shown surface. When compared to the last surface graph, the ringing phenomenon is absent in FD solution. The ringing is unwanted. Despite the limitations of FD technique at least we can appreciate the method in some problems.

◆ Example 3

A particular plane based graphing may also be wanted. Say in example 1 we wish to graph $z(0.8cm, y)$ versus y.

Now the $z(x,y)=\sum_{k=1}^{15} c_k \sin a_k x \sinh a_k y$ reduces to one dimensional computing because $z(0.8cm, y)=\sin a_k x \sum_{k=1}^{15} c_k \sinh a_k y$. No two dimensional grid is necessary. Only y directed variation can be generated by a row or column matrix by choosing the same resolution and harmonic variation:

```
y=0:0.05:1.5;
Z=0;
for k=1:2:15
        ak=k*pi/2;
        ck=40/pi/k/sinh(1.5/2*pi*k);
        Z=Z+sin(ak*0.8)*ck*sinh(ak*y);
end
```

The last Z this time is a row matrix which keeps the samples of $z(0.8cm, y)$. Having found the data, appendix E quoted plot can be exercised along with earlier labeling inclusion:

```
plot(y,Z)
xlabel('y spacing in cm')
ylabel('z(0.8cm,y) in Volt')
```

Figure 5.3(d) is the outcome from above executions.

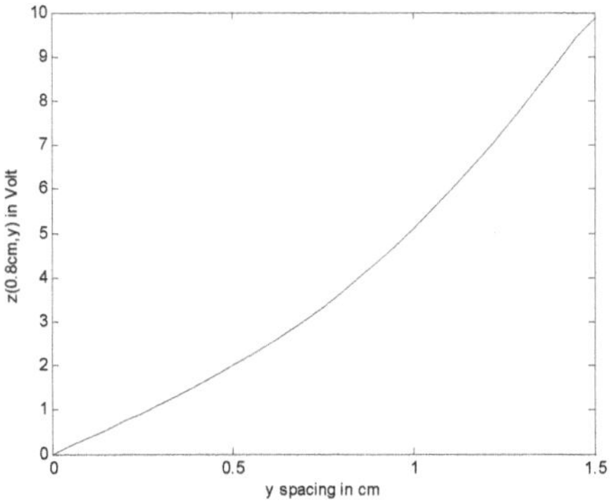

Figure 5.3(d) Graph of harmonic $z(0.8cm, y)$ versus y

♦ Example 4

Plane based graphing also happens in FD computing. Most FD computed results are in a rectangular matrix form. So to say, select the particular row or column from the rectangular matrix and graph that. In example 2 the fine $z(x, y)$ samples are available in the workspace zn. Say in example 2 we wish to graph $z(0.8cm, y)$ versus y too.

The rows and columns of zn refer to y and x directions respectively. Since we are looking for $z(0.8cm, y)$, we have to select a particular column. The x interval is $0 \le x \le 2cm$ subject to $\Delta x = 0.05cm$. The question is how to decide which column? The answer is $\frac{x - x_{start}}{\Delta x} + 1$ or $\frac{0.8-0}{0.05} + 1 = 17$. That is the 17th column corresponds to $z(0.8cm, y)$. Let us pick it (assuming zn is at the workspace) by:

```
zy=zn(:,17);
```

The zy is a user-chosen variable which retains the samples of $z(0.8cm, y)$ from FD computing. The y variation is needed for the plotter:

```
y=0:0.05:1.5;
```

Call the plotter by:

```
plot(y,zy)
```

Include labels by:

```
xlabel('y spacing in cm')
ylabel('z(0.8cm,y) in Volt')
```

Figure 5.3(e) shows the graph.

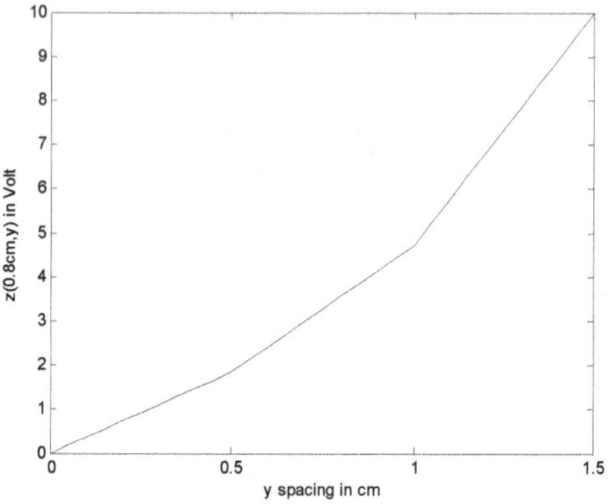

Figure 5.3(e) Graph of finite difference $z(0.8cm, y)$ versus y

◆ Example 5

What if we wish to plot the solutions of examples 3 and 4 together?

In example 3 the $z(0.8cm, y)$ is available in **Z**, so is in **zy** for example 4. After that generate the y variation by:

```
y=0:0.05:1.5;
```

Call the plotter with following input arguments:

```
plot(y,zy,y,Z)
```

Label inclusion is carried out by:

```
xlabel('y spacing in cm')
ylabel('z(0.8cm,y) in Volt')
```

In order to differentiate the solution we may use the command **legend** as follows:

```
legend('FD','Harmonic')
```

The input texts of **legend** are user-supplied. MATLAB displays the curves as color.

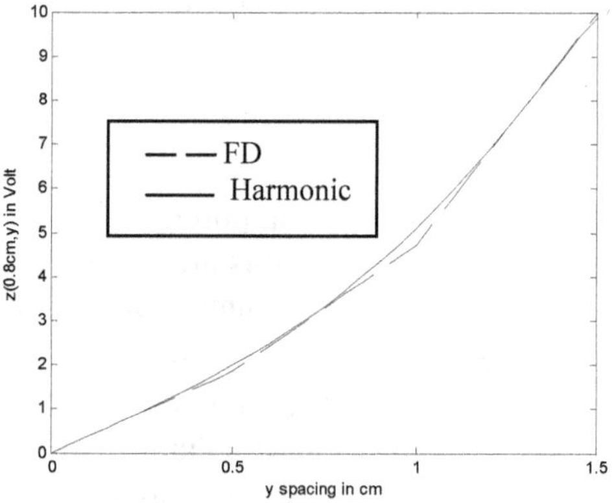

Figure 5.3(f) Graphs of finite difference and harmonic solutions together

Figure 5.3(f) depicts the comparison. By inspection the harmonic and FD solutions are very close indeed.

That brings an end to this chapter.

Exercises

1. A rectangular area is defined by $0 \le x \le 1$ and $-1 \le y \le 1$. Analyze the grid points on Δx =0.2 and Δy =0.5. Sketch the grid points in perspective.
2. Assuming regular grid, exercise finite difference coordinate to express the following PDEs by discrete derivative terms: (a) $4y^2\frac{\partial z}{\partial x}+\frac{\partial z}{\partial y}=x+y$ (b) $\frac{\partial^2 z}{\partial x^2}+\frac{\partial z}{\partial x}\frac{\partial z}{\partial y}=2+xy$ (c) $\frac{\partial^2 z}{\partial x^2}+\frac{\partial^2 z}{\partial y^2}=\sin(x+y)$ (d) $\frac{\partial^2 z}{\partial x^2}+\frac{\partial^2 z}{\partial y^2}+6\frac{\partial z}{\partial x}-8\frac{\partial z}{\partial y}-11z=2x+e^{-2x-y}$ (e) $\frac{\partial^2 z}{\partial x^2}+4\frac{\partial^2 z}{\partial x \partial y}+4\frac{\partial^2 z}{\partial y^2}=0$.
3. Exercise relative grid arrangement to express the PDEs of question 2 by discrete derivative terms.
4. What essential grid points do we need to write the regular FD molecular equation for each PDE in question (2)?
5. A triangular domain is defined by x =0, y =0, and $\frac{x}{3}+\frac{y}{5}\le 1$. Analyze the grid points on Δx =0.6 and Δy =1. Sketch the grid points in perspective.
6. A circular domain is defined by $x^2+y^2 \le 9$. Analyze the grid points on Δx =1 and Δy =1. Sketch the grid points in perspective.
7. Solve the PDE $\frac{\partial z}{\partial x}+x\frac{\partial z}{\partial y}=5x-y$ employing FD technique over the domain of question (1) where the boundary condition is $z_B(0,y)=10V$, $z_B(x,-1)=10V$, $z_B(1,y)=10V$, and $z_B(0<x<1,1)=0V$.
8. Solve the Poisson's equation $\frac{\partial^2 z}{\partial x^2}+\frac{\partial^2 z}{\partial y^2}$=0.1 employing FD technique over the domain of question (5) where the boundary condition is $z_B(0<x<3,0)=15^0C$, $z_B(0,0<y<5)=15^0C$, and $z_B(x,y)=0^0C$ along the inclined line.
9. Solve the Laplace equation $\frac{\partial^2 z}{\partial x^2}+\frac{\partial^2 z}{\partial y^2}$=0 employing FD technique on boundary condition of question (7) over the domain of question (1).
10. Solve the Laplace equation employing FD technique on boundary condition of question (8) over the domain of question (5).
11. Solve the elliptic PDE $5\frac{\partial^2 z}{\partial x^2}+5\frac{\partial^2 z}{\partial y^2}-2\frac{\partial z}{\partial x}-2\frac{\partial z}{\partial y}+3z=4x+y$ employing FD technique on boundary condition of question (8) over the domain of question (5).
12. Solve the Laplace equation employing FD technique over the domain of question (6) where the boundary condition is as follows: $60V$ on the periphery and $0V$ at the center.

13. Obtain the harmonic solution of Laplace equation up to the 17th harmonic over rectangular domain formed by $0 \le x \le 1cm$ and $0 \le y \le 0.75cm$ where the boundary condition is stated as follows: $z(0,0 \le y \le 0.75cm) = 0V$, $z(0 \le x \le 1cm,0) = 0V$, $z(1,0 < y < 0.75cm) = 50V$, and $z(0 \le x \le 1,0.75cm) = 0V$. Choose the spatial resolution as $\Delta x = \Delta y = 0.25\ cm$. Also obtain the FD solution.
14. In problem (13) the step sizes are reduced to $\Delta x = \Delta y = 0.125\ cm$. Starting from the FD result, obtain the solution considering two dimensional bilinear interpolation.
15. Graph the harmonic solution of problem (13) as a surface by choosing $\Delta x = \Delta y = 0.025\ cm$.
16. In problem (14) choose $\Delta x = \Delta y = 0.025\ cm$ and graph the FD solution as a surface.
17. Referring to problems (15) and (16), graph $z(0.5cm, y)$ versus y for harmonic and FD solutions together.
18. In problem (17) now graph $z(x, 0.5cm)$ versus x.

Answers:

(1) There are 6 and 5 grid points along x and y directions assuming 0 start and m and n vary from 0 to 5 and from 0 to 4 respectively. Figure E.5(a) shows the grid points in perspective. FD equation is not affected by relative positional change of m and n. Upper left corner coordinate is (0,–1).

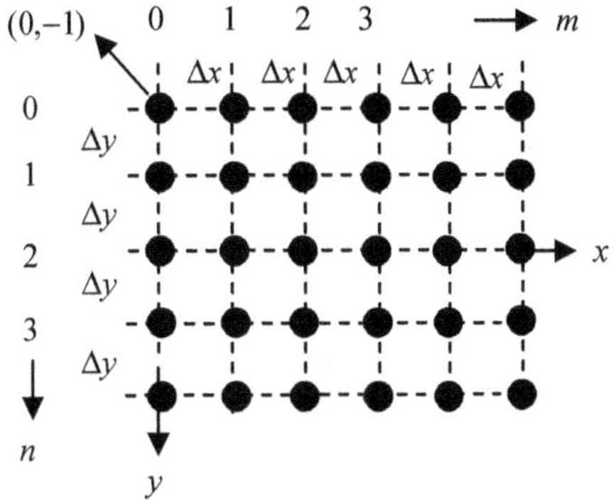

Figure E.5(a) Discretizing the domain of question 1

hint: section 5.2

(2) (a) $$4y^2[m,n]\frac{z[m+1,n]-z[m-1,n]}{2\Delta x}+\frac{z[m,n+1]-z[m,n-1]}{2\Delta y}=x[m,n]+y[m,n]$$

(b) $$\frac{z[m+1,n]-2z[m,n]+z[m-1,n]}{(\Delta x)^2}+\frac{z[m+1,n]-z[m-1,n]}{2\Delta x}\times$$
$$\frac{z[m,n+1]-z[m,n-1]}{2\Delta y}=2+x[m,n]y[m,n]$$

(c) $$\frac{z[m+1,n]-2z[m,n]+z[m-1,n]}{(\Delta x)^2}+\frac{z[m,n+1]-2z[m,n]+z[m,n-1]}{(\Delta y)^2}=$$
$$\sin(x[m,n]+y[m,n])$$

(d) $$\frac{z[m+1,n]-2z[m,n]+z[m-1,n]}{(\Delta x)^2}+\frac{z[m,n+1]-2z[m,n]+z[m,n-1]}{(\Delta y)^2}+$$
$$6\frac{z[m+1,n]-z[m-1,n]}{2\Delta x}-8\frac{z[m,n+1]-z[m,n-1]}{2\Delta y}-11z[m,n]=$$
$$2x[m,n]+e^{-2x[m,n]-y[m,n]}$$

(e) $$\frac{z[m+1,n]-2z[m,n]+z[m-1,n]}{(\Delta x)^2}+$$
$$\frac{z[m+1,n+1]-z[m+1,n-1]-z[m-1,n+1]+z[m-1,n-1]}{\Delta x\Delta y}+$$
$$4\frac{z[m,n+1]-2z[m,n]+z[m,n-1]}{(\Delta y)^2}=0$$

hint: section 5.2

(3) (a) $4y^2[m,n]\dfrac{right-left}{2\Delta x}+\dfrac{down-up}{2\Delta y}=x[m,n]+y[m,n]$

(b) $\dfrac{right-2\times center+left}{(\Delta x)^2}+\dfrac{right-left}{2\Delta x}\times\dfrac{down-up}{2\Delta y}=2+x[m,n]y[m,n]$

(c) $\dfrac{right-2\times center+left}{(\Delta x)^2}+\dfrac{down-2\times center+up}{(\Delta y)^2}=\sin(x[m,n]+y[m,n])$

(d) $\dfrac{right-2\times center+left}{(\Delta x)^2}+\dfrac{down-2\times center+up}{(\Delta y)^2}+$

$$6\frac{right-left}{2\Delta x}-8\frac{down-up}{2\Delta y}-11z[m,n]=2x[m,n]+e^{-2x[m,n]-y[m,n]}$$

(e) $\dfrac{right-2\times center+left}{(\Delta x)^2}+\dfrac{Upper\ left+Lower\ right-Upper\ right-Lower\ left}{\Delta x\Delta y}$

$$+4\frac{down-2\times center+up}{(\Delta y)^2}=0$$

hint: section 5.2

(4) (a) $[\bullet \quad p \quad \bullet]$ for $\dfrac{\partial z}{\partial x}$ and $\begin{bmatrix}\bullet\\ p\\ \bullet\end{bmatrix}$ for $\dfrac{\partial z}{\partial y}$

(b) $[\bullet \quad p \quad \bullet]$ for $\dfrac{\partial z}{\partial x}$ and $\dfrac{\partial^2 z}{\partial x^2}$ and $\begin{bmatrix}\bullet\\ p\\ \bullet\end{bmatrix}$ for $\dfrac{\partial z}{\partial y}$

(c) $[\bullet \quad p \quad \bullet]$ for $\dfrac{\partial^2 z}{\partial x^2}$ and $\begin{bmatrix}\bullet\\ p\\ \bullet\end{bmatrix}$ for $\dfrac{\partial^2 z}{\partial y^2}$

(d) $[\bullet \quad p \quad \bullet]$ for $\dfrac{\partial z}{\partial x}$ and $\dfrac{\partial^2 z}{\partial x^2}$ and $\begin{bmatrix}\bullet\\ p\\ \bullet\end{bmatrix}$ for $\dfrac{\partial z}{\partial y}$ and $\dfrac{\partial^2 z}{\partial y^2}$

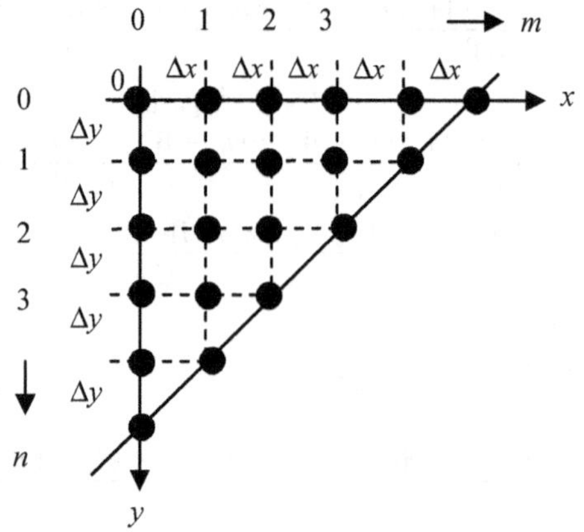

Figure E.5(b) Triangular area of problem 5 in FD domain

(e) $[\bullet \quad p \quad \bullet]$ for $\dfrac{\partial^2 z}{\partial x^2}$,

$\begin{bmatrix} \bullet \\ p \\ \bullet \end{bmatrix}$ for $\dfrac{\partial^2 z}{\partial y^2}$, and $\begin{bmatrix} \bullet & & \bullet \\ & p & \\ \bullet & & \bullet \end{bmatrix}$

for $\dfrac{\partial^2 z}{\partial x \partial y}$

hint: section 5.2

(5) Figure E.5(b), coincidentally all grid points are on the edge and no unequal spacing is among the grid points.
hint: section 5.2

(6) Figure E.5(c). Grid points with unequal spacing evolve.

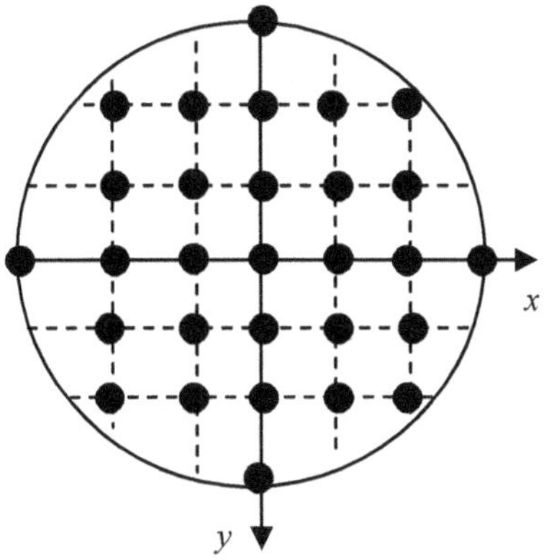

Figure E.5(c) Circular area of problem 6 in FD domain

Grid point coordinates within the domain:

along line $y=0$:

(–3,0), (–2,0), (–1,0), (0,0), (1,0), (2,0), (3,0),

along line $y=-1$:

(–2,–1), (–1,–1), (0,–1), (1,–1), (2,–1),

along line $y=-2$:

(–2,–2), (–1,–2), (0,–2), (1,–2), (2,–2),

along line $y=1$:

(–2,1), (–1,1), (0,1), (1,1), (2,1),

along line $y=2$:

(–2,2), (–1,2), (0,2), (1,2), (2,2),

lowest and highest:

(0,–3), (0,3),

Grid points with unequal spacing causing from intersection:

along line $y=-1$:

$(-2\sqrt{2},-1)$, $(2\sqrt{2},-1)$,

along line $y=-2$:

$(-\sqrt{5},-2)$, $(\sqrt{5},-2)$,

along line $y=1$:

$(-2\sqrt{2},1)$, $(2\sqrt{2},1)$,

along line $y=2$:

$(-\sqrt{5},2)$, $(\sqrt{5},2)$,

along line $x=-1$:

$(-1,-2\sqrt{2})$, $(-1,2\sqrt{2})$,

along line $x=-2$:

$(-2,-\sqrt{5})$, $(-2,\sqrt{5})$,

along line $x=1$:

$$(1,-2\sqrt{2}),\ (1,2\sqrt{2}),\text{ and}$$

along line $x=2$:

$$(2,-\sqrt{5}),\ (2,\sqrt{5}).$$

hint: section 5.2

(7) With the grid point labeling of figure E.5(d), the solution is as follows: $z_1=8.3983\,V$, $z_2=10.7505\,V$, $z_3=9.2525\,V$, $z_4=12.4137\,V$, $z_5=8.1191\,V$, $z_6=10.9117\,V$, $z_7=8.9032\,V$, $z_8=13.2889\,V$, $z_9=2.0017\,V$, $z_{10}=10.8495\,V$, $z_{11}=4.3475\,V$, and $z_{12}=13.9863\,V$ where peripheral round circles indicate $z=10\,V$ with the exception $z_{13}=z_{14}=z_{15}=z_{16}=0\,V$.

hint: sections 5.2 and 5.3

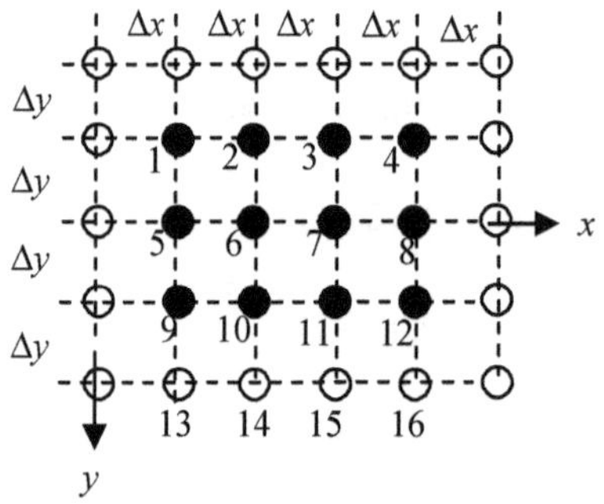

Figure E.5(d) Labeling for FD solution of problem (7)

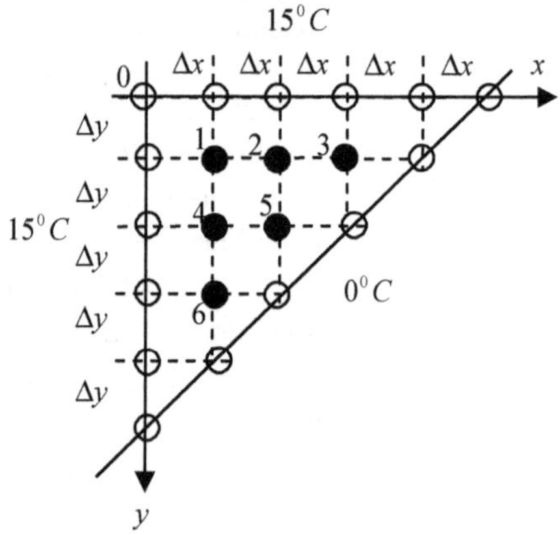

Figure E.5(e) Labeling for FD solution of Poisson's equation

(8) With the grid point labeling of figure E.5(e), the solution is as follows: $z_1=12.0793\,^0C$, $z_2=8.9820\,^0C$, $z_3=5.2743\,^0C$, $z_4=9.7490\,^0C$, $z_5=4.7598\,^0C$, and $z_6=6.7918\,^0C$.

hint: sections 5.2 and 5.3

(9) With the grid point labeling of figure E.5(d), the solution is as follows: $z_1=9.9039\,V$, $z_2=9.8456\,V$, $z_3=9.8456\,V$, $z_4=9.9039\,V$, $z_5=9.5722\,V$, $z_6=9.3263\,V$, $z_7=9.3263\,V$, $z_8=9.5722\,V$, $z_9=8.1041\,V$, $z_{10}=7.2699\,V$, $z_{11}=7.2699\,V$, and $z_{12}=8.1041\,V$ where peripheral round circles indicate $z=10\,V$ with the exception $z_{13}=z_{14}=z_{15}=z_{16}=0\,V$.

hint: sections 5.2 and 5.3

(10) With the grid point labeling of figure E.5(e), the solution is as follows: $z_1=12.1109\,^0C$, $z_2=9.0209\,^0C$, $z_3=5.3018\,^0C$, $z_4=9.7796\,^0C$, $z_5=4.7894\,^0C$, and $z_6=6.8091\,^0C$.

hint: sections 5.2 and 5.3

(11) With the grid point labeling of figure E.5(e), the solution is as follows: z_1=15.2740 ^0C, z_2=13.0327 ^0C, z_3= 8.1814 ^0C, z_4=12.9935 ^0C, z_5=7.8647 ^0C, and z_6= 8.7957 ^0C.

hint: sections 5.2 and 5.3

(12) With the grid point labeling of figure E.5(f), the solution is as follows: z_1=56.032 V, z_2= 52.064 V, z_3=49.4953 V, z_4 =52.064 V, z_5=56.032 V, z_6 =52.064 V, z_7=42.9586 V, z_8 =33.8531 V, z_9=42.9586 V, z_{10}=52.064 V, z_{11}=49.4953 V, z_{12}=33.8531 V, z_{14}=33.8531 V, z_{15}= 49.4953 V, z_{16}=52.064 V, z_{17}=42.9586 V, z_{18}=33.8531 V, z_{19}= 42.9586 V, z_{20}=52.064 V, z_{21}=56.032 V, z_{22}=52.064 V, z_{23}=49.4953 V, z_{24}=52.064 V, and z_{25}=56.032 V.

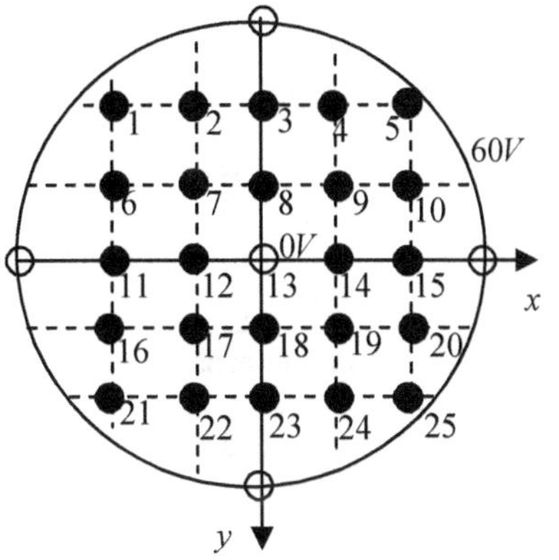

Figure E.5(f) Labeling for FD solution on circular area

Grid point 13 is excluded in FD equation writing. Laplace equation is simplified to $right-2\times center+left+down-2\times center+up$ =0 for the nodes 3, 7, 8, 9, 11, 12, 14, 15, 17, 18, 19, and 23 since $\Delta x=\Delta y$. Again for the unequally spaced nodes we have the FD equation $\frac{right-2\times center+left}{(\Delta x_1+\Delta x_2)^2}+\frac{down-2\times center+up}{(\Delta y_1+\Delta y_2)^2}$ =0 which applies to the nodes 1, 2, 4, 5, 6, 10, 16, 20, 21, 22, 24, and 25. The Δx_1, Δx_2, Δy_1, or Δy_2 can be 1, $\sqrt{8}-2$, or $\sqrt{5}-2$ for the unequally spaced nodes.

hint: sections 5.2 and 5.3

(13) Figure E.5(g) depicts the domain in perspective along with the grid point labeling. The analytical harmonic solution is given by $z(x,y)=\sum_{k=1}^{17} c_k \sinh b_k x \sin b_k y$ where

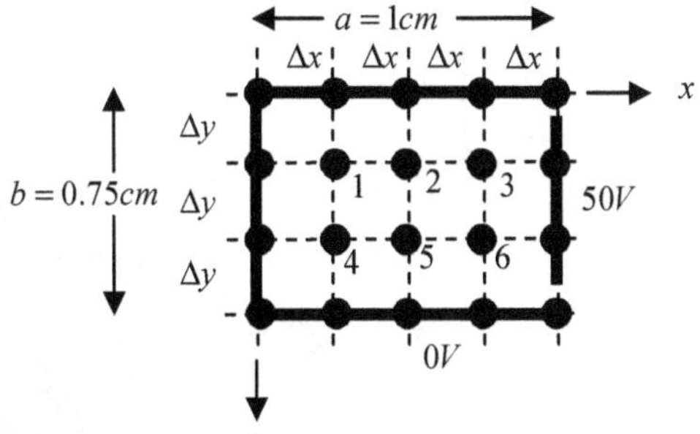

Figure E.5(g) Discretizing the domain of problem (13)

$b_k = \dfrac{k\pi}{b}$ and $c_k = \dfrac{200}{\pi k \sinh\left(\dfrac{a}{b}\pi k\right)}$ with odd k. The $z(x,y)$ samples from harmonic solution are in the sequel:

$$\begin{bmatrix} 0 & 0 & 0 & 0 & 0 \\ 0 & 2.0896 & 6.6876 & 19.2620 & 47.9682 \\ 0 & 2.0896 & 6.6876 & 19.2620 & 47.9682 \\ 0 & 0 & 0 & 0 & 0 \end{bmatrix}.$$

The FD counterpart is

$$\begin{bmatrix} 0 & 0 & 0 & 0 & 0 \\ 0 & 2.381 & 7.1429 & 19.0476 & 50 \\ 0 & 2.381 & 7.1429 & 19.0476 & 50 \\ 0 & 0 & 0 & 0 & 0 \end{bmatrix}.$$

hint: section 5.4

(14) The interpolated FD solution is

$$\begin{bmatrix} 0 & 0 & 0 & 0 & 0 & 0 & 0 & 0 & 0 \\ 0 & 0.5952 & 1.1905 & 2.3810 & 3.5714 & 6.5476 & 9.5238 & 17.2619 & 25 \\ 0 & 1.1905 & 2.3810 & 4.7619 & 7.1429 & 13.0952 & 19.0476 & 34.5238 & 50 \\ 0 & 1.1905 & 2.3810 & 4.7619 & 7.1429 & 13.0952 & 19.0476 & 34.5238 & 50 \\ 0 & 1.1905 & 2.3810 & 4.7619 & 7.1429 & 13.0952 & 19.0476 & 34.5238 & 50 \\ 0 & 0.5952 & 1.1905 & 2.3810 & 3.5714 & 6.5476 & 9.5238 & 17.2619 & 25 \\ 0 & 0 & 0 & 0 & 0 & 0 & 0 & 0 & 0 \end{bmatrix}.$$

hint: section 5.5

(15) Figure E.5(h) hint: section 5.6

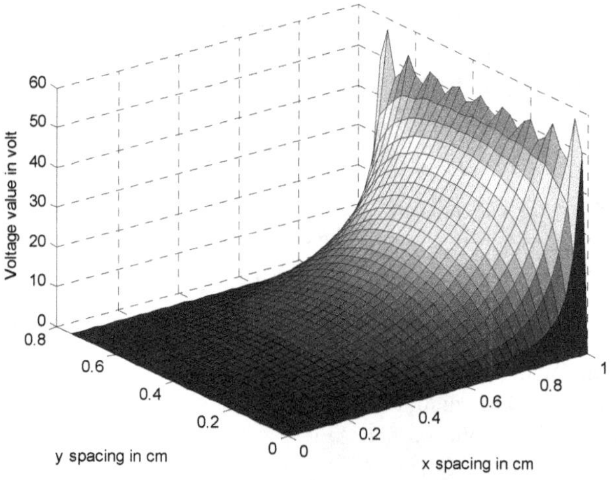

Figure E.5(h) PDE harmonic solution as a surface

(16) Figure E.5(i) hint: section 5.6

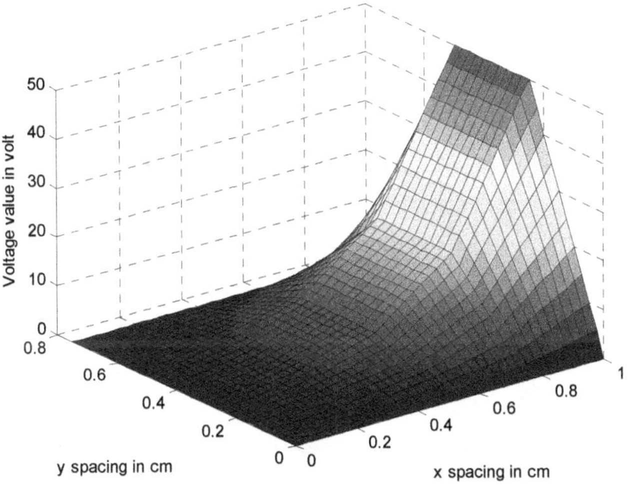

Figure E.5(i) FD solution of PDE as a surface

(17) Figure E.5(j) hint: section 5.6

(18) Figure E.5(k) hint: section 5.6

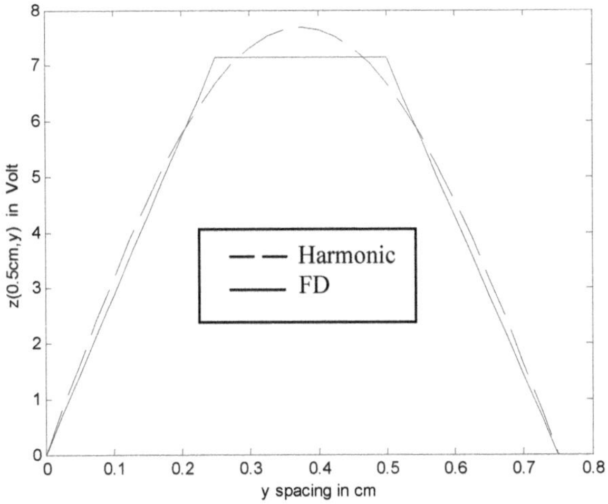

Figure E.5(j) Graph of $z(0.5cm, y)$ versus y

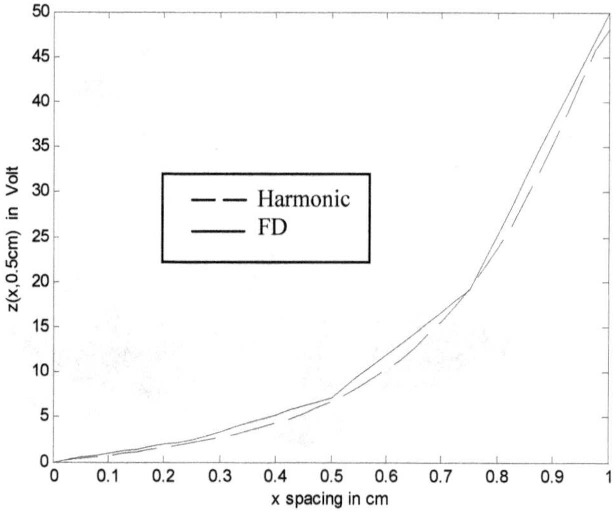

Figure E.5(k) Graph of $z(x,0.5cm)$ versus x

Appendices

Appendix A

Applications on finite difference

Finite difference finds its application in numerous science and engineering problems. Each discipline engages particular approach while applying the finite difference but computing fundamental is similar. In the sequel we demonstrate examples sampling from diversified applications.

A.1 Capacitor voltage and current

Capacitor is an element often found in electrical circuits. Think about your mobile, you must have a charger, right? Inside the charger there must be a capacitor to filter the electricity your mobile draws from the power system. Figure A.1(a) depicts the schematic representation of a capacitor which may have some voltage v_C and current i_C. The relationship between voltage and current as a function of time is given as follows:

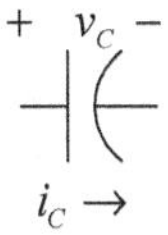

Figure A.1(a) A capacitor

$i_C = C\dfrac{dv_C}{dt}$ when v_C is known and

$v_C = \dfrac{1}{C}\int i_C\,dt$ when i_C is known where C is the capacitance.

The standard units of C, i_C, and v_C are Farad (F), Ampere (A), and Volt (V) respectively. We wish to show how FD is applied in computing and graphing of i_C or v_C. Let us see the following examples.

Example 1:

The capacitance C=33 μF contains a current i_C=0.01 e^{-t} mA over the time interval $0 \le t \le 50m\sec$. Calculate v_C at $t = 50m\sec$.

The $\dfrac{1}{C}\int i_C\,dt$ is approximated as $\dfrac{\Delta t}{C}\Sigma i_C$ (section 2.3). Let us choose some discretization step or in other words the number of samples (say 101) along t interval and generate the t samples as a row matrix in standard unit:

>>dt=50/100; ↵ ← dt⇔ Δt, dt is user-chosen, $\Delta t = 50m\sec/100$

>>t=[0:dt:50]*1e-3; ↵ ← t⇔ t, t is user-chosen, holds t samples in sec

The i_C samples we generate by the scalar code (appendix B):

>>ic=0.01*exp(-t)*1e-3; ↵ ← ic⇔ i_C, ic is user-chosen, holds i_C samples in A

Implementation of $\dfrac{\Delta t}{C}\Sigma i_C$ takes place by:

```
>>vc=dt*1e-3*sum(ic)/33e-6 ↵
```
← vc⇔ v_C , vc is user-chosen, all quantities are in standard unit

```
vc =

          0.0149
```

As the return indicates, v_C is $0.0149\,V$.

Example 2:

The capacitance $C = 33\,mF$ contains a voltage $v_C = 10\,e^{-t}\,V$ over the time interval $0 \le t \le 5\,\text{sec}$. Graph the v_C along with i_C in two different traces employing FD technique.

Let us follow the symbology of example 1 and choose 1001 samples:

```
>>dt=5/1000; ↵
>>t=0:dt:5; ↵
>>vc=10*exp(-t); ↵
```

Therefore the v_C samples are available in vc. Here we have two dissimilar quantities, v_C and i_C which can be best graphed by the subplot of appendix E hence v_C versus t we get by:

```
>>subplot(211), plot(t,vc) ↵
```

The i_C is approximated as $C\dfrac{\Delta v_C}{\Delta t}$ and we may consider the divided difference of section 2.4 for the computing and execute that by:

```
>>ic=33e-3*diff(vc)/dt; ↵
```

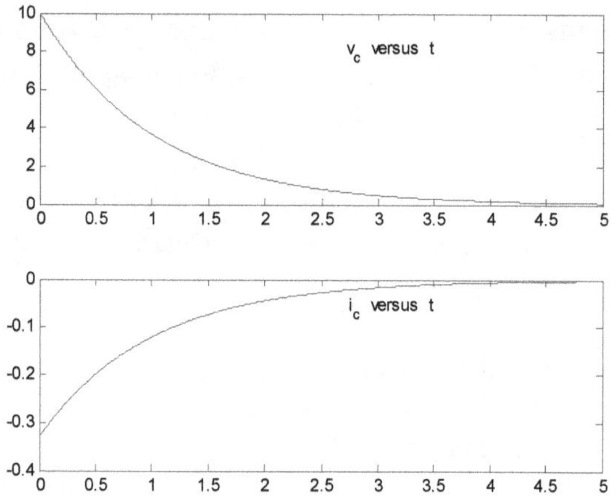

Figure A.1(b) Plots of v_C and i_C versus t

From section 2.4 we know that in forward dividend difference computing, total sample number is reduced by 1. Since plotter needs identical sample number on t and i_C, we discard the last sample of t as follows:

```
>>t(end)=[ ]; ↵
```

Then call the plotter:

```
>>subplot(212),plot(t,ic) ↵
```

In order to include label one at a time, execute the following mouse driven texts:

```
>>gtext('v_c versus t') ↵
```

Bring your mouse pointer on the upper graph and click the activated crosshair. Similar inclusion on the lower curve is done by:

```
>>gtext('i_c versus t') ↵
```

That results the figure A.1(b).

A.2 Cantilever beam deflection

The deflection of a cantilever beam is computed in civil engineering problems. Figure A.1(c) depicts the representation of a cantilever beam whose deflection equation is given by $\frac{d^2y}{dx^2} = -\frac{px^3}{6LEI}$ and where the related parameters are

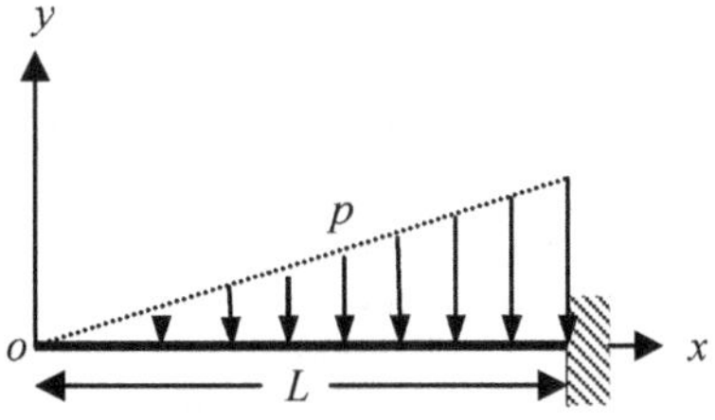

Figure A.1(c) A cantilever beam

L: cantilever beam length in meter,
I: moment of inertia in meter^4,
y: transverse deflection in meter,
x: horizontal distance from the tip of the beam in meter,
E: modulus of elasticity in Newton/meter^2, and
p: maximum intensity of a triangular load on the beam in Newton/meter.

We demonstrate two examples related to the deflection.

Example 1:

Find the deflection y of the beam subject to p=23 N/m, I= 500 m^4, L=1.2 m, and E=10^4 N/m^2 considering step size Δx=0.2 m over $0 \le x \le 1.2$ m where $y(0)$=0.05 m and $y(1.2\,m)$=0.

We solved one similar problem in section 4.2 so let us jump into the process.

Related FD equation is $\frac{y[m+1]-2y[m]+y[m-1]}{(\Delta x)^2} = -\frac{px^3}{6LEI}$.

The samples of dependent variable are as follows: y_0, y_1, y_2, y_3, y_4, y_5, and y_6, out of which y_0=0.05 m and y_6=0. Knowing so and maintaining symbology of section 4.2, the FD equations and their codes are in the sequel.

FD equations:

at x=0.2 or for y_1 : $\frac{y[2]-2y[1]+0.05}{0.2^2}=-\frac{23\times0.2^3}{6\times1.2\times10^4\times500}$,

at x=0.4 or for y_2 : $\frac{y[3]-2y[2]+y[1]}{0.2^2}=-\frac{23\times0.4^3}{6\times1.2\times10^4\times500}$,

at x=0.6 or for y_3 : $\frac{y[4]-2y[3]+y[2]}{0.2^2}=-\frac{23\times0.6^3}{6\times1.2\times10^4\times500}$,

at x=0.8 or for y_4 : $\frac{y[5]-2y[4]+y[3]}{0.2^2}=-\frac{23\times0.8^3}{6\times1.2\times10^4\times500}$, and

at x=1 or for y_5 : $\frac{0-2y[5]+y[4]}{0.2^2}=-\frac{23\times1^3}{6\times1.2\times10^4\times500}$ and

MATLAB commands:

```
>>e1='(y2-2*y1+0.05)/0.2^2=-23*0.2^3/6/1.2/1e4/500'; ↵
>>e2='(y3-2*y2+y1)/0.2^2=-23*0.4^3/6/1.2/1e4/500'; ↵
>>e3='(y4-2*y3+y2)/0.2^2=-23*0.6^3/6/1.2/1e4/500'; ↵
>>e4='(y5-2*y4+y3)/0.2^2=-23*0.8^3/6/1.2/1e4/500'; ↵
>>e5='(0-2*y5+y4)/0.2^2=-23*1^3/6/1.2/1e4/500'; ↵
>>s=solve(e1,e2,e3,e4,e5); ↵
>>sd=[s.y1 s.y2 s.y3 s.y4 s.y5]; ↵
>>double(sd) ↵

ans =

      0.0417    0.0333    0.0250    0.0167    0.0083
        ↑         ↑         ↑         ↑         ↑
       y[1]      y[2]      y[3]      y[4]      y[5]
```

In the last execution the **sd** is a user-chosen variable which holds the solution as a row matrix in symbolic form.

Example 2:

Plot the bending moment and deflection of example 1 quoted beam over the given interval.

The bending moment M is given by $M=-\frac{px^3}{6L}$. This is a graphical problem. We can employ **ezplot** (appendix E) to graph M versus x. Since two graphs of dissimilar quantities are involved, exercising **subplot** is a better option:

```
>>subplot(211), ezplot('-23*x^3/6/1.2',[0 1.2]) ↵
```

Graphics window shows the M versus x like the upper part of figure A.1(d). The next is the y versus x. The y samples are available in **sd** in symbolic form except y_0=0.05 and y_6=0. All y samples as a row matrix (appendix C.3) we form as follows:

```
>>y=[0.05 double(sd) 0]; ↵
```

Hence y holds all y samples but the x samples are not at the workspace so generate them by:

```
>>x=0:0.2:1.2; ↵
```

Appendix E cited **plot** brings about the second graph:

```
>>subplot(212), plot(x,y) ↵
```

Above execution returns the output as seen in the lower part of figure A.1(d). Appendix A.1 mentioned **gtext** is exercised to include the user-supplied label:

```
>>gtext('M versus x') ↵
>>gtext('y versus x') ↵
```

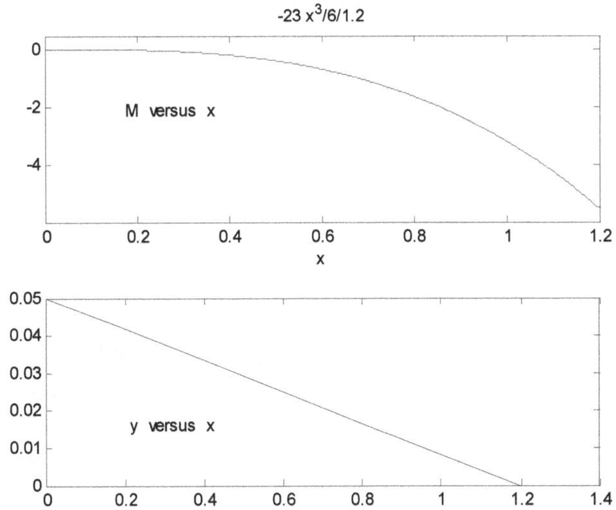

Figure A.1(d) Bending moment and deflection variations of a cantilever beam

A.3 Resistance and capacitance in an electromagnetic system

Many electromagnetic systems possess resistance which is dependent on geometry of the system. Here we present some example illustrating the resistance calculation by FD approach.

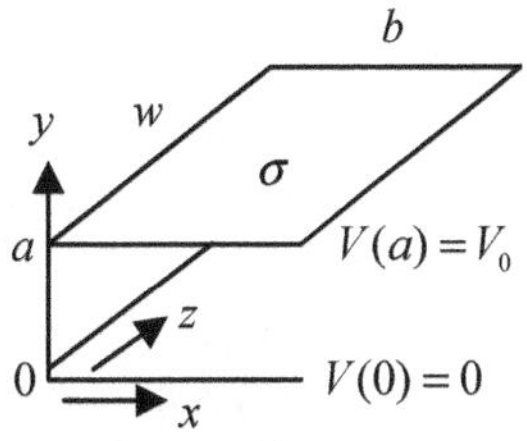

Figure A.1(e) A constant boundary voltage along y of an electromagnetic system

Figure A.1(e) shows a rectangular structure in which a plate or electrode is located on $y=a$ plane. Another identical plate is on the plane $y=0$. The two plates contain voltages V_0 and 0 respectively. Breadth and width of each plate are b and w respectively. Resistance between the two plates is given by $R=\frac{V_0}{\oint \sigma \overline{E} \circ d\overline{S}}$ where σ is the conductivity of the plates in $mho/meter$, $\overline{E}$ is the electric field between the plates in $Volt/meter$, R is the resistance in ohm, $d\overline{S}$ is the elementary surface vector, and $\oint \overline{E} \circ d\overline{S}$ is the closed surface integral. The vectorial dot product indicates $d\overline{S}$ and $\overline{E}$ must be in the same direction in order to get some integrational value. Usually electric field is given or found from Laplace equation so we are bypassing field finding discussion because that is beyond the scope of the text. Let us see the following computing examples.

Example 1:

Evaluate the resistance of electromagnetic system in figure A.1(e) on $V_0=100\,V$, $a=1cm$, $b=5cm$, $w=3cm$, and $\sigma=$ 20 $mho/meter$.

Assuming the electric field is uniform between the two plates, we have $\overline{E}=-\frac{V_0}{a}\overline{a}_y$ (negative sign is just an electrical engineering convention). The $d\overline{S}$ is normally outward from the surface which is $dxdz\ \overline{a}_y$ for the top plate. Even though the integral is closed, we consider only the top plate because for the other surfaces the contributions are zero. However the expression for R simplifies to $\frac{V_0}{\sigma \int_{z=0}^{w} \int_{x=0}^{b} E dx dz}$ where $E=-\frac{V_0}{a}$. In finite difference approximation (section 3.5) we have $R=\frac{V_0}{\sigma \Delta x \Delta z \sum_z \sum_x E}$.

We need to choose the sample numbers along x and z directions say 251 and 301 respectively. Enter the parameters in standard unit (e.g. $1cm$ or $10^{-2}m$ is 1e-2 in MATLAB term, appendix B):

>>a=1e-2; b=5e-2; w=3e-2; s=20; ↵ ← a⇔a, b⇔b, w⇔w, s⇔σ

Step sizes are computed by:

>>dz=w/300; dx=b/250; ↵ ← dz⇔Δz and dx⇔Δx

Only z directed z samples we get by:

>>z=0:dz:w; ↵

Only x directed x samples we get by:

>>x=0:dx:b; ↵

Grid points on x - z domain are obtained as:

>>[Z,X]=meshgrid(z,x); ↵

```
>>V=100; ↵          ← V⇔V0
```

The E is constant and its samples are generated on x - z domain or exactly at grid points by:

```
>>E=-V/a*ones(size(Z)); ↵
```

In last implementation matrix size of **Z** or **X** is identical – we get that by the command **size** and sample generation of E happens likewise (appendix C.8) hence resistance computing is carried out by:

```
>>R=V/s/dx/dz/sum(sum(E)) ↵

R =
        -0.3309
```

From above return the expected resistance is 0.3309 ohm ignoring the negative sign. All workspace variables for example **E** are user-chosen.

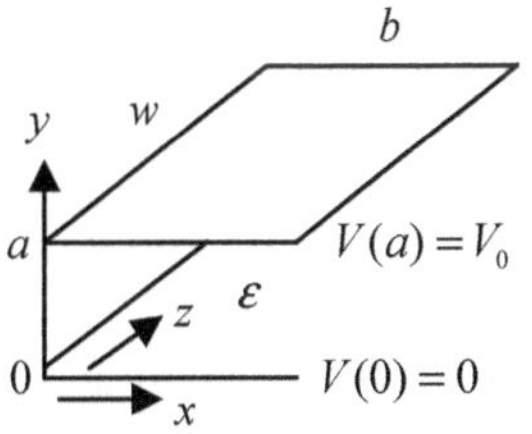

Figure A.1(f) Example 1 electromagnetic system forms a capacitance

Example 2:

In example 1 now the electromagnetic system forms a capacitance by filling the plates with a material (see figure A.1(f)) whose permittivity ε is $12\,pF/m$ (pF/m means $picoFarad/meter$). Compute capacitance of the electromagnetic system.

Capacitance between the plates is given by $C=\dfrac{\varepsilon\oint \overline{E}\circ d\overline{S}}{V_0}$ where the symbols have example 1 mentioned meanings. The simplified form of capacitance expression is $C=\dfrac{\varepsilon\int_{z=0}^{w}\int_{x=0}^{b} Edxdz}{V_0}$ where the finite difference counterpart is $C=\dfrac{\varepsilon\Delta x\Delta z\sum_z\sum_x E}{V_0}$. All executions of example 1 are applicable here until the computing of **E**, then conduct the following at the command prompt:

```
>>e=12e-12; ↵       ← e⇔ε , e is user-chosen

>>C=e*dx*dz*sum(sum(E))/V ↵       ← exercising C = εΔxΔzΣzΣxE / V0

C =
        -1.8132e-012
```

As the return shows, the capacitance is $1.8132\times10^{-12}F$ or $1.8132pF$ ignoring the negative sign.

Example 3:

Uniform field may not happen always. Suppose the field is $\overline{E}=-\frac{V_0(x+z)}{b+w}\overline{a}_y$. The modified command you only need is E=-V/(b+w)*(X+Z); in ongoing computing which would result R= 66.1805 *ohm* and C=0.0091 *pF* in examples 1 and 2 respectively.

A.4 Dynamics in a mechanical system

A mechanical system possesses certain characteristics for example mass, stiffness, and viscosity. In mechanical engineering problems it is a common analysis technique that a certain force is applied to a given system and its dynamics for example displacement, velocity, acceleration, etc are sought.

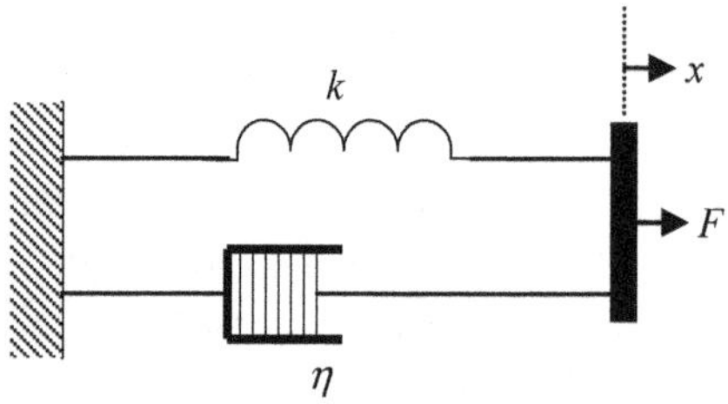

Figure A.1(g) A mechanical system subject to a force F

Adjacent figure A.1(g) illustrates one mechanical system in which only stiffness k (in Newton/meter) and viscosity η (Newton-sec/meter) are present. An external force F is exerted on the system. Constitutive equation of the dynamics is given by $\eta\frac{dx}{dt}+kx=F$ where x is the displacement of the mechanical system based on the reference indicated in the figure and t is the time.

Following example presents some computing and graphing on above mechanical system.

Example:

A constant force 20 N at t=0sec is applied to the mechanical system of figure A.1(g). Obtain the displacement x assuming initially relaxed condition on Δt=0.2sec over $0 \le t \le 2\sec$ where η=20 $N.\sec/meter$ and k=10 $N/meter$. Also plot the displacement and velocity of the system over $0 \le t \le 6\sec$.

The constitutive equation is $20\frac{dx}{dt}+10x=20$. We wish to apply the built-in solver ode23 of MATLAB as explained in chapter 4 to solve this problem.

Initially relaxed means $x(0)=0$. The rearranged equation is $\frac{dx}{dt}=1-x/2$. Adjacent text box shows the function file required to

```
Function file:
function dx=f(t,x)
dx=1-x/2;
```

solve the problem. Save the file by the name **f** at the workspace and call the solver as follows:

```
>>[t x]=ode23('f',[0:0.2:2],0); ↵
>>[t x] ↵                ← To see t and x data side by side

ans =
         0         0
    0.2000    0.1903
    0.4000    0.3626
    0.6000    0.5184
    0.8000    0.6594
    1.0000    0.7870
    1.2000    0.9024
    1.4000    1.0069
    1.6000    1.1014
    1.8000    1.1869
    2.0000    1.2643
       ↑         ↑
       t         x
```

The displacement and velocity are x and $\frac{dx}{dt}$ respectively. When we graph the quantities, larger step sizes do not bring a smooth curve that is why reduce the step size (say 0.01) and reexecute the solver.

```
>>[t x]=ode23('f',[0:0.01:6],0); ↵
```

For $\frac{dx}{dt}$ we apply forward divided difference of section 2.4 and graph the two traces with the help of **plot**. Along with that **subplot** is used to get two dissimilar traces:

```
>>subplot(211), plot(t,x) ↵
```

You can add the horizontal and vertical axes labels say **Time** and

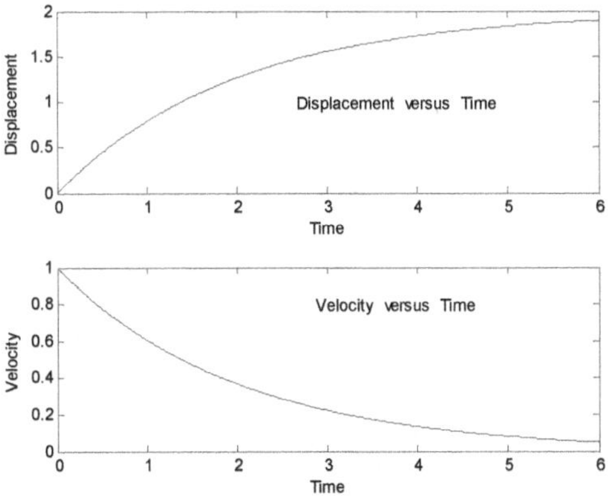

Figure A.1(h) Displacement and velocity of the mechanical system

Displacement respectively by:

```
>>xlabel('Time') ↵
>>ylabel('Displacement') ↵
```

Since forward difference causes to reduce the sample number by one, we discard the last time sample by:

```
>>t(end)=[ ]; ↵
```

If diff(x)/0.01 is exercised, we get the samples of $\frac{dx}{dt}$ so the velocity is graphed by:

```
>>subplot(212), plot(t,diff(x)/0.01) ↵
```

Include axes labeling by:

```
>>xlabel('Time') ↵
>>ylabel('Velocity') ↵
```

Like appendix A.1, the user selected label is added by:

```
>>gtext('Displacement versus Time') ↵
>>gtext('Velocity versus Time') ↵
```

With all these we ended up with the figure A.1(h).

Finite difference has wide variety of applications; we provided some flavor in this introductory text. Important aspect of the computing is identify the involved mathematical operation such as differentiation, summation, integration or other and apply the appropriate function or tool what we addressed in various chapters.

Appendix B

Coding in MATLAB

MATLAB executes the code of an expression in terms of string which is the set of keyboard characters placed consecutively. One distinguishing feature of MATLAB is that the workspace variable itself is a matrix. The strings adopted for computation are divided into two classes – scalar and vector. The scalar computation results the order of the output matrix same as that of the variable matrix. On the contrary, the order for the vector computation is determined in accordance with the matrix algebra rules. Some symbolic functions and their MATLAB counterparts are presented in table B.1. The operators for arithmetic computations are as follows:

addition	+
subtraction	–
multiplication	*
division	/
power	^

The operation sequence of different operators in a scalar or vector string observes the following order:

enclosing braces	( )	first,
power operator	^	then,
division operator	/	next,
multiplication operator	*	after that,
addition operator	+	then, and
subtraction operator	–	finally.

The syntax of the scalar computation urges us to use .*, ./, and .^ in lieu of *, /, and ^ respectively. The operators *, /, and ^ are never preceded by . for the vector computation. The vector string is the MATLAB code of any symbolic expression or function often found in mathematics. In the sequel we present some examples on writing an expression in MATLAB.

◆ Write MATLAB codes both in scalar and vector forms on following functions

$A.\ \sin^3 x \cos^5 x$ $\quad B.\ 2+\ln x$ $\quad C.\ x^4+3x-5$ $\quad D.\ \dfrac{x^3-5}{x^2-7x-7}$

$E.\ \sqrt{|x^3|+\sec^{-1} x}$ $\quad F.\ (1+e^{\sin x})^{x^2+3}$ $\quad G.\ \dfrac{\cosh x+3}{\sqrt{\dfrac{x+4}{\log_{10}(x^3-6)}}}$

$H.\ \dfrac{1}{(x-3)(x+4)(x-2)}$ $\quad I.\ \dfrac{1}{1+\dfrac{1}{1+\dfrac{1}{x}}}$ $\quad J.\ \dfrac{a}{x+a}+\dfrac{b}{y+b}+\dfrac{c}{z+c}$

$K.\ \dfrac{u^2v^3w^9}{x^4y^7z^6}$

In tabular form, they are coded as follows:

Example	String for scalar computation	String for vector computation
A	sin(x).^3.*cos(x).^5	sin(x)^3*cos(x)^5
B	2+log(x)	2+log(x)
C	x.^4+3*x-5	x^4+3*x-5
D	(x.^3-5)./(x.^2-7*x-7)	(x^3-5)/(x^2-7*x-7)
E	sqrt(abs(x.^3)+asec(x))	sqrt(abs(x^3)+asec(x))
F	(1+exp(sin(x))).^(x.^2+3)	(1+exp(sin(x)))^(x^2+3)
G	(cosh(x)+3)./sqrt((x+4)./log10(x.^3-6))	(cosh(x)+3)/sqrt((x+4)/log10(x^3-6))
H	1./(x-3)./(x+4)./(x-2)	1/(x-3)/(x+4)/(x-2)
I	1./(1+1./(1+1./x))	1/(1+1/(1+1/x))
J	a./(x+a)+b./(y+b)+c./(z+c)	a/(x+a)+b/(y+b)+c/(z+c)
K	u.^2.*v.^3.*w.^9./x.^4./y.^7./z.^6	u^2*v^3*w^9/x^4/y^7/z^6

Finite difference programming circumstance dictates the type of code – whether scalar or vector should be employed.

Table B.1 Some mathematical functions and their MATLAB counterparts

Mathematical notation	MATLAB notation	Mathematical notation	MATLAB notation	Mathematical notation	MATLAB notation
$\sin x$	sin(x)	$\sin^{-1} x$	asin(x)	π	pi
$\cos x$	cos(x)	$\cos^{-1} x$	acos(x)	A+B	A+B
$\tan x$	tan(x)	$\tan^{-1} x$	atan(x)	A–B	A–B
$\cot x$	cot(x)	$\cot^{-1} x$	acot(x)	A×B	A*B
$\operatorname{cosec} x$	csc(x)	$\sec^{-1} x$	asec(x)	e^x	exp(x)
$\sec x$	sec(x)	$\operatorname{cosec}^{-1} x$	acsc(x)	A^B	A^B
$\sinh x$	sinh(x)	$\sinh^{-1} x$	asinh(x)	$\ln x$	log(x)
$\cosh x$	cosh(x)	$\cosh^{-1} x$	acosh(x)	$\log_{10} x$	log10(x)
$\operatorname{sech} x$	sech(x)	$\operatorname{sech}^{-1} x$	asech(x)	$\log_2 x$	log2(x)
$\operatorname{cosech} x$	csch(x)	$\operatorname{cosech}^{-1} x$	acsch(x)	Σ	sum
$\tanh x$	tanh(x)	$\tanh^{-1} x$	atanh(x)	Π	prod
$\coth x$	coth(x)	$\coth^{-1} x$	acoth(x)	$\lvert x \rvert$	abs(x)
10^A	1e*A* e.g. 1e3	10^{-A}	1e-*A* e.g. 1e-3	$\sqrt{x}$	sqrt(x)

* In the six trigonometric functions for example sin(x), the x is in radian. If the x is in degree, we use sind(x). The other five functions also have the syntax cosd(x), tand(x), cotd(x), cscd(x), and secd(x) when the x is in degree. The default return from asin(x) is in radian, if you need the return to be in degree, use the command asind(x). Similar degree return is also possible from acosd(x), atand(x), acotd(x), asecd(x), and acscd(x).

Numerical examples to point out the difference between scalar and vector computations are in the following.

We have the matrices $A=\begin{bmatrix}3 & 5\\ 7 & 8\end{bmatrix}$, $B=\begin{bmatrix}5 & 2 & 1\\ 0 & 1 & 7\end{bmatrix}$, and $C=\begin{bmatrix}3 & 2 & 9\\ 4 & 0 & 2\end{bmatrix}$. The scalar computation is not possible between the matrices A and B because of their unequal order, nor is between the matrices A and C for the same reason. On the contrary the scalar multiplication can be conducted between the B and C for having the same order, which is $B.*C=\begin{bmatrix}15 & 4 & 9\\ 0 & 0 & 14\end{bmatrix}$(element by element multiplication).

Matrix algebra rule says that any matrix A of order $M\times N$ can only be multiplied with another matrix B of order $N\times P$ so that the resulting matrix has the order $M\times P$. For the last paragraph cited A and B, we have M=2, N=2, and P=3 and obtain the vector-multiplied matrix as $A\times B=$ $\begin{bmatrix}3\times5+5\times0 & 3\times2+5\times1 & 3\times1+5\times7\\ 7\times5+8\times0 & 7\times2+1\times8 & 7\times1+8\times7\end{bmatrix}=\begin{bmatrix}15 & 11 & 38\\ 35 & 22 & 63\end{bmatrix}$, which has the MATLAB code A*B not A.*B. Similar interpretation follows for the operators * and /.

Whenever writing the scalar codes A.*B, A./B, and A.^B, we make it certain that both the A and B are identical in matrix size. The 3*A means all elements of matrix A are multiplied by 3 and we do not use 3.*A. Also do we not use A./3 but do A/3. The signs + and - are never preceded by the operator . in scalar codes. The command 4./A means 4 is divided by all elements in A. The A.^4 means power on all elements of A is raised by 4 and so on.

❖ Scale factors or units

In science and engineering physical quantity measurement always requires the understanding of units. Measured unit of a physical quantity can be far apart from the standard unit very often in the power of 10 that is why scale factors are important. Table B.2 presents the engineering scale factor units and their MATLAB equivalences.

Table B.2 Engineering unit scale factors and their MATLAB counterparts

Scale factor	Symbol	As power of 10	MATLAB code
giga	G	10^9	e9
mega	M	10^6	e6
kilo	K	10^3	e3
milli	m	10^{-3}	e-3
micro	μ	10^{-6}	e-6
nano	n	10^{-9}	e-9
pico	p	10^{-12}	e-12

For example the time 10.7 $m\sec$ is coded as 10.7e-3. Again a distance of 4.7 km is entered by writing 4.7e3 in standard unit.

Appendix C

MATLAB functions/statements for finite difference study

While working on finite difference problems in MATLAB, we come across lots of built-in MATLAB functions or programming statements. In order to employ these elements for FD analysis, we need to understand their input and output argument types and purpose of the elements. Functions or program elements exercised in the text with brief descriptions are in the following.

C.1 Comparative and logical operators

Comparative operators are used for comparison on two scalar elements, one scalar and one matrix elements, or two identical size matrix elements. There are six comparative operators as presented in table C.1.

Table C.1 Equivalence of comparative operators

Comparative operation	Mathematical notation	MATLAB notation
equal to	$=$	==
not equal to	$\neq$	~=
greater than	$>$	>
greater than or equal to	$\geq$	>=
less than	$<$	<
less than or equal to	$\leq$	<=

The output of expression pertaining to the comparative operators is logical – either true (indicated by 1) or false (indicated by 0). For example when A=3 and B=4, the comparisons A=B, $A\neq B$, A>B, $A\geq B$, $A<B$, and $A\leq B$ should be false(0), true(1), false(0), false(0), true(1), and true(1) respectively. We implement these comparative operations as presented in table C.2.

Table C.2 Scalar comparative operation

>>A=3; B=4; ↵ >>A==B ↵ ans = 0 >>A~=B ↵ ans = 1	>>A>B ↵ ans = 0 >>A>=B ↵ ans = 0	>>A<B ↵ ans = 1 >>A<=B ↵ ans = 1

There are two operands A and B in table C.2, each of which is a single scalar. Each of the operands can be a matrix in general. In that case the logical decision takes place element by element on all elements in the matrix. For instance if A=$\begin{bmatrix} 5 & 8 \\ 5 & 7 \end{bmatrix}$ and B=$\begin{bmatrix} 2 & 1 \\ -2 & 9 \end{bmatrix}$, A>B should be $\begin{bmatrix} 5>2 & 8>1 \\ 5>-2 & 7>9 \end{bmatrix}=$ $\begin{bmatrix} 1 & 1 \\ 1 & 0 \end{bmatrix}$. Again if the A happens to be a scalar (say A=4), the single scalar is compared to all elements in the B therefore A≤B should be $\begin{bmatrix} 4\leq 2 & 4\leq 1 \\ 4\leq -2 & 4\leq 9 \end{bmatrix}=$

$\begin{bmatrix} 0 & 0 \\ 0 & 1 \end{bmatrix}$. In a similar fashion the B also operates on A however the scalar and matrix related comparative implementation is presented in the table C.3.

Some basic logical operations are NOT, OR, and AND. The characters ~, |, and & of the keyboard are adopted for the logical NOT, OR, and AND respectively. In all logical outputs the 1 and 0 stand for true and false respectively. All logical operators apply to the matrices in general. For the matrix A= $\begin{bmatrix} 0 & 0 \\ 0 & 1 \end{bmatrix}$, NOT(A) operation should provide $\begin{bmatrix} 1 & 1 \\ 1 & 0 \end{bmatrix}$ (see table C.4). The logical OR and AND operations on the like positional elements of the two matrices A= $\begin{bmatrix} 1 & 1 \\ 0 & 1 \end{bmatrix}$ and B= $\begin{bmatrix} 0 & 1 \\ 1 & 1 \end{bmatrix}$ must return $\begin{bmatrix} 1 & 1 \\ 1 & 1 \end{bmatrix}$ and $\begin{bmatrix} 0 & 1 \\ 0 & 1 \end{bmatrix}$ respectively. Table C.4 shows both implementations.

Table C.3 Scalar and matrix comparative operations

when A and B are matrices,	when A is scalar and B is matrix,
>>A=[5 8;5 7]; ↵ >>B=[2 1;-2 9]; ↵ >>A>B ↵ ans = 1 1 1 0	>>A=4; ↵ >>B=[2 1;-2 9]; ↵ >>A<=B ↵ ans = 0 0 0 1

Table C.4 Basic logical operations on matrix elements

for NOT(A) operation,	for A OR B,	for A AND B,	for A XOR B,
>>A=[0 0;0 1]; ↵ >>~A ↵ ans = 1 1 1 0	>>A=[1 1;0 1]; ↵ >>B=[0 1;1 1]; ↵ >>A|B ↵ ans = 1 1 1 1	>>A&B ↵ ans = 0 1 0 1	>>xor(A,B) ↵ ans = 1 0 1 0

If the A or the B is a single 1 or 0, it operates on all elements of the other.

Sometimes we need to check the interval of the independent variable of mathematical functions for instance $-6 \le x \le 8$. The interval is split in two parts $-6 \le x$ and $x \le 8$. In terms of the logical statement one expresses the $-6 \le x \le 8$ as (-6<=x)&(x<=8).

There is no operator for the XOR logical operation instead the MATLAB function xor syntaxed by xor(A,B) implements the operation as presented in the table C.4.

C.2 Simple if/if-else/nested if syntax

Conditional commands are exercised by the if-else statements (reserve words). Also comparisons and checkings may need if-else statements. We can have different if-else structures namely simple-if, if-else, or nested-if depending on programming circumstances, some of which we discuss in the following.

Simple if

The program syntax of simple-if is as follows:

```
if logical expression
        Executable MATLAB command(s)
end
```

Logical expression usually requires the use of comparative operators which are explained in appendix C.1. If the logical expression beside the if is true, the command between the if and end is executed otherwise not. In tabular form a simple-if implementation is as follows:

Example: If $x \geq 1$, we compute $y = \sin x$. When $x = 2$, we should see $y = \sin 2 =$ 0.9093.	Executable M-file:
	x=2;
	if x>=1
	y=sin(x);
	end
		Steps: Save the statements in a new M-file (section 1.3) by the name test and execute the following:
		>>test ↵
			Check from the command window after running the M-file:
			>>y ↵
			
			y =
			0.9093

If-else

General program syntax for the if-else structure is as follows:

```
if logical expression
        Executable MATLAB command(s)
else
        Executable MATLAB command(s)
end
```

If the logical expression beside the if is true, the command between if and else is executed else the command between else and end is executed. In tabular form, an if-else-end implementation is the following:

Example: When $x = 1$, we compute $y = \sin\frac{x\pi}{2}$ =1 otherwise $y = \cos\frac{x\pi}{2}$ =0.	Executable M-file:
	x=1;
	if x==1
	
	y=sin(x*pi/2);
	else
	
	y=cos(x*pi/2);
	end
		Steps: Save the statements in a new M-file by the name test and execute the following:
		>>test ↵
			Check from the command window after running the M-file:
			>>y ↵
			
			y =
			1

If we had x=2; in the first line of M-file in last exercise, we would see y= $\cos\pi$ =−1.

Nested-if

The third type of if structure is the nested-if whose general program syntax is attached in the right side text box. Clearly the syntax takes care of multiple logical expressions which we demonstrate by one example as shown in the following table.

```
if logical expression
        Executable MATLAB command(s)
elseif logical expression
        Executable MATLAB command(s)
            ⋮
elseif logical expression
        Executable MATLAB command(s)
else
        Executable MATLAB command(s)
end
```

Example: The best example can be taking the decision of grades out of 100 based on the achieved number of a student. The grading policy is stated as if the achieved number of a student is greater than or equal 90, greater than or equal to 80 but less than 90, greater than or equal to 70 but less than 80, greater than or equal to 60 but less than 70, greater than or equal to 50 but less than 60, and less than 50, then the grade is decided as A, B, C, D, E, and F respectively.	Executable M-file: N=77; if N>=90 g='A'; elseif (N<90)&(N>=80) g='B'; elseif (N<80)&(N>=70) g='C'; elseif (N<70)&(N>=60) g='D'; elseif (N<60)&(N>=50) g='E'; else g='F'; end	In the executable M-file, the N and g refer to the number achieved and the grade respectively. If the number N is 77, the grade g should be C. Any character is argumented under the single inverted comma. Steps: Save the left statements in a new M-file by the name test and execute the following: >>test ↵	Check from the command window after running the M-file: >>g ↵ g = C

C.3 Data accumulation

Sometimes it is necessary that we perform appending operation on an existing matrix at MATLAB workspace.

Appending rows

Assume that the $A=\begin{bmatrix}1 & 3 & 5\\ 2 & 6 & 8\\ 9 & 5 & 0\\ 4 & 7 & 8\end{bmatrix}$ is formed by appending two row matrices [9 5 0] and [4 7 8] with the matrix $B=\begin{bmatrix}1 & 3 & 5\\ 2 & 6 & 8\end{bmatrix}$.

We first enter the matrix B (section 1.3) into MATLAB and append one row after another by using the command as presented below:

for entering B,

```
>>B=[1 3 5;2 6 8] ↵

B =

     1     3     5
     2     6     8
```

for appending the first row,

```
>>B=[B;[9 5 0]] ↵

B =

     1     3     5
     2     6     8
     9     5     0
```

for appending the second row,

```
>>A=[B;[4 7 8]] ↵

A =

     1     3     5
     2     6     8
     9     5     0
     4     7     8
```

The command B=[B;[9 5 0]] in above execution says that the row [9 5 0] is to be appended with the existing B (inside the third bracket) and that the result is again assigned to B. You can append as many rows as you want. The important point is the number of elements in each row that is to be appended must be equal to the number of columns in the matrix B.

♦ Appending columns

Suppose $C=\begin{bmatrix}1 & 3 & 5 & 9 & 3\\ 2 & 6 & 8 & 0 & 1\\ 9 & 5 & 0 & 1 & 9\end{bmatrix}$ is formed by appending two column matrices $\begin{bmatrix}9\\0\\1\end{bmatrix}$ and $\begin{bmatrix}3\\1\\9\end{bmatrix}$ with matrix $D=\begin{bmatrix}1 & 3 & 5\\ 2 & 6 & 8\\ 9 & 5 & 0\end{bmatrix}$. We get the matrix D into MATLAB and append one column after another as follows:

for entering D,

```
>>D=[1 3 5;2 6 8;9 5 0] ↵

D =

     1     3     5
     2     6     8
     9     5     0
```

for appending the first column,

```
>>D=[D [9 0 1]'] ↵

D =

     1     3     5     9
     2     6     8     0
     9     5     0     1
```

for appending the second column,

```
>>C=[D [3 1 9]'] ↵

C =

     1     3     5     9     3
     2     6     8     0     1
     9     5     0     1     9
```

The column matrix [9 0 1]' and D in above execution has one space gap within the third bracket. In the second of above implementation, the resultant matrix is again assigned to D. Append as many columns as you want just remember that the number of elements in each column that is to be appended must be equal to the number of rows in the matrix D.

♦ Data accumulation by using the two appending techniques

Suppose initially there is nothing in the f matrix, which in MATLAB we write by the statement f=[ ]; (an empty matrix is assigned to f). An empty matrix does not have any size and completely empty, it follows the null symbol ∅ of matrix algebra. Let us say k=2 and perform the assignment as follows:

```
>>f=[ ]; k=2; ↵
```

Now if we execute f=[f k] time and again first f=[f k] returns 2, second f=[f k] returns [2 2], third f=[f k] returns [2 2 2], and so on. This is called row directed data accumulation. Column directed data accumulation occurs by executing f=[f;k] each time.

The demonstrated k is just a scalar but it can be a return from some function, row matrix, or column matrix.

C.4 For-loop syntax

A for-loop performs similar operations for a specific number of times and must be started with the for and terminated by an end statements. Following the for there must be a counter. The counter of the for-loop can be any variable that counts integer or fractional values depending on the increment or decrement. If the MATLAB command statements between the for and end of a for-loop are few words lengthy, one can even write the whole for-loop in one line. The programming syntax and some examples on the for-loop are as follows:

♦ **Program syntax**

for *counter*=starting value:increment or decrement of the counter value:final value

Executable MATLAB command(s)

end

♦ **Example 1**

Our problem statement is to compute $y = \cos x$ for $x = 10^0$ to 70^0 with the increment 10^0. Let us assign the computed values to some variable y where y should be [$\cos 10^0$ $\cos 20^0$ $\cos 30^0$ $\cos 40^0$ $\cos 50^0$ $\cos 60^0$ $\cos 70^0$]=[0.9848 0.9397 0.866 0.766 0.6428 0.5 0.342].

In the programming context, y(1) means the first element in the row matrix y, y(2) means the second element in the row matrix y, and so on. MATLAB code for the $\cos x$ is cosd(x) where x is in degree. The for-loop counter expression should be k=1:1:7 or k=1:7 to have the control on the position index in the row matrix y (because there are 7 elements or indexes in y). Since the computation needs 10 to 70, one generates that by writing k*10. Following is the implementation:

Executable M-file:

```
for k=1:1:7
        y(k)=cosd(k*10);
end
```

Or, as a one line:

```
for k=1:1:7 y(k)=cosd(k*10); end
```

Steps we need:
Open a new M-file (section 1.3), type the executable M-file statements in the M-file editor, save the editor contents by the name **test** in your working path, and call the **test** as shown below.

```
>>test ↵
>>y ↵

y =
        0.9848 0.9397  0.8660  0.7660   0.6428  0.5000   0.3420
```

❖ Example 2

A for-loop helps us accumulate data (appendix C.3) controlled by the consecutive loop index. In this example we accumulate some data row directionally according to the for-loop counter index.

For $k=1$, 2, and 3, we intend to accumulate the k^2 side by side. At the end we should be having [1 4 9] assigned to some variable f – this is our problem statement.

for the right shifting,	for the left shifting,
`>>f=[ ]; for k=1:3 f=[f k^2]; end ↵`	`>>f=[ ]; for k=1:3 f=[k^2 f]; end ↵`
`>>f ↵`	`>>f ↵`
`f =`	`f =`
`1 4 9`	`9 4 1`

The for-loop for the accumulation is presented above. The accumulation may occur as right or left shifting. Corresponding to the right shifting, the vector code (appendix B) for k^2 is k^2. The statement f=[ ]; means that an empty matrix is assigned to f outside the for-loop but at the beginning. The k variation in our problem is put as the for-loop counter. How the for-loop accumulates is shown below:

When k=1, f=[f k^2]; returns f=[[ ] 1^2]; ⇒ f=1;
When k=2, f=[f k^2]; returns f=[1 2^2]; ⇒ f=[1 4];
When k=3, f=[f k^2]; returns f=[1 4 3^2]; ⇒ f=[1 4 9];

The accumulation is happening from the left to the right. A single change provides the shifting from the right to the left which is f=[k^2 f];. The complete code and its execution result are also shown above by the heading 'for the left shifting'.

❖ Example 3

Another accumulation can be column directed that is we wish to see the output like $\begin{bmatrix} 1 \\ 4 \\ 9 \end{bmatrix}$ in example 2.

We just insert the row separator of a rectangular matrix (done by the operator ;) in the command f=[f k^2];. Again the shifting can happen either from the up to down or from the down to up. Both implementations are shown below:

for the down shifting,
```
>>f=[ ]; for k=1:3 f=[f;k^2]; end ↵
>>f ↵

f =
     1
     4
     9
```

for the up shifting,
```
>>f=[ ]; for k=1:3 f=[k^2;f]; end ↵
>>f ↵

f =
     9
     4
     1
```

◆ **Example 4**

Many FD problems need writing multiple for-loops. Usually one loop is for one dimensional function, two loops are for two dimensional function, and so on. One dimensional function data takes the form of a row or column matrix.

Suppose we have the one dimensional data as y=[9 6 7 4 6]. We wish to access to every data in y. A single for-loop helps us conduct that as shown below:

```
>>y=[9 6 7 4 6]; for k=1:length(y) v=y(k); end ↵
```

First we assign the data to workspace y as a row matrix. The command length finds the number of elements in the row matrix y. The y(k) means the k-th element in the y which we assign to workspace v (any user-chosen variable). Every single data of the y is available sequentially in the v. The contents of y can be a column matrix too.

C.5 Finding the maximum/minimum numerically

Given a matrix, one finds the maximum element from the matrix by using the command max (min for the minimum). Let us say we have three matrices $R=[1\ \ -2\ \ 3\ \ 9]$, $C=\begin{bmatrix}23\\-20\\30\\8\end{bmatrix}$, and $A=\begin{bmatrix}2 & 4 & 7\\-2 & 7 & 9\\3 & 8 & -8\end{bmatrix}$ whose maxima are 9, 30, and 9 (from all elements in the matrix) and minima are –2, –20, and –8 respectively. We find the maxima first entering (section 1.3) the respective matrices as follows:

for the row matrix,
```
>>R=[1 -2 3 9]; ↵
>>max(R) ↵

ans =
     9
>>min(R) ↵

ans =
    -2
```

for the column matrix,
```
>>C=[23;-20;30;8]; ↵
>>max(C) ↵

ans =
    30
>>min(C) ↵

ans =
   -20
```

for the rectangular matrix,
```
>>A=[2 4 7;-2 7 9;3 8 -8]; ↵
>>max(max(A)) ↵

ans =
     9
>>min(min(A)) ↵

ans =
    -8
```

Font equivalence is maintained by using the same letter for example A⇔ A in last implementation. If the matrix is a row or column one, we apply one max or min. For a rectangular matrix, the max or min separately operates on each column that is why two max or min functions are required. The functions are equally applicable on decimal number elements.

In the row matrix R, the maximum 9 is occurring as the fourth element in the matrix. Suppose we also intend to find the position index (that is 4) of the maximum element in the R. Now we need two output arguments – one for the maximum and the other for its index. Its implementation is shown in the right side attached text box of this paragraph in which the two output arguments M and I correspond to the maximum and its integer index respectively.

```
for index finding in R,
>>[M,I]=max(R) ↵

M =
        9
I =
        4
```

The function min also keeps this type of integer index returning option in a similar fashion.

C.6 Matrix data rounding and remainder after integer division

As the title articulates we introduce truncation or rounding and remainder after integer division of matrix elements in this subappendix (font equivalence is maintained by using the same letter for example R⇔ R).

♦ Truncating matrix elements

Built-in function fix discards the fractional parts of a matrix elements regardless of the magnitude and returns the integer parts on all elements in the matrix when the matrix is its input argument. Let us say we have the row matrix R=[1.2578 −9.3445 −8.9999] which should return [1 −9 −8] following the removal of the fractional parts and we carry out the implementation as follows:

```
>>R=[1.2578 -9.3445 -8.9999]; ↵   ← We assigned the row matrix to
                                      the workspace R
>>V=fix(R) ↵                      ← Truncated elements are
                                      assigned to V as a row matrix
V =
        1 -9 -8
```

If the R were a rectangular matrix, the command would be applied equally on all elements in the matrix.

♦ Rounding matrix elements

Any fractional number can be rounded to its nearest integer by using the command round which means if the fractional part of the number is greater than or equal to 0.5, it is taken as 1 and if it is less than 0.5, it is taken as 0. Referring to C=[1.5001 −9.5000

```
for rounding the C elements:
>>C=[1.5001 -9.5000 -8.4999]; ↵
>>V=round(C) ↵

V =
        2 -10 -8
```

−8.4999], rounding operation on all elements in C should provide us [2 −10 −8] whose implementation is presented in attached text box of this paragraph and the rounded elements are held in V. The C can be a rectangular matrix in general.

♦ **Remainder after integer division**

When an integer is divided by another integer, there is no fractional part in the integer division for example the integers 3 and 2 provide the quotients $\frac{2}{3}=0$ and $\frac{3}{2}=1$. Remainder after integer division is found by the command rem which basically computes integer−divider×quotient. When 2 is divided by 3, we should get 2−3×0=2 as the remainder after the integer division. Similarly 3 by 2 should provide us 1. Again the same operation on all elements of $A=\begin{bmatrix} 2 & 9 \\ -56 & -5 \\ 6 & 76 \\ 3 & 2 \end{bmatrix}$ by −3 should return $\begin{bmatrix} 2 & 0 \\ -2 & -2 \\ 0 & 1 \\ 0 & 2 \end{bmatrix}$. Also the same operation for the like positional elements of dividend $D=\begin{bmatrix} 2 & 3 & 4 \\ 7 & 9 & 2 \end{bmatrix}$ and divider $B=\begin{bmatrix} 3 & 4 & 2 \\ -3 & 2 & 3 \end{bmatrix}$ should return us $\begin{bmatrix} 2 & 3 & 0 \\ 1 & 1 & 2 \end{bmatrix}$. All these are presented below (every result is assigned to V):

when 2 divided by 3,	when A is divided by -3,	like positional elements of D divided by B,
>>V=rem(2,3) ↵ V = 2 when 3 divided by 2, >>V=rem(3,2) ↵ V = 1	>>A=[2 9;-56 -5;6 76;3 2]; ↵ >>V=rem(A,-3) ↵ V = 2 0 -2 -2 0 1 0 2	>>D=[2 3 4;7 9 2]; ↵ >>B=[3 4 2;-3 2 3]; ↵ >>V=rem(D,B) ↵ V = 2 3 0 1 1 2

C.7 Position indexes of matrix elements with conditions

MATLAB command find looks for the position indexes of matrix elements subject to some logical condition whose general format is [R C]= find(condition) where the indexes returned to the R and C are meant to be for the row and column directions respectively. The R and C are user-chosen workspace variables. Let us consider $A=\begin{bmatrix} 11 & 10 & 11 & 10 \\ 12 & 10 & -2 & 0 \\ -7 & 17 & 1 & -1 \end{bmatrix}$ which we enter by the following:

>>A=[11 10 11 10;12 10 -2 0;-7 17 1 -1]; ↵ ← A is assigned to A

We would like to know what the position indexes of A where the elements are greater than 10 are. In matrix A the left-upper most element has the position index (1,1). The elements of A being greater than 10 have the position indexes (1,1), (2,1), (3,2), and (1,3). MATLAB finds the required index in accordance with columns. Placing the row and column indexes vertically, we have $\begin{bmatrix}1\\2\\3\\1\end{bmatrix}$ and $\begin{bmatrix}1\\1\\2\\3\end{bmatrix}$ respectively. The output arguments R and C of the find receive these two column matrices respectively. The input argument of the find must be a logical statement, any element in A greater than 10 is written as $A>10$ (appendix C.1). The position indexes are found as shown in the right side attached text box.

where elements of A are greater than 10,

```
>>[R C]=find(A>10) ↵

R =

     1
     2
     3
     1

C =

     1
     1
     2
     3
```

where elements of $A=10$:

```
>>[R C]=find(A==10) ↵

R =
     1
     2
     1
C =
     2
     2
     4
```

where elements of $A\le 0$:

```
>>[R C]=find(A<=0) ↵

R =
     3
     2
     2
     3
C =
     1
     3
     4
     4
```

for the row matrix D:

```
>>D=[-10 34 1 2 8 4]; ↵
>>R=find(D>=8) ↵

R =
     2     5
```

for the column matrix E:

```
>>E=[-2 8 -2 7]'; ↵
>>C=find(E~=-2) ↵

C =
     2
     4
```

To exercise more conditions, what are the position indexes in the matrix A where the elements are equal to 10? The answer is (1,2), (2,2), and (1,4). Again the position indexes where the elements are less than or equal to zero are (3,1), (2,3), (2,4), and (3,4).

The comparative operators $>$, $<$, $\ge$, $\le$, and $\ne$ have the MATLAB counterparts >, <, >=, <=, and ~= respectively.

So far we considered a rectangular matrix for demonstration on position index finding. Let us see how the find works for a row or column matrix. Let us take $D=[-10 \quad 34 \quad 1 \quad 2 \quad 8 \quad 4]$ from which we find the position indexes of the elements where they are greater than or equal to 8. Obviously they are the 2nd and 5th elements. Here we do not need to place two output arguments to the find.

Again let us find the position indexes of the elements in column matrix $E=\begin{bmatrix}-2\\8\\-2\\7\end{bmatrix}$ where the elements are not equal to –2. The 2nd and 4th elements are not equal to –2.

The output of **find** is a row one for the row matrix input and a column one for the column matrix input.

Presented middle in the last page are the executions on all these conditional findings.

C.8 Matrix of ones, zeroes, and constants

MATLAB built-in commands **ones** and **zeros** implement user-defined matrix of ones and zeroes respectively. Each function conceives two input arguments, the first and second of which are the required numbers of rows and columns respectively. Let us say we intend to form the matrices $A=\begin{bmatrix}1&1&1\\1&1&1\\1&1&1\\1&1&1\end{bmatrix}$, $B=\begin{bmatrix}1&1&1\\1&1&1\\1&1&1\end{bmatrix}$, and $C=\begin{bmatrix}1&1&1&1\\1&1&1&1\end{bmatrix}$. Their orders are 4×3, 3×3, and 2×4 respectively and the implementations are as follows:

for A,
```
>>A=ones(4,3) ↵

A =
     1     1     1
     1     1     1
     1     1     1
     1     1     1
```

for B,
```
>>B=ones(3) ↵

B =
     1     1     1
     1     1     1
     1     1     1
```

for C,
```
>>C=ones(2,4) ↵

C =
     1     1     1     1
     1     1     1     1
```

Either the number of rows or columns will do if the matrix is a square. For the row and column matrices of ones for example of length 6, the commands would be **ones(1,6)** and **ones(6,1)** respectively.

Formation of the matrix of zeroes is quite similar to that of the matrix of ones. Replacing the function **ones** by **zeros** does the formation. Matrix of zeroes like $A=\begin{bmatrix}0&0&0\\0&0&0\\0&0&0\\0&0&0\end{bmatrix}$, $B=\begin{bmatrix}0&0&0\\0&0&0\\0&0&0\end{bmatrix}$, and $C=\begin{bmatrix}0&0&0&0\\0&0&0&0\end{bmatrix}$ (whose orders are 4×3, 3×3, and 2×4) we form by the commands **A=zeros(4,3)**, **B=zeros(3)**, and **C=zeros(2,4)** respectively. A row and a column matrices of 6 zeroes are formed by the commands **zeros(1,6)** and **zeros(6,1)** respectively.

A matrix of constants is obtained by first creating a matrix of ones of the required size and then multiplying by the constant number. For example the matrix $\begin{bmatrix}0.2&0.2&0.2\\0.2&0.2&0.2\\0.2&0.2&0.2\\0.2&0.2&0.2\end{bmatrix}$ is generated by the command **0.2*ones(4,3)**.

C.9 Summing matrix elements

MATLAB function sum adds all elements in a row, column, or rectangular matrix when the matrix is its input argument. Example matrices are $R=[1\ \ -2\ \ 3\ \ 9]$, $C=\begin{bmatrix}23\\-20\\30\\8\end{bmatrix}$, and $A=\begin{bmatrix}2&4&7\\-2&7&9\\3&8&-8\end{bmatrix}$ whose all element sums are 11, 41, and 30 for the R, C, and A respectively. We execute the summations as follows (font equivalence is maintained by using the same letter for example A⇔ A):

Sum for the row matrix,	Sum for the column matrix,	Sum for the rectangular matrix,
>>R=[1 -2 3 9]; ↵	>>C=[23 -20 30 8]'; ↵	>>A=[2 4 7;-2 7 9;3 8 -8]; ↵
>>sum(R) ↵	>>sum(C) ↵	>>sum(sum(A)) ↵
		ans =
ans =	ans =	30
11	41	

For a rectangular matrix, two functions are required because the inner sum performs addition over each column and the result is a row matrix. The outer sum provides addition over the resulting row matrix.

The function is operational on real, complex, and even symbolic variable like x or y.

C.10 Random sample generators

There are many random generators embedded in MATLAB, two of which are addressed.

Uniformly distributed random variable:

Function unifrnd (abbreviation for <u>uni</u>formly <u>f</u>ractional <u>r</u>a<u>nd</u>om) generates samples of uniformly distributed continuous random variable X from user-defined range $A \le X \le B$ where $B > A$. One of the syntaxes in the function is unifrnd(A , B) for example any fractional value over $-4 \le X \le 5$ is generated by:

```
>>X=unifrnd(-4,5) ↵     ← X is user-chosen variable that holds the value

X =
        -2.2373
```

The random numbers in row, column, or rectangular matrix are generated by four input arguments with the syntax unifrnd(A , B ,user-required row number,user-required column number). Let us see the following generation:

Generation of a column matrix X of length 4 in which every element is between –4 and 5:

```
>>X=unifrnd(-4,5,4,1) ↵
```

```
X =
        4.0428
       -3.4790
       -0.8242
        1.3456
```

Generation of a row matrix X of length 4 in which every element is between –4 and 5:

```
>>X=unifrnd(-4,5,1,4) ↵

X =
       -0.3486   4.4192   4.2521  -0.3076
```

Generation of a rectangular matrix X of order 2×3 in which every element is between –4 and 5:

```
>>X=unifrnd(-4,5,2,3) ↵

X =
        3.3185  -2.7500  -2.2115
       -3.9112  -2.1751   1.4341
```

When you execute the commands, these output numbers may not appear in the command window due to randomness of generation but the numbers will be between the defined range that is for sure. A row and a column matrices of length 4 have the rectangular matrix dimensions 1×4 and 4×1 which we used in the generation of above random numbers respectively. The fractional value means the generation is in continuous sense. The term uniform means any value between –4 and 5 is equally likely.

Gaussian random variable:

Samples of Gaussian random variable from user-supplied mean μ and standard deviation σ we implement by the function normrnd (abbreviation for <u>norm</u>al <u>rand</u>om number). The function in general provides matrix based Gaussian random numbers for which the common syntax is normrnd(μ,σ,user-required row number,user-required column number). It should be noted that the random number might appear from $-\infty$ to $+\infty$ theoretically but with more likelihood towards the user-given mean. However following is the example on sample generation of the random numbers:

Generation of a single Gaussian number X of mean μ=2 and standard deviation σ=4:

```
>>X=normrnd(2,4,1,1) ↵

X=
        6.2671
```

Generation of a row matrix X of length 4 in which every element is a Gaussian random number with μ=2 and σ=4:

```
>>X=normrnd(2,4,1,4) ↵
```

```
X =
        -3.3447  4.8573  8.4942  -0.7671
```

Generation of a column matrix X of length 3 in which every element is a Gaussian random number with μ=2 and σ=4:

```
>>X=normrnd(2,4,3,1) ↵

X =
          7.1610
          4.6744
          6.7634
```

Generation of a 3×3 rectangular matrix X in which every element is a Gaussian random number with μ=2 and σ=4:

```
>>X=normrnd(2,4,3,3) ↵

X =
          5.4320  -3.7639   4.7600
          7.0160   4.2846   5.2625
         -4.3749   0.4005   4.8476
```

The sample so generated is for continuous sense random variable.

A normal random number has μ=0 and σ=1 which is just a special case of the Gaussian random number.

Uniform random integers:

In this sort of generation mainly we need the discrete integers and the command we apply is randint with the syntax randint(user-required row number, user-required column number, integer range as a two element row matrix but first the lower bound and then the upper bound).

For instance a uniformly distributed single random integer n within the range $-4 \le n \le 3$ is generated by using the command n=randint(1,1,[-4 3]) where n is user-chosen variable which keeps the generated integer. The first two input arguments of randint must be 1 and 1 because a single element has matrix dimension 1×1. Again n=randint(2,3,[-4 3]) generates random integers of matrix size 2×3 in which every element of n is in between –4 and 3.

C.11 Matrix manipulations

New matrices can be formed from the matrix we have at workspace of MATLAB. We pick a portion of the matrix by using colon operator (:).

Let us see some coloning by first assigning the row matrix A=[2 4 3 –10 0 9 73 29 –31 50] to the workspace variable A:

```
>>A=[2 4 3 -10 0 9 73 29 -31 50]; ↵
```

Suppose we wish to form a matrix B where B will be the second, third, and ninth element of A i.e. B=[4 3 –31]:

```
>>B=A([2 3 9]) ↵
```
← The input argument of A is a row matrix indicating position indices

```
B =
        4    3  -31      ← B holds the required matrix
```

A matrix C is to be formed from the third through the eighth elements of A i.e. C=[3 −10 0 9 73 29]. We execute the following:

```
>>C=A(3:8) ↵      ← The input argument 3:8 indicates the third through eighth

C =
        3  -10    0    9   73   29       ← C holds the required matrix
```

What if we have a column matrix like $D=\begin{bmatrix}2\\4\\5\\-10\\0\\6\\73\\7\\-31\\50\end{bmatrix}$, we enter the matrix into MATLAB workspace as follows:

```
>>D=[2 4 5 -10 0 6 73 7 -31 50]'; ↵         ← D holds the D
```

We wish to form a matrix E from the tenth and the seventh elements of D i.e. $E=\begin{bmatrix}50\\73\end{bmatrix}$ and F from the first five elements of D i.e. $F=\begin{bmatrix}2\\4\\5\\-10\\0\end{bmatrix}$ and do so by:

formation of matrix E,

```
>>E=D([10 7]) ↵

E =
       50
       73
```

formation of matrix F,

```
>>F=D(1:5) ↵

F =
        2
        4
        5
      -10
        0
```

Now we present how the coloning of a rectangular matrix is accomplished. Let us input the $G=\begin{bmatrix}8 & 64 & 27 & 56 & 98 & 43 & 4\\-64 & 216 & 729 & 40 & 12 & 23 & 568\\678 & -90 & 70 & 61 & 67 & 445 & 3\\1 & 47 & 45 & 72 & 34 & -5 & -7\\3 & 87 & 82 & 29 & 10 & -16 & -59\end{bmatrix}$ to G by the following:

```
>>G=[8 64 27 56 98 43 4;-64 216 729 40 12 23 568;678 ... ↵
     -90 70 61 67 445 3;1 47 45 72 34 -5 -7;3 87 82 29 10 -16 -59] ↵
```

```
G =                                                    ← G holds the G
     8    64    27    56    98    43     4
   -64   216   729    40    12    23   568
   678   -90    70    61    67   445     3
     1    47    45    72    34    -5    -7
     3    87    82    29    10   -16   -59
```

In last command the last word of the first line is 678. After typing 678 we leave one space by pressing spacebar and then type three dots from the keyboard. These three dots mean continuation of any MATLAB command. Press Enter key and type the other matrix elements of the row which were interrupted. The three dots (...) are called ellipsis.

Required matrix elements from G are shown by elements inside the dotted box in the following.

Matrix H is to be formed from the second and the fourth columns of G:

$$\begin{bmatrix} 8 & 64 & 27 & 56 & 98 & 43 & 4 \\ -64 & 216 & 729 & 40 & 12 & 23 & 568 \\ 678 & -90 & 70 & 61 & 67 & 445 & 3 \\ 1 & 47 & 45 & 72 & 34 & -5 & -7 \\ 3 & 87 & 82 & 29 & 10 & -16 & -59 \end{bmatrix}$$

Matrix K is to be formed from the third and the fifth rows of G:

$$\begin{bmatrix} 8 & 64 & 27 & 56 & 98 & 43 & 4 \\ -64 & 216 & 729 & 40 & 12 & 23 & 568 \\ 678 & -90 & 70 & 61 & 67 & 445 & 3 \\ 1 & 47 & 45 & 72 & 34 & -5 & -7 \\ 3 & 87 & 82 & 29 & 10 & -16 & -59 \end{bmatrix}$$

Matrix L is to be formed from the fourth through seventh columns of G:

$$\begin{bmatrix} 8 & 64 & 27 & 56 & 98 & 43 & 4 \\ -64 & 216 & 729 & 40 & 12 & 23 & 568 \\ 678 & -90 & 70 & 61 & 67 & 445 & 3 \\ 1 & 47 & 45 & 72 & 34 & -5 & -7 \\ 3 & 87 & 82 & 29 & 10 & -16 & -59 \end{bmatrix}$$

Matrix M is to be formed from the third through fifth rows of G:

$$\begin{bmatrix} 8 & 64 & 27 & 56 & 98 & 43 & 4 \\ -64 & 216 & 729 & 40 & 12 & 23 & 568 \\ 678 & -90 & 70 & 61 & 67 & 445 & 3 \\ 1 & 47 & 45 & 72 & 34 & -5 & -7 \\ 3 & 87 & 82 & 29 & 10 & -16 & -59 \end{bmatrix}$$

Matrix N is to be formed from the intersection of the third through fifth rows and the fourth through seventh columns of G:

$$\begin{bmatrix} 8 & 64 & 27 & 56 & 98 & 43 & 4 \\ -64 & 216 & 729 & 40 & 12 & 23 & 568 \\ 678 & -90 & 70 & 61 & 67 & 445 & 3 \\ 1 & 47 & 45 & 72 & 34 & -5 & -7 \\ 3 & 87 & 82 & 29 & 10 & -16 & -59 \end{bmatrix}$$

Formations of the required H, K, L, M, and N assigned to respective workspace variables are presented in the sequel:

for the formation of H,

```
>>H=G(:,[2 4]) ↵

H =
    64    56
   216    40
   -90    61
    47    72
    87    29
```

for the formation of N,

```
>>N=G(3:5,4:7) ↵

N =
    61    67   445     3
    72    34    -5    -7
    29    10   -16   -59
```

for the formation of M,

```
>>M=G(3:5,:) ↵

M =
   678   -90    70    61    67   445     3
     1    47    45    72    34    -5    -7
     3    87    82    29    10   -16   -59
```

for the formation of K,

```
>>K=G([3 5],:) ↵

K =
   678   -90    70    61    67   445     3
     3    87    82    29    10   -16   -59
```

for the formation of L,

```
>>L=G(:,4:7) ↵

L =
    56    98    43     4
    40    12    23   568
    61    67   445     3
    72    34    -5    -7
    29    10   -16   -59
```

Summarizing all, we exercise the commands matrix name(desired row/rows,:), matrix name(:,desired column/columns), and matrix name(desired row/rows, desired column/columns) for selecting row, column, and submatrix from any existing matrix respectively.

C.12 Matrix data flipping

Usually two kinds of matrix data flipping are practiced in finite difference study (font equivalence is maintained by using the same letter for example A⇔A and the flipped data is assigned to workspace F, which is a user-chosen variable).

❖ Flipping from the left to right

Flipping from the left to right of a row or rectangular matrix is performed by the command **fliplr** (abbreviation for flipping from left to right). Suppose we have a row matrix R=[2 4 3 −4 6 9 3 7 10]. If you flip the elements of R from the left to right, the resulting matrix should be [10 7 3 9 6 −4 3 4 2]. For a rectangular matrix, the flipping operation from left to right takes place over each column that is turning the first column to the last, the second column to the second from the last, and so on. Considering $A = \begin{bmatrix} 4 & 23 & 85 & 34 \\ 5 & 43 & 41 & 87 \\ 8 & 65 & 76 & 71 \end{bmatrix}$, just mentioned flipping should return

$\begin{bmatrix} 34 & 85 & 23 & 4 \\ 87 & 41 & 43 & 5 \\ 71 & 76 & 65 & 8 \end{bmatrix}$. Both implementations are exercised as follows:

Left to right flipping on the row matrix,

```
>>R=[2 4 3 -4 6 9 3 7 10]; ↵
>>F=fliplr(R) ↵

F =
  10  7   3   9   6  -4   3   4   2
```

Left to right flipping on rectangular matrix,

```
>>A=[4 23 85 34;5 43 41 87;8 65 76 71]; ↵
>>F=fliplr(A) ↵

F =
         34   85   23    4
         87   41   43    5
         71   76   65    8
```

Since a column matrix has only one column, no change to the column matrix is brought about by the fliplr.

❖ Flipping from up to down

The function flipud (abbreviation for flipping from up to down) flips the elements of a column or rectangular matrix from up to down. Flipping the column matrix $C=\begin{bmatrix} 4 \\ 7 \\ 8 \\ 3 \\ 1 \end{bmatrix}$ from up to down results the matrix $\begin{bmatrix} 1 \\ 3 \\ 8 \\ 7 \\ 4 \end{bmatrix}$. Flipping from up to down of a rectangular matrix happens over each row for example $D=\begin{bmatrix} 4 & 23 & 85 \\ 5 & 43 & 41 \\ 8 & 65 & -1 \\ 3 & 12 & 13 \end{bmatrix}$ becomes $\begin{bmatrix} 3 & 12 & 13 \\ 8 & 65 & -1 \\ 5 & 43 & 41 \\ 4 & 23 & 85 \end{bmatrix}$ due to the flipping. No change occurs to a row matrix when the flipud is applied on it. Both examples are implemented as follows:

Up to down flipping on the column matrix,

```
>>C=[4 7 8 3 1]'; ↵
>>F=flipud(C) ↵

F =
        1
        3
        8
        7
        4
```

Up to down flipping on the rectangular matrix,

```
>>D=[4 23 85;5 43 41;8 65 -1;3 12 13]; ↵
>>F=flipud(D) ↵

F =
      3   12   13
      8   65   -1
      5   43   41
      4   23   85
```

Appendix D

Algebraic equation solver

By virtue of master function solve, we find the solution of a single or multiple algebraic equations when the equations are its input arguments. The notion of the solution is symbolic and a substantial number of simultaneous linear, algebraic, or trigonometric equations can be solved by using the solve. The common syntax of the implementation is solve(equation-1, equation-2, ... so on in vector string form – appendix B, unknowns of the equations separated by a comma but put under quote).

The return from solve is in general a structure array which is beyond the discussion of the text (reference 12). Very briefly a structure array is composed of several members. In order to view the solution from the solve, one needs to call a member of the array. If s is a structure array and u is one of its members, we call the member by the command s.u. One can assign the s.u to some other workspace variable if it is necessary. Following points must be considered while using the solve:

(a) We solve equations related to variables which have power 1 or more. One variable equation of power 1 for example $2x-7=5x$ is written as 2*x-7=5*x in code form, two variable equations $7x+y-7=0$ and $2y+4=5x$ are written as 7*x+y-7=0 and 2*y+4=5*x respectively, and so on.

(b) Since the solution approach is completely symbolic, we enter rational value of the equation coefficient in case of decimal data for example the equation $2.4x-7.5=5x$ had better be written as 24*x/10-75/10=5*x.

(c) The i or j is unit imaginary number in MATLAB. Such use sometimes turns the solve non-executable. If any variable i is in the equations, we use a dummy variable for example c.

(d) The return from solve is usually in rational form for instance 24/10 instead of 2.4. If we need the decimal value, we employ the command double on the return.

(e) The equations are assigned under quote while entering as input arguments to the solve or assigning to some variables.

Let us go through the solution finding on following three examples.

♦ Example 1

The solution of the equation $2x+7=9x$ is $x=1$ which we wish to find. We execute the following for the solution at the command prompt:

```
>>s=solve('2*x+7=9*x','x') ↵

s =
```

```
1
```

The s in last execution is any user-chosen variable. The s=1 return indicates the $x=1$ solution. The independent variable in given equation is x that is why the second input argument of solve is 'x'.

♦ Example 2

The equation set $\begin{Bmatrix} 6x-y=-8 \\ 9x=8y+5 \end{Bmatrix}$ has the solution $x=-\frac{23}{13}$=–1.7692 and $y=-\frac{34}{13}$=–2.6154 and our objective is to obtain the solution.

The given two equations have the codes 6*x-y=-8 and 9*x=8*y+5 respectively. The related variables in the two equations are x and y therefore we carry out the following at the command prompt:

```
>>s=solve('6*x-y=-8','9*x=8*y+5','x','y') ↵

s =

        x: [1x1 sym]
        y: [1x1 sym]
```

The s in above execution is also any user-chosen variable. The solve returns the solution to the s. As we mentioned earlier, the return from solve is a structure array and its members are the x and y (related variables in given equations). The return is an object (called symbolic object, indicated by the sym) rather than data. Should we pick the solution of x and y from the s, we need to exercise the commands s.x and s.y respectively. Let us see what we obtain as the solution:

For the x value:

```
>>s.x ↵

ans =

-23/13
>>double(s.x) ↵

ans =
        -1.7692
```

For the y value:

```
>>s.y ↵

ans =

-34/13
>>double(s.y) ↵

ans =
        -2.6154
```

The result is as expected. We could have assigned the return to some variable for example s.x or double(s.x) to a by writing a=s.x or a=double(s.x).

♦ Example 3

For multiple equations it is not feasible that we enter all equations as one line to solve. Instead we first assign the given equations to some user-chosen variables and then call the solve with these variable names as the input arguments. The equation set $\{x-y-3.2z+2u=-8,\ 8.5y-7z+u=5,\ x-4y+2z=76,\ -3.4x+6z+7u=-12\}$ has the solution $u=$

$\frac{29598}{1387}$ =21.3396, $x=\frac{348525}{2774}$ =125.6399, $y=\frac{95869}{2774}$ =34.5598, and $z=\frac{245775}{5548}$ =44.2997 which we find by exercising ongoing function and symbology as follows:

```
>>e1='x-y-32*z/10+2*u=-8'; ↵            ← assigning the first equation to e1
>>e2='85*y/10-7*z+u=5'; ↵               ← assigning the second equation to e2
>>e3='x-4*y+2*z=76'; ↵                  ← assigning the third equation to e3
>>e4='-34*x/10+6*z+7*u=-12'; ↵          ← assigning the fourth equation to e4
>>s=solve(e1,e2,e3,e4,'x','y','z','u') ↵ ← calling the solve on e1, e2, e3, and e4

s =                         ← s holds the solution as a structure array
      u: [1x1 sym]          ← u is a member of s
      x: [1x1 sym]          ← x is a member of s
      y: [1x1 sym]          ← y is a member of s
      z: [1x1 sym]          ← z is a member of s
```

The e1, e2, e3, and e4 are all user-chosen variables in above. The next step is to see the values returned by the solve:

for the rational value of x:

```
>>s.x ↵

ans =

348525/2774
```

for the rational value of y:

```
>>s.y ↵

ans =

95869/2774
```

for the rational value of z:

```
>>s.z ↵

ans =

245775/5548
```

for the rational value of u:

```
>>s.u ↵

ans =

29598/1387
```

for the decimal value of x:

```
>>double(s.x) ↵

ans =
        125.6399
```

for the decimal value of y:

```
>>double(s.y) ↵

ans =
        34.5598
```

for the decimal value of z:

```
>>double(s.z) ↵

ans =
        44.2997
```

for the decimal value of u:

```
>>double(s.u) ↵

ans =
        21.3396
```

When we assign the equations, we use the quote but inside the solve the assignees do not have quote for example e1 not 'e1'. All four values as a four element row matrix are seen by:

```
>>[s.x s.y s.z s.u] ↵

ans =

[ 348525/2774,  95869/2774, 245775/5548,  29598/1387]
```

All four values in decimal form as a row matrix are seen as follows:

```
>>double([s.x s.y s.z s.u]) ↵

ans =
        125.6399   34.5598   44.2997   21.3396
```

Obviously the return is in the order we typed in.

Appendix E

Some graphing functions of MATLAB

One of MATLAB's nicest features is you can have your graphics drawn while programming finite difference related problems. There are so many easy accessible built-in graphics functions that one finds it very interesting when the input-output argumentation style of these functions is understood. Some graphing functions which we applied frequently in previous chapters are addressed for syntax details in the sequel.

❖ y versus x data

The command plot graphs y versus x data. Let us say we have the attached (on the right side in this paragraph) tabular data. We intend to graph these data as y versus x graph.

Tabular data of y versus x type:							Command to graph the y vs x data:
x	-6	-4	0	4	5	7	>>x=[-6 -4 0 4 5 7]; ↵ >>y=[9 3 -3 -5 2 0]; ↵ >>plot(x,y) ↵
y	9	3	-3	-5	2	0	

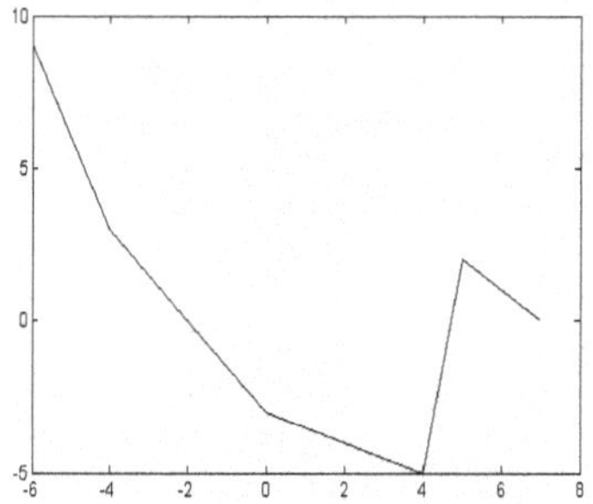

Figure E.1(a) y vs x plot of the tabular data

Commands to graph the data are also presented beside the tabular data on the right side in the last paragraph. We first assign the x and y data to workspace x and y (some user-chosen variables) respectively and then call the command plot to see the figure E.1(a). The plot has two input arguments, the first and second of which are the x and y data both as a row or column matrix of identical size respectively.

In order to graph the mathematical expression by using the plot, one first needs to calculate the functional values by using the scalar code (appendix B) and then applies the command. During the calculation, computational step selection is mandatory which is completely user-defined.

For instance we wish to graph the function $f(x)=x^2-x+2$ over $-2 \le x \le 3$.

Let us choose some x step say 0.1. The x vector as a row matrix is generated by x=-2:0.1:3; (section 1.3). At every element in x vector, the functional value is computed and assigned to workspace f by f=x.^2-x+2;. The f is any user-chosen variable. Now we call the grapher as plot(x,f) to see the trajectory (not shown for space reason).

The command plot just draws the graph, no graphical features such as x axis label or title are added to the graph. It is the user who is supposed to add these graphical features.

♦ Multiple y data versus common x data

The plot keeps many options, one of which is just discussed. We graph several y data versus common x data with the help of the same plot but with different number of input arguments. Let us choose the right side attached table for the graphing. We intend to plot the y_1, y_2, and y_3 data on common x data. To do so,

Tabular data for multiple y versus common x:

x	-6	-4	0	4	5	7
y_1	9	3	-3	-5	2	0
y_2	0	-2	1	0	5	7.7
y_3	-1	2	8	1	0	-3

```
>>x=[-6 -4 0 4 5 7]; ↵          ← Assigning the x data as a row matrix to x
>>y1=[9 3 -3 -5 2 0]; ↵         ← Assigning the y1 data as a row matrix to y1
>>y2=[0 -2 1 0 5 7.7]; ↵        ← Assigning the y2 data as a row matrix to y2
>>y3=[-1 2 8 1 0 -3]; ↵         ← Assigning the y3 data as a row matrix to y3
>>plot(x,y1,x,y2,x,y3) ↵        ← Applying the command plot
```

The plot now has six input arguments – two for each graph, the first and second of which are the common x data and y data to be plotted respectively. If there were four y data, the command would be plot(x,y1,x,y2,x,y3,x,y4). Once the data is plotted for several y, identifying the y traces is obvious and which is carried out by the command legend. The command legend('y1', 'y2','y3') puts identifying marks/colors among various graphs. The input argument of the legend is any user-given word but under quote and separated by a comma. The number of y traces must be equal to the number of input arguments of the legend. We gave the names y1, y2, and y3 for the three y traces respectively. In doing so, we end up with the figure E.1(b). You can even move the legend on the plot area by using the mouse. You see all graphics throughout the text as black and white because we did not include color graphics in the text (for expense reason). But MATLAB displays figures in color plots, which you can easily identify.

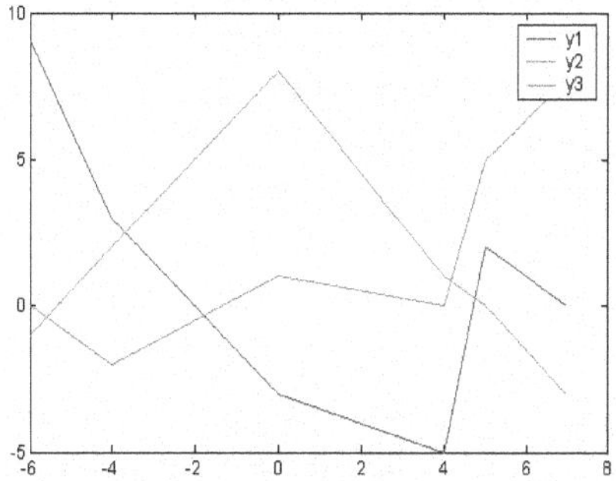

Figure E.1(b) Multiple y vs x for the tabular data

Another situation can be that we have several functions and intend to plot those on common x variation. For instance we wish to graph $y_1 = x^3 - x^2 + 4$ and $y_2 = x^2 - 7x - 5$ over the common $-1 \le x \le 3$.

Under these circumstances, the step selection of the x data is compulsory. Without calculating the functional values of given y curves, we can not graph the functions for which we exercise the scalar code. Let us choose the x step as 0.1. We first generate the common x vector as a row matrix by writing x=-1:0.1:3; and then calculate the y_1 and y_2 (y1⇔y_1 and y2⇔y_2) data by writing y1=x.^3-x.^2+4; y2=x.^2-7*x-5; and eventually the graph appears by executing plot(x,y1,x,y2), graph is not shown for space reason. Thus you can graph three or more functions.

◆ Functions of the form $y = f(x)$

If any function is of the form $y = f(x)$ and the $f(x)$ versus x is to be graphed, the built-in **ezplot** is the best option which uses a syntax ezplot(functional vector code under quote according to appendix B, interval bounds as a two element row matrix) where the first and second elements in the row matrix are the beginning and ending bounds of the interval respectively. The **ezplot** graphs $y = f(x)$ in the default interval $-2\pi \le x \le 2\pi$ when no interval description is argumented.

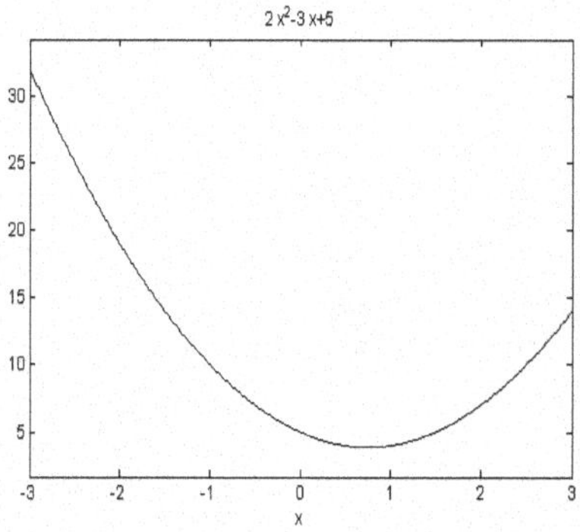

Figure E.1(c) Plot of $y = 2x^2 - 3x + 5$ versus x over $-3 \le x \le 3$

We intend to graph the function $y = 2x^2 - 3x + 5$ over the interval $-3 \le x \le 3$. We first give $2x^2 - 3x + 5$ MATLAB vector code and then assign that to y as follows:

```
>>y='2*x^2-3*x+5'; ↵
```

In above implementation the y is any user-chosen variable. The interval $-3 \le x \le 3$ is entered by [-3 3]. To obtain the plot of y in the given interval, we execute the following at the command prompt:

```
>>ezplot(y,[-3,3]) ↵
```

Above command results the figure E.1(c).

◆ Multiple graphs in the same window

The function subplot splits a figure window in subwindows based on the user definition. It accepts three positive integer numbers as the input arguments, the first and second of which indicate the number of subwindows in the horizontal and the number of subwindows in the vertical directions respectively. For example 22 means two subwindows horizontally and two subwindows vertically, 32 means three subwindows horizontally and two subwindows vertically, ... and so on. The third integer in the input argument numbered consecutively offers control on the subwindows so generated. If the first two digits are 32, there should be 6 subwindows and they are numbered and controlled by using 1 through 6. When you plot some graph in a subwindow, as if you are handling an independent figure window.

Commands for the figure E.1(d):

>>subplot(121) ↵ ← It handles the first graph
>>ezplot('x') ↵ ← Plotting $y = x$
>>subplot(122) ↵ ← It handles the second graph
>>ezplot('exp(-x)') ↵ ← Plotting $y = e^{-x}$

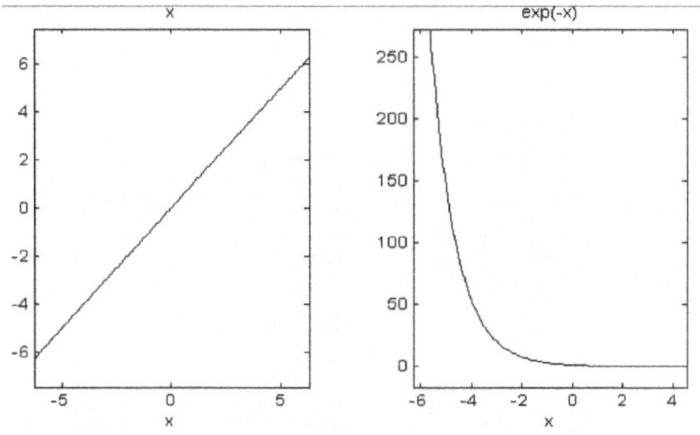

Figure E.1(d) Plots of $y = x$ and $y = e^{-x}$ side by side in the same window

We wish to graph $y = x$ and $y = e^{-x}$ side by side as two different plots by using earlier mentioned **ezplot** but in the same window. If we imagine the subfigures as matrix elements, we have a figure matrix of size 1×2 (one row and two columns). That is why the first two integers of the input argument of **subplot** should be 12. Attached commands in the upper right text box of last paragraph show the figure E.1(d). The third integers 1 and 2 in the **subplot** give the control on the first and second subfigures respectively.

As another example we wish to plot $y = x$ and $y = e^{-x}$ in the upper row and only $y = (1 - e^{-x})$ in the lower row subfigures in the same window whose implementation needs above attached text box commands and whose final output is the figure E.1(e). We are supposed to have four figures when the integer input argument of **subplot** is 22 (two for rows and two for columns). The arguments 221, 222, 223, and 224 provide handle on the four

Commands for the figure E.1(e):

>>subplot(221) ↵ ← Subfigure selection for $y = x$
>>ezplot('x') ↵ ← Plotting $y = x$
>>subplot(222) ↵ ← Subfigure selection for $y = e^{-x}$
>>ezplot('exp(-x)') ↵ ← Plotting $y = e^{-x}$
>>subplot(212) ↵ ← Subfigure selection for $y = (1 - e^{-x})$
>>ezplot('1-exp(-x)') ↵ ← Plotting $y = (1 - e^{-x})$

figures consecutively. The figures could have been plotted on 223 and 224 are absent so we ignore them. The argument 21 creates two subfigures (two rows and one column) handled by 211 and 212, but 211 is absent so we ignore that too.

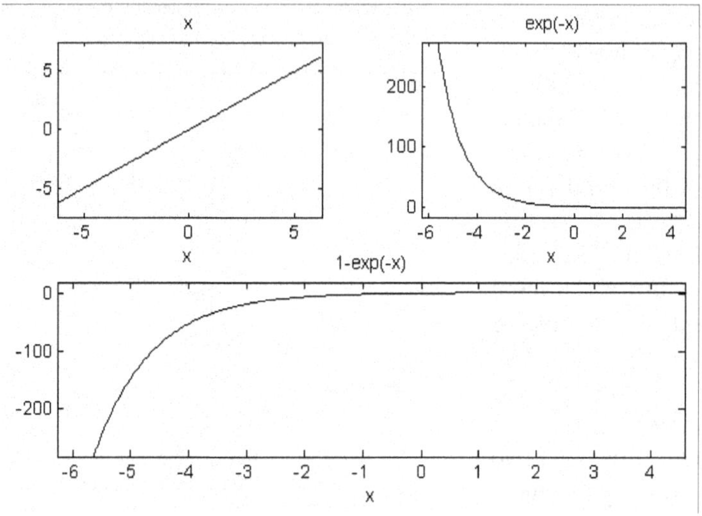

Figure E.1(e) Plots of $y=x$ and $y=e^{-x}$ in the upper row and $y=(1-e^{-x})$ in the lower row in the same window

Let us see the input arguments of **subplot** for different subfigures (each third brace set [ ] is one subfigure in the following tabular representation) as follows:

Subfigures needed	First two input integers of **subplot**	Third input integer of **subplot**	Commands we need
[ ] [ ] [ ] [ ]	22	[1] [2] [3] [4]	subplot(221) subplot(222) subplot(223) subplot(224)
[ ] [ ] [ ]	22 for upper two (lower two remain empty) 21 for the lower one (upper one remains empty)	[1] [2] [2]	subplot(221) subplot(222) subplot(212)
[ ] [ ] [ ]	21 for the upper one (lower one remains empty) 22 for the lower two (upper two remain empty)	[1] [3] [4]	subplot(211) subplot(223) subplot(224)
[ ] [ ] [ ]	22 for the left two (right two remain empty) 12 for the right one (left one remains empty)	[1] [2] [3]	subplot(221) subplot(223) subplot(122)
[ ] [ ] [ ]	22 for right two (left two remain empty) 12 for the left one (right one remains empty)	[1] [2] [4]	subplot(222) subplot(224) subplot(121)

Appendix F

Creating a function file

A function file is a special type of M-file (section 1.3) which has some user-defined input and output arguments. Both arguments can be single or multiple. The first line in a function file always starts with the reserve word **function**. A function file must be in your working path or its path must be defined in MATLAB. Depending on problem, a function file is written by the user and can be called from the MATLAB command prompt or from another M-file. For convenience, long and clumsy programs are split into smaller modules and these modules are written in a function file. The basic structure of a function file is as follows:

MATLAB Prompt → function file

>> g =call f ⟹ $\underbrace{g(y_1, y_2, ...y_m)}_{\text{output arguments}} = \underbrace{f(x_1, x_2, x_3, ...x_n)}_{\text{input arguments}}$

We present following examples for illustration of function files keeping in mind that the arguments' order and type of the caller and function file are identical.

Example 1

Let us say the computation of $f(x) = x^2 - x - 8$ is to be implemented as a function file. When $x = -3$ and $x = 5$, we should be having 4 and 12 respectively.

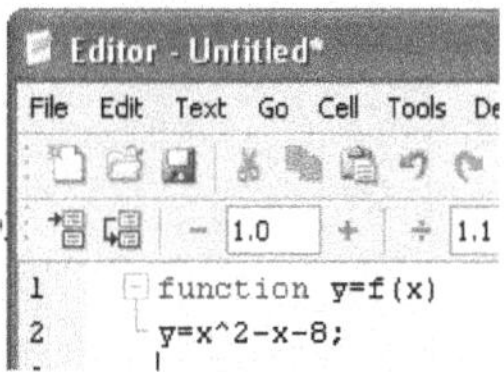

Figure F.1(a) Single input – single output function file

The vector code (appendix B) of the function is x^2-x-8 assuming scalar x and obviously the x is for x. We have one input (which is x) and one output (which is $f(x)$). Open a new M-file editor, type the codes of figure F.1(a) exactly as they appear in the M-file, and save the file by the name f. The assignee y and independent variable x can be any variable of your choice, which are the output and input arguments of the function respectively. Again the file and function name f can be any user-chosen name only the point is the chosen function or file name should not exist in MATLAB. Let us call the function f(x) to verify the programming as shown in the right side text box. You can write dozens of MATLAB executable statements in the file but whatever is assigned to the last y returns the function f(x) to g. Writing the = sign between the y and f(x) in the function file is compulsory.

Calling for example 1:

>>g=f(-3) ↵ ← call $f(x)$ for $x = -3$

```
g =
    4
```

for $x = 5$,

```
>>g=f(5) ↵

g =
    12
```

Example 2

Example 1 presents one input-one output function how if we handle multiple inputs and one output? The input argument variables are separated by commas in a function file. A three variable function $f(x_1, x_2, x_3) = x_1^2 - 2x_1x_2 + x_3^2$ is to be computed by a function file. The input arguments (assuming all scalar) are x_1, x_2, and x_3 and the output argument is the functional value of the function. The x_1 is written as x1, and so is the others. Follow the M-file procedure of example 1 but the code should be as shown in figure F.1(b). Let us inspect the function (with the specific x_1=3, x_2=4, and x_3=5, the output value of the three variable function must be $f(3,4,5) = 3^2 - 2\times3\times4 + 5^2 = 10$) as presented in the text box below.

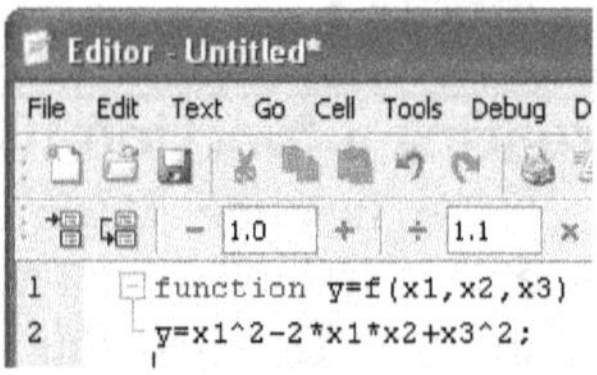

Figure F.1(b) Multiple inputs – single output function file

Calling for example 2: when input arguments are all scalar:

```
>>g=f(3,4,5) ↵        ← calling f(x1, x2, x3) for x1=3, x2=4, and x3=5

g =
        10
```

Calling for the example 2: when input arguments are all column matrix:

```
>>x1=[2 3 4]'; ↵    ← x1 values are assigned to x1 as a column matrix
>>x2=[-2 2 5]'; ↵   ← x2 values are assigned to x2 as a column matrix
>>x3=[1 0 3]'; ↵    ← x3 values are assigned to x3 as a column matrix
>>f(x1,x2,x3) ↵     ← calling f(x1, x2, x3) using column matrix input arguments

ans =
          13
          -3
         -15
```

The function not only works for the scalar inputs but also does for matrices in general for example a set of input argument values are $x_1 = \begin{bmatrix} 2 \\ 3 \\ 4 \end{bmatrix}$, $x_2 = \begin{bmatrix} -2 \\ 2 \\ 5 \end{bmatrix}$, and $x_3 = \begin{bmatrix} 1 \\ 0 \\ 3 \end{bmatrix}$ for which the $f(x_1, x_2, x_3)$ values should be $\begin{bmatrix} 13 \\ -3 \\ -15 \end{bmatrix}$ respectively. The computation needs the scalar code (appendix B) of $f(x_1, x_2, x_3)$ regarding x_1, x_2, and x_3. The modified second line statement of the figure F.1(b) now should be y=x1.^2-2*x1.*x2+x3.^2;. On making the modification and saving the file, let us carry out the commands which are placed in above text box of this page too. If it is necessary, the output can be assigned to user-supplied workspace variable v by writing v=f(x1,x2,x3) at the command prompt. The return from the function file also follows the same input matrix order. If the input arguments of f(x1,x2,x3) are rectangular matrix, so is the output. The input arguments of the function file do not have to be the mathematics symbol. Suppose x_1=ID, x_2=Value, and x_3=Data, one could have written the first and second lines of the function file in the figure F.1(b) as function y=f(ID,Value, Data) and y=ID.^2-2*ID.*Value+ Data.^2; respectively.

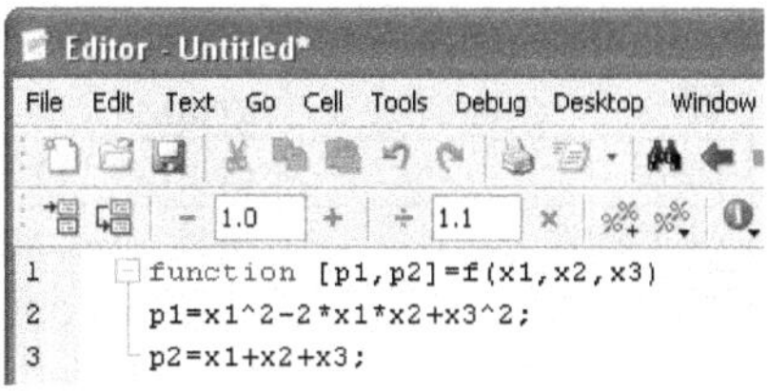

Figure F.1(c) Function file for three input and two output arguments

Example 3

To illustrate a multi-input and multi-output function file, let us consider that p_1 and p_2 are to be found from three variables x_1, x_2, and x_3 (all are scalars) employing the expressions $p_1 = x_1^2 - 2x_1x_2 + x_3^2$ and $p_2 = x_1 + x_2 + x_3$ whose function file (type the codes in a new M-file editor and save the file by the name f) is presented in figure F.1(c).

Choosing x_1=4, x_2=5, and x_3=6, one should get p_1=12 and p_2=15 for which right side text box commands are conducted at the command prompt. More than one output arguments (which are here p_1 are p_2 and represented by p1 and p2 respectively) are separated by commas and placed inside the third bracket following the word function in figure F.1(c).

Function file calling for the example 3:

>>[p1,p2]=f(4,5,6) ↵ ← calling the function file f for p_1 and p_2 using x_1=4, x_2=5, and x_3=6

```
p1 =
        12
p2 =
        15
```

When we call the function from the command prompt, the output argument writing is similar to that of the function file (that is why we write [p1,p2] as output arguments at the command prompt). The output argument variable names do not have to be p1 and p2 and can be any name of user's choice. If there were three output arguments p_1, p_2, and p_3, the output arguments in the function file would be written as [p1,p2,p3] and their calling would happen in a like manner.

Note: We saved different function files by the same name f just for simplicity and maintaining unifying approach. By this action any previously saved file by the name f disappears. What we suggest is save the function file by other name like f1 and call accordingly for instance the first line of figure F.1(c) would be function [p1,p2]=f1(x1,x2,x3) and calling would take place as [p1,p2]=f1(4,5,6) for the last illustration.

Appendix G
MATLAB functions exercised in the text

Function name	Purpose	Page
bar	graphs 1D FD data using bars	34
bar3	graphs 1D FD data using 3D bars	35
clabel	includes contour label in a drawn plot	74
contour	graphs contour plot from a rectangular or sampled $f(x,y)$ matrix data	74
diff	determines finite difference numerically	24
double	turns any symbolic data to double precision value or decimal	193
end	terminates the execution of a for-loop or if-else checking	176
eval	evaluates a function	113
ezcontour	draws contour i.e. line of constant values from an expression which is of the type $f(x,y)$	70
ezcontourf	similar operation as **ezcontour** does	70
ezmesh	similar operation as **ezsurf** does	71
ezplot	draws y versus x type graph from y expression and x interval	198
ezsurf	draws surface plot of $f(x,y)$ versus x and y from expression	71
find	determines the element position in a matrix subject to condition	23
flipud	flips 1D FD column data from up to down	55
for-end	beginning and ending statements of a for-loop	29
gradient	determines finite difference numerically according to MATLAB definition	63
gtext	includes user-defined texts in a drawn graph	163
hold	built-in word for retaining the last figure window	113
imshow	displays mapped rectangular matrix data as a gray image	76
interp1	computes interpolated values based on 1D FD data	31

Continuation of the last table:

Continuation of the last table:

Function name	Purpose	Page
subplot	divides a figure window into subwindows according to user-definition	112
sum	sums all elements in a row or column matrix	22
surf	graphs surface plot from a rectangular or sampled $f(x,y)$ matrix data	75
xlabel	includes x or horizontal label in a drawn graph	145
xlsread	reads data from microsoft excel file	20
ylabel	includes y or vertical label in a drawn graph	145
zeros	generates matrix of zeroes	62
zlabel	includes z or third dimension label in a drawn graph	145

References

[1] W. Yu, X. Yang, Y. Liu, R. Mittra, and A. Muto, "*Advanced FDTD Methods: Parallelization, Acceleration, and Engineering Applications*", 2011, Artech House, Norwood, MA.

[2] J. J. Tuma, "*Handbook of Numerical Calculations in Engineering*", 1989, McGraw-Hill, Inc., New York.

[3] P. Monk, "*Finite Element Methods for Maxwell's Equations*", 2003, Oxford University Press, Oxford.

[4] M. Nuruzzaman, "*Tutorials on Mathematics to MATLAB*", 2003, AuthorHouse, Bloomington, Indiana.

[5] Duffy, Dean G., "*Advanced Engineering Mathematics with MATLAB*", Second Edition, 2003, Chapman & Hall, CRC, Boca Raton.

[6] Shampine, Lawrence F. and Reichelt, Mark W., "*The MATLAB ODE Suite*", 1996, The Math-Works, Inc., Natick, MA.

[7] Peter V. O'Neil, "*Advanced Engineering Mathematics*", Third Edition, 1991, Wadsworth Publishing Company, Belmont, California.

[8] Serge Lang, "*Calculus of Several Variables*", Second Edition, 1979, Addison–Wesley Publishing Company.

[9] B. G. Pachpatte, "*Integral and Finite Difference Inequalities and Applications*", First Edition, 2006, Elsevier, Amsterdam, The Netherlands.

[10] A. R. Mitchell and D. F. Griffiths, "*The Finite Difference Method in Partial Differential Equations*", 1980, John Wiley & Sons Ltd, New York.

[11] D. V. Griffiths and I. M. Smith, "*Numerical Methods for Engineers: A Programming Approach*", 1991, Blackwell Scientific Publications, London.

[12] M. Nuruzzaman, "*Technical Computation and Visualization in MATLAB for Engineers and Scientists*", February, 2007, AuthorHouse, Bloomington, Indiana.

[13] D. M. Etter, "*Engineering Problem Solving with MATLAB*", 1993, Prentice Hall, Englewood Cliffs, N. J.

[14] Gander, Walter. and Hrebicek, Jiri., "*Solving Problems in Scientific Computing Using MAPLE and MATLAB*", 1997, Third Edition, Springer Verlag, New York.

[15] Biran, Adrian B and Breiner, Moshe, "*MATLAB for Engineers*", 1997, Addison Wesley, Harlow, Eng.

Subject Index

www.ingramcontent.com/pod-product-compliance
Lightning Source LLC
Chambersburg PA
CBHW071424050326
40689CB00010B/1970

* 9 7 8 1 4 8 4 8 4 5 3 8 7 *